Elementary Mathematics and Language Difficulties

Elementary Mathematics and Language Difficulties

A Book for
Teachers, Therapists and Parents

Eva Grauberg

Consulting Editor: Professor Margaret Snowling
University of York

Whurr Publishers Ltd
London

British Library Catalogue in Publication data

A catalogue record for this book is available from the
British Library.

ISBN 1 86156 048 6

Printed and bound in the UK by Athenaeum Press Ltd,
Gateshead, Tyne & Wear

Contents

Preface

'Elementary Mathematics and Language Difficulties' is written for teachers, therapists and parents who are trying to help children experiencing combined difficulties in language and elementary mathematics. It may also be helpful for teacher trainers as a means to initiate discussion based on what individual children said and did, and for mainstream teachers to provide guidelines for systematic work in areas such as mental arithmetic.

The book is written not from the perspective of a linguist or a mathematician but, rather, from the standpoint of a teacher with a keen interest in methods and with many years' experience in teaching children in mainstream education and in a special school for children with language impairment. It addresses three questions:

- What are the specific learning features of children with language difficulties?
- Which are the critical points in the mathematical syllabus where such features lead to difficulties?
- What can be done?

The first part of the book outlines the characteristics of these children, looks at relevant research, and provides suggestions for dealing with the children's problems. Three distinctive features are discussed in detail: weakness in symbolic understanding, weakness in organizational skills, and memory weakness. Other features discussed more briefly are: problems with relative concepts, weakness in auditory discrimination, and difficulties with social interaction.

The second part is primarily intended for reference purposes: it explores some of the suggestions made in the first part in greater depth, and provides details that are often needed for practical application.

The suggestions made here are not intended to constitute a structured curriculum for children with language difficulties. They are meant to increase a carer's repertoire of methods for dealing with the difficulties (the term 'carer', as used here, refers not only to the qualified teachers and language therapists professionally responsible for the education of these children, but also to teachers in a wider sense: classroom assistants, parents, grandparents, neighbours or even an older capable child). In each case the carer should assess how appropriate a suggestion seems for a specific situation.

In a predetermined curriculum structure the diversity of language-impaired children is often not sufficiently allowed for. I have emphasized such diversity and tried to account for its threefold roots: the differences in the impairment itself, the variety in the combinations of impairments, and the different ways in which individual children can compensate for their deficiencies. In spite of such diversity it does, however, seem possible to specify general aims and to work selectively within a syllabus where questions of methods are left open.

I think that the approaches outlined here will be suitable for a wide range of children, from those with severe language disorders to children with milder forms of impairment or even to children in mainstream education with temporary language problems. Anything suggested for a 'special child' should also make sense for a 'normal' one, although the latter may not need all of the steps proposed. Similarly, the book covers an age range from the preschool years to pupils aged 14 who are still experiencing specific difficulties with basic mathematical concepts. Most of the activities described are adaptable to whole class, group and individual work.

In general, the suggestions for teaching favour a 'holistic' approach, in the sense that the term was used, for instance, by the German-American psychologist Wertheimer (1966) and his associates. The aim is to present problems in a way which facilitates the visual perception of 'a good gestalt' (configuration) and which will lead to the establishment of well-structured images. The approach focuses on 'wholes' and 'sub-wholes'. It starts by looking at the relations between parts rather than at their sequential order. Such a 'holistic/visual' approach is meant to counteract 'sequential/verbal' deficiencies; thus the teaching is generally geared to a learning style that has often been termed 'right hemispheric'. (For different interpretations of this relevant but difficult concept, and for mathematical learning styles related to it see Krutetskii, 1976; Wheatley, 1977; Fidelman, 1985; Bath, Chinn and Knox, 1986; Globerson and Zelniker, 1989; Robinson 1992.)

I try, throughout, to find ways that give children extra time to learn. Some of my suggestions might seem to have the effect of 'slowing children down' rather than accelerating their performance. This is quite deliberate. All visual processing tends to be relatively slow. Experience has shown that the child who has difficulty in one area (language) is often limited in coping with new learning in another (mathematics). This seems to be due to an 'overloading' of the cognitive processing system rather than to low general ability (cf. Johnston, 1992). The child needs time for guided reflection, for active pauses, for mental 'mulling over', for slowly abandoning scaffolds, and for reaching more conscious levels of understanding (cf. Karmiloff-Smith, 1992).

Teachers and researchers in this field both aim to help children who experience difficulties with cognitive functioning. Their interests are the same. Both are troubled by the current state of theory (cf. Johnston, 1992), but whereas the researcher has time to stop and think, and can calmly and honestly state that there is a 'temporary plateau' (as does Judith Johnston with regard to research into the causes of language impairment in children), the teacher has to act – the children are there to be taught and cannot be sent home until the waters are clear. It is the teacher's lot to act confidently despite doubts about the theoretical basis of what he or she is doing. The suggestions in this book might go some way to help with this daunting task.

I am grateful to the researchers in the field, without whom our teaching would be the poorer. On a more personal level, my thanks go to Walter Grauberg and Corinne Haynes for their more than professional help, to Anni Satow and Gary Thomason for their help with the figures, and to the publishers who were willing to publish a book about teaching in the UK today which mentions the National Curriculum only once.

Finally, I would like to thank the following publishers and authors for permission to reproduce figures and longer passages of text: Blackwell Ltd (Figure 1.12, 1.14 and text by M. Hughes); Multilingual Matters Ltd. (quotation from R. Da Costa); Association of Teachers of Mathematics (quotation from M. Walter).

Note: Throughout the book the female pronoun 'she' will be used for the carer, and the male pronoun 'he' for the language-impaired child; this seems to reflect the relative proportion of both in special language units and in schools.

Part One

Features of Children with Language Difficulties: Consequences for Learning and Teaching Elementary Mathematics

Chapter 1
Weakness in Symbolic Understanding

INTRODUCING THE FEATURE

Among all the features that can be observed in language-impaired children, a weakness in symbolic understanding is probably the most general. It is an elusive, vague and deep-seated problem. The feature is also one that the language-impaired child shares to some extent with many young children without language difficulties (see, for instance, Hughes, 1986; Anghileri, 1995). And, on a different level, it may even be shared by adults.

However, we are talking here mainly about children who are seriously handicapped by this condition and who do not seem to be able to take the first step in symbolic understanding. They seem to have difficulty in grasping the basic idea that something can 'stand for' something else; they may, for instance, fail to come to terms with the notion that one coin (such as a two-penny piece) can stand for two other coins.

Such children are most probably learning-impaired in a wider sense, but they are often found in special language units and in special schools for children with language impairments. This happens because at an early age their language problem seems the most obvious of their many difficulties; it is also the one considered the most devastating for further learning. Although a weakness in symbolic understanding rarely seems to occur in isolation but mostly in combination with other kinds of learning problems, it may be possible to identify certain groups where this weakness is most prominent.

'Asymbolic dysphasics'

It has been suggested (Benton, 1978) that it may be possible to identify a group of 'asymbolic dysphasic' children as different from other dysphasic groups. Since the mid-1980s there has been interest in children who are described as having 'pragmatic' language problems

3

(McTear and Conti-Ramsden, 1991) or 'semantic' ones, or both, without being autistic (Rapin and Allen, 1983). Among these are often children who seem to have specific difficulties with symbols. They can learn to use symbols such as letters and numbers quite efficiently, but they will use them strictly as they have learned them, being almost unable to see them just as useful constructs which have no meaning as such, but only 'stand for meaning'. Such children will often be able to read fluently; they may even be 'hyperlexic' (i.e. they have an almost compulsive drive to read whatever written material appears in front of them), but they will not be able to *relate* the text they have read to some obvious situations.

They have a strong tendency to take words literally. One example is a boy of 12 to whom the teacher had explained something. She finished her explanations with the question: 'Is it clear now?' The pupil's serious response was to look out of the window to find out whether the sky was clear.

In their early years such children might attract the clinician's attention because of an obvious lack of ability to join in symbolic play. Later they will stand out because of their inability to understand even the simplest joke. They seem unable to grasp any 'let's pretend' situation, whether it be explicit as in role-play or implicit as in literature. They seem to live in a dreamlike situation, where the details are exact and clear but where the parts fail to relate in a meaningful way.

In number work they may excel in learning mechanical number procedures. They will have no problems when asked to do 'sums' with the numbers written in the conventional vertical arrangement. If the same sum is written horizontally (325 + 250), however, they will not know what to do. A child may have been using written methods of addition successfully for some time, but one day he will interpret '11' as '2'. In general, such children will have difficulty in applying acquired number skills to new situations.

Delay in language development

Children with a severe delay in language development form another large group of language-impaired children who may show signs of bewilderment when dealing with symbols used in elementary mathematics. Unless they are introduced very carefully to the most commonly used symbols, they could give up trying to understand mathematics at a very early age.

These children usually give a general impression of being uninterested. This may take various forms depending on the temperament of the specific child. They may react with anxious attempts just to please the teacher, carefully trying to do as they are told but showing by their mistakes that they do not understand the meaning of their work; they may show signs of fatigue the moment number work starts; they may try to 'leave the field' and let themselves be distracted; or they may protest in more dramatic forms. In general, things don't seem to make sense to them, and this feeling may become automatically linked to any further mathematical activity.

Such children have probably not reached a stage of language development where they can use word labels sufficiently well in a symbolic way. They may, for instance, be able to understand that one can label a door, a chair, a ball (i.e. things that can be touched), but they may have difficulties in understanding how one can label an *action*, like 'adding' or 'taking away'.

CRITICAL POINTS IN THE ELEMENTARY MATHEMATICAL SYLLABUS

The following is a discussion of points in the early mathematics syllabus where a lack of symbolic understanding has been shown to lead to difficulties. These are:

> the diverse use of number words in the child's pre-school experience;
> the written recording of number work;
> place value and 'zero';
> relational signs: 'plus', 'minus', 'equal(s)';
> moncy;
> time.

The Diverse Use of Number Words in the Child's Pre-school Experience

What are the problems?

'False friends'

Recent research suggests the possibility that children are born with an innate sense of number, partly shared with animals, which enables them to count with a system that does not rely on the positional relationship of number words (Starkey, Spelke and Gelman, 1990; Wynn, 1992a,b; cf. also Donlan, 1993). Thus they may be equipped with a counting system very different from the one they are trying to learn (at school or before).

Also, on a level easier to observe, a child will hardly ever start school mathematics without previously having encountered some number words or number figures in all kinds of 'strange' contexts.

These two factors may turn out to be 'false friends'. In the first case children will have difficulty in accommodating their own, more global and non-verbal working symbol system into the dawning new system of verbal school counting – which is 'surely not a trivial process', as Wynn (1992c) says. And in the second case their previous encounters with number words will have occurred in situations which are also hard to relate to school counting: they may, for instance, know that one can 'live' in a number because one can live in Number 5; that one can 'go along' a number because one can go along the M6 motorway, and that one can even 'be' a number because one can be five. All this will make it difficult for them to understand the use of numbers in a specific mathematical sense, as labels for a certain quantity.

The counting game

The child may be able to sing a happy number song: 'One, two, three-four-five, once I caught a fish alive' where the expression, 'one, two, three' is probably no more to him than 'eenie, meenie, minie, mo' (cf. Ginsburg, 1989: 23). He may even have learned the 'counting game', which means, from his point of view, 'one says something (like "one-two-three") and one points to some things (preferably lined-up things)'. This game can lead, perhaps to the child's surprise, to extraordinary adult approval as long as one follows a set pattern. This pattern must not be changed, otherwise approval will change to one of those strange signs of disapproval that adults sometimes show: you don't jump into puddles; you hold your knife in the right hand; and after three comes four, always. It all seems unreasonable, but such is life for a young child. He may be left entirely on his own to work out the connection between the M6 motorway you travel along and the six he has to say after five and before seven.

Shifts of meaning

Most children can learn this 'counting game' quite well. But one day someone will ask 'how many?' The child may understand this as being just another counting-song task, but one where the last word matters. He might not realize that now he is expected to think of 'the lot' (numerosity). Assuming that there are four items to count, the person who has asked the question is now thinking of the last number in the counting sequence ('four') as a symbol for the value of the whole set, the 'total'. This means she is thinking in terms of the 'cardinality principle' (Gelman and Gallistel, 1978) rather than of the 'counting' or 'ordinal' meaning. But the child is still playing the counting game. At best, if he has used the counting game in connection with objects to point to, this may have given him some understanding of the stable sequence of counting words and the ordinal aspects. A shift from the established meaning of 'four' to a new and more complex meaning has to take place, all with the same symbol. This shift, the 'count-cardinal transition' (Fuson and Hall, 1983: 66), seems to be a real stumbling block for a child with a weakness in symbolic understanding; and it is not difficult to see why (cf. Fuson, 1991).

As already seen above, some uses of numbers must seem totally unrelated to a child. For instance, he might be expected to reply with 'five' to the question 'how many?' as well as to the question 'how old are you?' With 'how many?' he is supposed to consider a quantity of countable items in front of him and 'figure it out'; with 'how old are you?' he has to produce a memorized label because in no way can he think of past early years as countable items. Other uses will perhaps seem more related, such as counting (while pointing) up to a number and then naming the last number to satisfy the adult who asked 'how many?' However, the fact that here the two aspects (ordinal and cardinal) are linked in one activity can actually make matters more difficult in learning and teaching (cf. Piaget, 1952). For the child, it makes the difference less obvious: he uses one label for two different meanings; and for the teacher, the need for special teaching measures may be underestimated. Dantzig (1962: 8) has pointed out that we have learned to pass from one aspect of number to the other with such ease that the two aspects appear as one.

> For a full list and discussion of five diverse meanings of number words see Fuson and Hall (1983). For a lucid description of five counting principles (including the cardinality principle) see Gelman and Gallistel (1978: 77ff.); for a discussion of some of those principles see Bryant (1995: 10ff.) and Nunes and Bryant (1996: 23ff.).

Where to start

The first thing to realize is that problems exist and that they need special attention. In general, there seems to be a preference in Britain and America for number sequence and counting strategies in the early stages of mathematics. By contrast, central-European, east-European and Japanese traditions emphasize such aspects as quantity and 'subitizing' (i.e. the ability to recognize and to label small quantities without counting). In other words, they emphasize the cardinal aspect (cf. various chapters in Carpenter, Moser and Romberg, 1982; Hatano, 1982: 221; section 7 in Durkin and Shire, 1991; Bierhoff, 1996: 20).

The Anglo-American tradition of emphasizing counting strategies at the beginning normally makes the child at the pre- and infant-school level very familiar with counting rhymes, with finger counting, and the pointing/counting game. Thus the child's attention is drawn to the position of a number in the number line (i.e. to the sequential and ordinal aspect of number). However, this aspect may cognitively be more difficult than the cardinal aspect: the latter may be nearer to his 'innate' counting system; also it only involves matching a certain number symbol to a certain quantity, whereas the former involves, or should involve, matching *and* ordering of a quantity in a simultaneous action.

'Four' as a quantity can stand on its own; 'four' in the number line must come after three and before five (cf. Piaget, 1952). Furthermore, ordinal number names 'proper' ('sixth' as contrasted with 'six') are morphologically more complex, with their added suffix '-th', and this may be taken as an indication of a later development in history (Clark and Clark, 1977: 537).

I have suggested above that working with the ordinal aspect of number should involve *matching* as well as counting. When counting activities are limited to a verbal process that focuses on position (one says 'four' and points to 'the fourth'), as often happens, there is no matching between quantity and symbol: the child touches his chin with four different fingers and stops; or he points to the 'one-two-three-' fourth object lined up; or he points to the fourth symbol in the number line and forgets about the rest. This means that he uses the cardinal number word for what is strictly speaking an ordinal identification task. Even worse, if a child *does* think of a quantity when he arrives at the target number, it may be the wrong one (i.e. 'n − 1'). He may still be aware of 'three' (of the objects he has counted; or, on the number line, of the numerals to his left) while he covers the fourth with his chubby finger. Thus a child will chant 'four' and perceive 'three'. No wonder that one of the most common mistakes in adding and subtracting, when counting strategies are used, is a mistake by 'plus-or-minus-one' (cf. Starkey and Gelman, 1982; see also the section on teaching various number sequences in Chapter 3 below).

How can we help?

I suggest – keeping in mind the child who has difficulties with the simplest symbolic representations – that one starts teaching number by concentrating on the *cardinal* aspect, where the relationship between the linguistic form and the content is relatively simple and unambiguous: one says 'four' and one thinks of a 'set' of four. If the theories about an innate pre-verbal and more global counting system can be accepted, such a start might also be the way to link the two systems (cf. Grauberg, 1995: 42ff.).

This means that counting and the number line are set aside for a while. The initial task of teaching is to provide opportunities in which the child can become entirely familiar with a number symbol as it relates to *one* aspect of number – quantity (cf. Davydov, 1982; for a discussion of counting and the number line see Chapter 3 of this book).

Working with non-specific quantities and 'subitizing'

Before precisely specified quantities like 'three' or 'four' are introduced, it may be useful to work (or better still, 'to play about') with large non-specific quantities (e.g. 'a little bit', 'a few', 'a lot', 'the lot'). Working with such quantities will establish the habit of viewing a quantity and making a global numerical judgment about it without an attempt to count. This will perhaps foster the useful habit of 'subitizing' – of looking at a quantity *as a whole* when trying to determine its numerosity.

> The term 'subitizing' is derived from the Latin word 'subitus' (meaning 'sudden') and is related to the Italian word 'subito' (meaning 'immediately'). It was first used by Kaufman, Lord, Reese and Volkman (1949). An everyday example of subitizing would be: you need five glasses, you see four glasses on the table and know immediately that one is missing. Subitizing is normally more accurate and done with more confidence than estimating. The drawback is that it only works for small numbers, i.e. for *'The magical number 7, plus or minus 2'* (a memorable title of a paper by Miller, 1956 who used subitizing as one task among others when investigating the limits of information processing in humans). More recently, subitizing has been defined as 'the rapid preverbal or nonverbal estimation of numerosity' and as such includes the animal counting mechanism. (Gallistel and Gelman, 1993: 58; Dehaene, 1993; for a detailed analysis of the processes involved in subitizing see Mandler and Shebo, 1982.)

A well established habit of subitizing or looking at quantities as wholes will prove its usefulness later when cardinal meaning is introduced with the first specific quantities, namely those labelled with the number words 'one' to 'ten'.

The most natural way of learning the concept and vocabulary of quantity is perhaps to start with common non-count quantities like 'a little (bit of) water', 'a lot of sand'. This serves as a preparation for the next step: the use of non-specified quantities of countable items, like beans (a bag full), pumpkin pips (a heap of), leaves (masses of), shells (a lot of), wooden bricks (a few), little cubes (all, the lot), rods (some). At this stage, all materials are presented to the child in an unordered mass, and gradually, in a top-down way, the child will be led to the creation of order and to the specification of small subitized quantities: making a single line with beans (taking 'one' at a time), a double line (taking 'two' at a time) and so forth (see Chapter 2). Thus (allowing for some overlap) the didactic sequence is roughly:

(a) non-count quantities (e.g. some water);
(b) non-specified countable quantities (e.g. some beans);
(c) specified small (subitized) quantities (e.g. two, four counters).

The first step (i.e. experience with non-count quantities like sand, water and mashed potatoes in various amounts) will normally take place in pre-school years and perhaps all that is needed is extended vocabulary work. Therefore I will go straight to the second step.

Large non-specified countable quantities

This step needs large quantities of counters. Any counters can be used; the greater the variety, the better: new materials will make the situation new for children even if the mathematical task is the same.

Teaching at this stage will mainly consist of asking the child to pick out an imprecisely qualified quantity (e.g. putting 'a few beans in each pot', making 'a lot of heaps', 'getting some bricks each'). A detailed description of a lesson ('a few' 'a lot' 'the lot') is provided in Unit 1 to exemplify how such work can be done with emphasis on concept- and vocabulary-learning.

Two questions may arise. Firstly, is it a good idea to introduce related terms like 'a few' and 'a lot' together? We all know children with labelling problems who say 'tomorrow' when they mean 'yesterday' and who may say 'a few' when they mean 'a lot'. This is a rather fundamental point. I do not believe that introducing one word-meaning in isolation is always the best way – not even for children with language difficulties. We want the child to learn concepts, not just vocabulary. For this we need a backcloth of relational understanding. Concept formation involves isolating particular features of the concept from other features. One has to recognize boundaries, which means one needs to have something else in mind with which to link or contrast a newly learned word. When that is done, however, a consolidating period ought to follow where one term is practised at a time. Taking time over this step is particularly important with language-impaired children. Only after that, when all concepts and word labels involved are well established, can they be linked again. Thus *understanding* takes place in whole situations; *practice* is carried out element by element.

The second question relating to the teaching of non-specific quantities is whether there is an optimum sequence in which to introduce them. One criterion could be the order in which they appear in the speech of young children. For instance, 'some' appears much earlier than 'few' in frequency lists of words used by young children (Burroughs, 1970; Edwards and Gibbon, 1973). Another criterion is the experience gained by practitioners. For instance, a syllabus developed by teachers and speech therapists working in a school for language-impaired children included suggestions about the order in which to introduce non-specific quantities (for an adaptation of this syllabus see Unit 1; cf. also Hutt, 1986: 129, who lists 'all', 'some', 'more' and 'no' as the first basic quantity words she herself used in mathematical work with language-impaired children).

In the end, however, one hopes that teachers will appreciate both the usefulness of acquisition research and other teachers' experience without feeling constrained to follow them rigidly. I have found, for example, that in certain respects 'a few' with its limited reference to countable items, was easier to teach than 'some' with its broader, and therefore more ambiguous, over-used meanings (you can have 'a few bricks' but not 'a few sand'; you can have 'some bricks' as well as 'some sand'). As in the lesson described in Unit 1, it is often the particular classroom situation that determines what ought to be introduced next. Thus, if a situation lends itself to the introduction of 'the lot', one ought to make use of the situation and at least try teaching 'the lot' there and then. The chances are that a child will be able to learn a concept in a situation which is meaningful and emotionally satisfying, even if it is not strictly speaking the 'next step' in the order found through acquisition research.

Introducing specific quantities (1 to 10) as 'entities'

Let us remind ourselves: we are trying to help children who have problems with understanding number symbols. We are especially concerned that such children should learn to connect certain word labels which they may have used (or may have heard being used) in non-specific ways, with a specific mathematical meaning. We want the children to understand the cardinal number concept first, as the basis for further number work. This may mean discouraging the use of counting on the number line, since all too often this leads to perceiving a point in space rather than a quantity; or, worse, it may lead to verbal chanting devoid of any quantity meaning.

I suggest that specific quantities could be introduced by treating each number as an entity, a 'thing *per se*', rather than as a quantity which occupies a fixed position on the number line. For the time being, and with the asymbolic child in mind, I suggest treating a quantity as one would treat an apple, a door, or a car when a child is learning to speak and to read (i.e. as a 'thing' with certain properties, something that can be put in front of the child and that can be labelled). I am aware that, to some extent, one runs the risk of neglecting the abstract nature of a number by linking it too closely to a concrete quantity, but this seems a necessary first step. Martin Hughes (1986: 45) reports an interview with a boy called Ram (4 years 7 months) which illustrates this point well:

MH: What is three and one more? How many is three and one more?
Ram: Three and what? One what? Letter? I mean number?
      [We had earlier been playing a game with magnetic numerals and
      Ram is presumably referring to them here.]
MH: How many is three and one more?
Ram: One more what?
MH: Just one more, you know?
Ram: (Disgruntled) I *don't* know.

Only much later, after extensive activities with numbers in a variety of contexts, will the child be able to grasp the powerful abstract qualities of a number – which means the concept of 'two-ness', 'three-ness', 'n-ness'. Through his experience with many different materials, we want him to see what is common to all (the fact that there are, for instance, 'two' of each) and we want him to learn to ignore what is irrelevant (e.g. size, colour, feel).

The first number concept to be established after 'one' and the general 'more-than-one' ought probably to be 'two' – which means the basic concept of duality. We are thereby following the progression from the singular to the general plural and then on to the dual, a progression which is actually reflected in the grammatical forms of some foreign languages (cf. Clark and Clark, 1977: 537).

The teaching materials needed are unordered masses of different counters. These should be ordered by the child into long rows of pairs.

This activity ought to be repeated frequently, with different counters. Although doing the same thing over and over again may seem an unrewarding, repetitive task to an adult, in my experience the young child will not see it as such, as long as the materials are sufficiently varied. The teacher knows that the child is doing 'the same' in relation to her teaching objective, but for the child this is a different matter. Lining up cubes and lining up beans are different activities. The cubes are made of wood and feel like it; they have different bright colours and they stay nicely in their place where one puts them. Beans, however, are nothing like cubes. They have subtle colours with funny freckles; they have strange shapes; they feel slippery and tend to swivel and slide off their place. What a difference!

While the child is busy with these lining-up tasks, it is the role of the teacher (or other carer) to provide the verbal label 'two' over and over again. The most natural situation in which to do this seems to me the following: the teacher sits down with the children and joins in the fun; she too has a mass of counters and lines them up, constantly saying 'two, two'. At the same time she keeps an eye on the children and encourages them to take 'two in one go' rather than counting 'one, two', hoping that they will join in the chant 'two, two...' spontaneously. If not, the teacher can encourage them. In my experience there is nothing more enjoyable and probably nothing more effective than when the teacher outwardly gives up her role as an instructor and sits down with the children to join the activity, thereby providing a happy model. The effectiveness of teaching in such a situation seems almost proportional to the fun the teacher or carer can get out of the activity herself.

Through such activities one hopes that the label 'two' and the specific quantity 'two' will become linked, and that the concept of 'two' will become established first and foremost as a unit consisting of a certain verbal symbol and a certain quantity. In the end the children will have met the quantity meaning of 'two' more often than any other meaning. Thus the cardinal meaning of 'two' will become a familiar one, against which all the other diverse uses will seem exceptions.

The next practical step would probably be to introduce the number 'four' as the double of 'two': we are joining two pairs of counters. In accordance with the principle that one ought to introduce each number as an entity there is no need to go up the number scale, one by one, incrementally. The next number to introduce after 'four' could be 'eight', which means that one goes up the 'doubling line' rather than the conventional 'plus one' line (the latter must seem rather dull to a child with its monotonous adding of a miserable 'one'. Who at that age cares about unexciting small changes?) For more suggestions on how the first numbers may be introduced as entities rather than by the incremental 'plus one' sequence of the number line, see Chapter 3 and Unit 2.

The Written Recording of Number Work

So far we have concerned ourselves solely with the concept and the spoken number word. After all, as Karl Friedrich Gauss (1777–1855) said, it is 'not notations but notions' that matter (Stewart, 1995: 33). It will, however, become necessary or convenient to introduce written symbols at some stage. This is another critical point in the syllabus of elementary mathematics which again will have to be done with great care when working with children who have difficulties in symbolic understanding.

What are the problems?

His birthday card

A child, on his fifth birthday, may be introduced to written number symbols by a card with a pretty '5' on it. This is one of his 'false friends' he would have been better without. It may confuse him and be actually harmful to the learning process. What can he make of this strange combination of lines? He can hardly be expected to link it to a 'quantity' of years, most of which are blurred or completely lost from memory anyway.

Where is the 'f' in '5'?

Systematic school introduction to written number symbols may come at the same time as he is learning to write and to read. He may have just grasped the enormous idea that some combinations of rather uninteresting lines (letters) can stand for something else – something as juicy as 'apple' or as fascinating as 'tractor'. Now he has to cope with an additional set of symbols, number figures. And the more the child has already understood of the sound/symbol relation of letters, the more puzzling the number symbols must be. After all, where is the 'f' in '5' (Flegg, 1983: 281)?

The abstract nature of our Hindu-Arabic number symbols

Moreover, the number system to be introduced to the children is the sophisticated Hindu-Arabic system, invented for efficiency rather than for understanding. It is a brilliant but relatively late development that arose from the need for fast computations. This makes it highly inadequate as a teaching tool at the early stage, where one wants to introduce a child to general concepts of quantity and to very natural simple forms of computation. One is dealing here with a clash of two different stages of development: the child is at the beginning of his mathematical development, whereas the system is the result of centuries of sophistication. Thus it seems wrong to impose on children such a system which may be potentially more efficient but which they, at their stage of cognitive development, will find hard to understand (cf. Collins, 1982: 181).

There are other systems of recording numbers which seem superior for teaching. They also employ symbols, but iconic symbols, where there is still a visible relationship between sign and quantity. They are 'nearer to life' and can be seen as an intermediate step from the concrete to the abstract. As such they provide an almost indispensable help for children with problems in symbolic understanding.

How can we help?

Using written number words

My first suggestion might strike some readers as an odd detour, especially for children who have reading/writing difficulties and is certainly not advisable for all children. Nevertheless, it may make sense for *children with a weakness in symbolic understanding* to go directly from the spoken number word, with which the child is already familiar, to its written equivalent: instead of *saying* 'four' we *write* 'f-o-u-r', we spell it out just as we would spell 'car' 'c-a-r'.

Thus one treats a quantity in a familiar way: there is a written word for 'car', and there is a written word for a quantity of four. The children will become familiar with the notion that a quantity, like everything else, can be labelled in writing. And, as a welcome sideeffect, they will learn to read and write some useful words which they are bound to need in future work.

Early matching exercises, where a quantity is matched with a written symbol, can be carried out using word cards with 'four' rather than '4'. Using written number words for computation is of course highly impractical, but for the time being the children are not expected to do arithmetic. We are just trying to make them thoroughly familiar with the 'tools of the trade' – which are quantities. Only when children are thought ready to do more formal arithmetic should they be introduced to the use of conventional number figures.

These will then be recognized as a convenient kind of 'shorthand'. Some difficulty with mathematical symbols seems to diminish when the newcomer to the system experiences a *need* for a particular symbol (cf. Buxton, 1982: 219).

Exercises like

- matching quantity to quantity (e.g. four cubes to four dots)
- matching quantity to a written number word (e.g. four cubes to 'four') and later
- matching quantity to a number figure (e.g. four cubes to '4')

can all be practised again and again in a game which has proved very popular with quite an age range of children and is described as the 'ruler-game' in Unit 3.

Tallying

Another suggestion for work at this early stage of learning to write down number work is the use of non-Hindu-Arabic symbol systems. One such system is tallying. Others include counting rods, abaci and hieroglyphs.

Tallying is probably the most basic form of recording quantities and their changes. It can be done in many ways, with wooden bricks, sticks, straws, notches, knots, play matches, lines in sand and finally with lines on paper.

The main rule to observe is that one always tallies *something*, that is to say: something other than tally-sticks or tally-lines. Strange uses like II + II = IIII are to be avoided. There is no need for operational symbols like '+' and '='. Tallying is an additive system *per se*: if one adds an item, one just records it by adding a tally token.

This means that there should always be some items to be tallied, like the bunches of bananas on a ship (use, if you like, a recording of the fine and by now almost classic song by Harry Belafonte: 'Come Mr Tallyman, tally me bananas' when working with older children). Items to be tallied in the classroom could be chairs, tables, bottles of milk or smaller items; practically anything will do, and the more unusual it is the more fun it will be. Tallying activities could include:

- shells (How many broken ones? How many perfect ones? How many altogether? How many have you got? How many do I have?)
- kitchen roll middles, some cut in half (How many long ones? How many shorter ones? How many altogether?)

- How many sunny days in a term?
- How many bangs on the drum?

With the last two items one introduces a new concept: that of recording something in time rather than in space. Theoretically, this should pose problems. One is now dealing with fleeting matter, instead of something concrete that can be seen and touched. In practice, however, I have not experienced many problems when the recording of time events was introduced in the context of tallying. Any difficulty that arose seemed to be linked to a short memory span rather than to a lack of understanding time events as countable items.

Recording with tally-sticks or tally-lines should, in the end, be standardized by having the fifth tally cross the four preceding lines, either diagonally or horizontally (see Figure 1.1). Five thus becomes one's first larger unit of measure. Five seems a good number (a) because of the natural link to five fingers; (b) because it is half of ten and therefore a 'natural anchor point' in the decimal system (for five as a 'privileged anchor' cf. Yoshida and Kuriyama, 1991); and (c) because it is probably the largest quantity even a weaker child can recognize all at once (Miller, 1956).

If one then establishes the habit of always pairing two 'bundles of five' by writing them next to each other, one introduces 'ten' as a unit and thus prepares the child for our base-ten system. Twenty-eight would, for instance, be represented by groupings of 'five-five' (ten), 'five-five' (another ten) and a bundle of five plus three singles (8) (see Figure 1.1). Arranged in this way, the representation of a quantity can be seen and determined as a whole without counting. In other words, it can be subitized.

Figure 1.1: Quantity of 28 represented with tally-lines

Using a selection of coloured rods

Tallying can be followed and extended by work with a *selection* of coloured rods (e.g. Cuisenaire rods, Colour Factor rods, Stern rods;

see Unit 3). Thus one uses a recording system which is not historical like tallying, but which stems from requirements of teaching mathematics. Using at this stage only white 1 cm cubes ('ones'), yellow 5 cm rods ('fivers') and orange 10 cm rods ('tenners') one can again show 'five' in a privileged position. The selection corresponds to the tallying system of single lines (1), bundles (5), and pairs of bundles (10). It introduces the basic idea, so important later for understanding and handling money, that one can have a token which stands for more than one (a 'fiver' for five singles, a 'tenner' for two 'fives').

Now the children can learn the essential procedure of changing a group of small units into a bigger unit and vice versa (five white ones into one yellow 'five'; or two yellow 'fives' into one orange 'ten'). They will soon see the advantages of this: instead of building up an 'eight' with small fiddly one-cubes, they can take a yellow fiver and only have to bother with three small fiddly one-cubes. The abstract notion of a new 'token' will thus not bewilder the children but will make practical sense.

At this stage, recording some number work on paper could be done, if one so wishes, by using coloured pencils (yellow and orange). However, it should not just be a 'keep-them-occupied' activity: its purpose should be made clear to them: we write down what we have, so that we can refer to it later, which at this stage will probably mean 'to show Mum and Dad'.

A representation of 28 with these rods will look as shown in Figure 1.2 (for a full description of Cuisenaire rods and similar materials, together with suggestions for use and organization, see Unit 3).

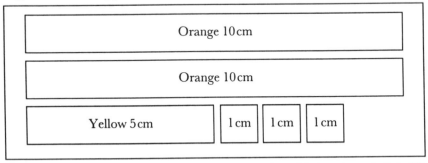

Figure 1.2: Quantity of 28 represented with a selection of Cuisenaire rods (1, 5, 10)

Introducing the structured 'field of 100' (Slavonic abacus)

To advance beyond Cuisenaire rods one can use the beads of a Slavonic abacus as tallies. Here 100 single beads are presented simultaneously as a structured 'field of 100' with groups of five and ten. The child can record any number up to 100 by pushing a bead or a group of beads to the other side. A representation of 28 on the

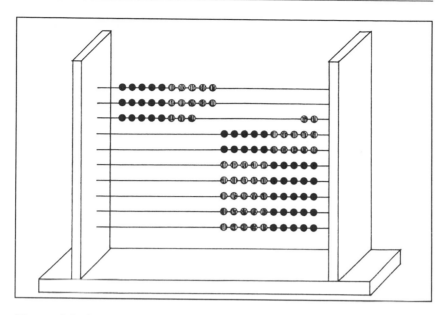

Figure 1.3: Quantity of 28 represented on the Slavonic abacus

Slavonic abacus will look as shown in Figure 1.3. Note the change of colour after five in both directions, an essential feature for instant recognition of quantities, but one which is hardly ever found in bead frames supplied by British firms. I will refer to this apparatus again and again. For a detailed description and suggestions of work with the Slavonic abacus see Unit 4.

If one wanted a more permanent record of a quantity tallied on the Slavonic abacus, teachers or children could translate the number shown on the abacus into a 'quantity picture' (see Figure 1.4). For work with 'quantity pictures' see Unit 4. Unit 4 also provides a description of how to make and work with a 'paper abacus', which is

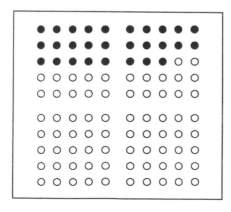

Figure 1.4: Quantity picture representing 28

an easily-made adaptation of the Slavonic abacus. For 'field of 100' work in all its forms see Chapter Two.

Using hieroglyphic symbols of ancient Egypt

A last suggestion for introducing developmentally suitable ways of recording quantities is to use the hieroglyphic system of ancient Egypt. This is another historical tool and has been found especially useful for older pupils who show a weakness in symbolic understanding and who have developed a feeling of failure when working with numbers: it provides them with a new start. Such a system puts mathematics into the context of history and geography and can thus raise the prestige of rather basic mathematical activities that might otherwise be rejected as 'baby stuff'.

The main advantage of this system is that the signs relate to the quantity which they represent. Moreover, the system can record even very high numbers without a place value and without the need for 'zero'. The shape of these symbols shows their charming origin (see Figure 1.5): 1000 is represented by a lotus flower, 100 by a coil of rope, 10 by a horseshoe-shaped cattle hobble and 1 by a tally-stick (cf. Menninger, 1969: 42 and 121; also Katan, 1985).

If the pupils are already familiar in a mechanical fashion with recording quantities through the Hindu-Arabic number system (i.e. our 'normal' way), one can use both systems simultaneously for some time by 'translating' from one system into the other and vice versa. The advantage of such a parallel use of both systems – one of which is more familiar but abstract, and the other new but more concrete – is that pupils are constantly reminded of the quantity they are record-

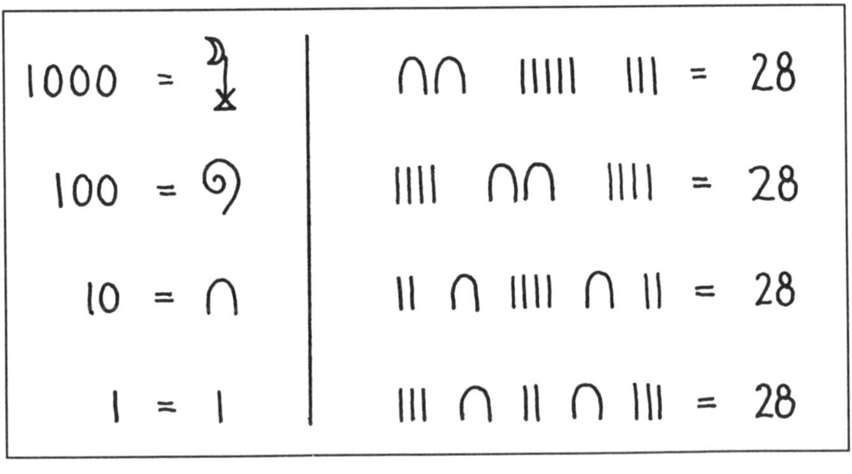

Figure 1.5: Hieroglyphic number symbols and some possible representations of 28

ing; they are not left at this critical learning stage with 'empty' signs which bear no visible relation to the quantity they represent. Detailed suggestions for work with hieroglyphic symbols (recording, matching, 'translating' as well as simple arithmetic) are given in Unit 3.

Place Value and 'Zero'

What are the problems?

'Place' as a sign for 'power'

So far we have dealt with signs which could be 'handled' or at least be written and be seen written. The idea of using 'place' as a symbol, is a major step forward into the abstract. In elementary mathematics 'place value' seems to be one of the last core concepts to be understood by learners. During the Second World War, Luria (1969) studied patients whose ability to work with numbers had been affected by localized forms of brain damage. He came to the conclusion that the concepts most likely to suffer first were those which had been acquired last; the ability to use 'place value' was among the very first losses such patients experienced (1969: 47).

Using 'place' as a 'value' is an extremely useful feature of advanced number systems, but it is a feature which one can only appreciate after working with cumbersome simpler systems first or when one has gained considerable experience and insight into the very abstract systems which use place value. Neither of these two conditions applies to a young child or to an older child lacking in symbolic understanding. Such children may well be bewildered by 'place' as a symbol of specific value, especially if a child is still at an age where he takes his teddy to bed with him: after all, his teddy does not acquire a sudden power of ten just by being shifted from one side to the other.

In our number system the use of place value starts with number 10. It seems incredible that we let children go straight on to 10 once they have learned to read and write the numbers 1 to 9, and that we get them to write the figure 10 using 1 and 0, as if there was nothing special about this and 10 was just another number. Unfortunately, verbally 'ten' is of course just another number; so are eleven and twelve. The English language does not reflect the structure of the system in the 'teens' (if we used 'system words' we would have to say 'onety, onety-one and onety-two' etc.) as, for instance, the Welsh, the Japanese and the Chinese languages do. In Welsh the counting system that is normally used (except for time, dates and age, where there is a special traditional counting system) follows the principle of ten, one-ten-one (11) one-ten-two (12) and so forth (Griffiths, 1982). This is similar to the Japanese and Chinese (ten-one = 11, ten-two = 12, etc.; cf. Hatano, 1982; Fuson and Kwon, 1991; Nunes and Bryant, 1996 : 45 ff.). In all cases 'ten' is given special recognition through the way it is used for the expression of the decimal system (for 'system words' see Unit 2).

The specific problems that can arise from an auditory confusion between the suffixes '-ty' and '-teen' are discussed in the section on weakness in auditory discrimination in Chapter 4.

Historically, as long as imperial measurements were used in England, there may have been some justification for ignoring the special significance of 'ten', since 'ten' does not carry a special function in the imperial system. If we want the child to understand and benefit from the *decimal* system, however, it seems essential to point out the special significance of ten as our normal 'measure' or 'base' unit, reflected in writing by the special combination of signs already used previously ('1' and '0' in a fixed order) rather than by a new sign.

However, at this stage children have often not yet been introduced to the zero sign. Even if this has been done and they know that a sign exists which looks like the letter 'O' and tells them that one 'hasn't got anything', are they then ready for 'number 10'? The answer is 'no': this knowledge does not help them when '1' and '0' are situated next to each other with a special place value meaning. For the child, 'one' (1) and 'nothing' (0) add up to 'one' (1); likewise, 1 (one 'stick') next to another 1 (another 'stick') makes 2 'sticks'; so why should 11 not make 2? (Or, as Eric, a 13-year-old boy of normal intelligence with asymbolic features asked: 'What's wrong with $1024 - 10 = 24$?').

'Zero' as a sign for 'nothing'

Understanding of the zero sign involves two aspects (cf. Hughes, 1986: 89). The first is that the child has to learn that it symbolizes the state of 'no quantity at hand', which is a unique state. Theoretically a quantity of nought is not very different from a quantity of – let us say – three: there is only a difference in magnitude, and both quantities exist among many possible ones. In practical terms, however, the situation is not so 'simple' for a child who is not likely to think in abstract terms.

Talking about a quantity of 'zero' does not make sense unless there is another quantity. There is no point in thinking of just 'nothing'. Thus the state of 'no quantity at hand' always goes together with an expectation that this state will change, or that there is another set which can be compared with the 'empty set' (labelled 'zero'). In other words, we can't have zero without context – at least not in elementary mathematics. If children have worked with the number line and have a mental representation of it, they will learn to think about zero as being a place on the very left of this line – the position before the 'start'.

The second, more difficult aspect of zero is that it is used as a place holder in a multi-digit number, as a signifier for the 'empty column'. In a place value system the same sign is used for units of different 'power', which makes the recording of such a system probably the most difficult and most critical point in early mathematics.

Moreover, the need for a zero sign only becomes obvious when the whole decimal system has been understood, which assumes familiarity with the numbers from 1 to 100 at least. Therefore children who are advancing in their number knowledge from 9 to 10 and then to 20 will have to work with a symbol whose usefulness evades them and whose significance is often not explained to them. Historically, 'zero' is a relatively late development. Pythagoras and his contemporaries – old and young – lived and thought and worked happily without it. It only became necessary when computation was done within the place value system and a symbol was needed for the 'empty column' (cf. Dantzig, 1962; Flegg, 1983).

Young children with difficulties in symbolic understanding may be able to use the sign for zero when they learn to work in a mechanical way with numbers from 1 to 20. This, however, should not lead us to assume that they have an understanding of zero. After all, 'zero' entails the understanding of a symbol which has the paradoxical function of being 'something that must be there to say that nothing is there' (Menninger, 1969: 400); it is a sign that literally 'signifies nothing'. Who has ever seen children – creatures of the 'here and now' – being interested in 'nothing'?

How can we help?

Delaying written work

The first suggestion is to delay written work generally, and certainly to avoid writing down anything with figures from our Hindu-Arabic decimal system, for as long as possible. I am thinking of years rather than months when dealing with children who have difficulty in understanding symbols. In reality it will probably mean as long as the teacher can bear the situation and justify it convincingly to the parents. Such a delay will not be a loss but a beneficial gain in oral work. Skemp (1982: 287) writes:

> In these important early years, it helps if we stay longer with spoken language. The connection between thought and spoken words is initially

much stronger than those between thoughts and written words or symbols. Spoken words are also much quicker and easier to produce. So, in the early years of learning mathematics, we may need to resist pressures for children to have 'something to show' in the form of pages of written work.

This was written with children who have no special difficulties in mind; how much more important it seems for children who have problems with symbols.

Making the advantages of our conventional system obvious

Delaying the use of conventional symbols does not mean that one will have to do without paper and pencil work. One can write down numbers with different 'transitional' methods that do not use place value (e.g. the hieroglyphic system mentioned above; or fully written number words if these are familiar; or systems invented by the children themselves). This can lead to an abundance of quite advanced mathematical activities. In the end, after having happily laboured with safe and easy but cumbersome systems, our conventional way of recording may be introduced as the brilliant time- and effort-saving invention it really is.

Using different familiar systems in parallel with our conventional system

It is advisable to use two kinds of system for some time – like the hieroglyphic one and our conventional Hindu-Arabic one – in parallel. By comparing the two, children can gain insight into the advantages and disadvantages of each, and thus obtain a better understanding of the conventional one, which they are going to use in the end on a higher level. It also ensures that children still have a visible quantity/sign relationship in front of them – as a safety net in case they 'get lost' in the abstract. Adding let's say, 41 to 28 in the two systems will show that one system is 'safe', easy to check, visually attractive, but clumsy to operate, whereas the other system is elegant, time-saving like writing in shorthand, but rather risky because one can't actually *see* what one is doing (see Figure 1.6).

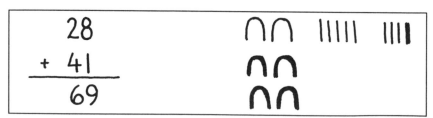

Figure 1.6: Adding 41 to 28 in two systems

In employing such methods, one is perhaps responding to Resnicks's still challenging conclusion that the way forward in mathematics instruction should be to devise methods that 'help students to explicitly link meaning and procedure' (1982: 136).

Using Roman numerals

Another suggestion relates more specifically to the understanding of place value. The use of place value in our system is especially sophisticated, since it depends on the place of a figure in a sequence of variable length. We can prepare children for this to some extent by first making them familiar with an easier place value system: that of the Roman numbers, which they may have seen on church towers or other clocks. Place value is handled here in a simpler way, since it has a fixed point of reference, a middle. It is based on units of one, five and ten. A unit sign put to the right means an increase, a sign to the left a decrease, so 4, 5, 6 are written IV, V, VI. Although being familiar with such a system will not help directly with understanding our conventional system, it will convey, in a very simple way, the fundamental idea that 'place' can be used to signify a value (cf. Grauberg, 1986).

Introducing zero with a game

Hughes has shown that under the right conditions children as young as 4 years can grasp the idea of a zero sign to label an 'empty set'. He describes the following experiment which I summarize (Hughes, 1986: 64 ff.). Four identical tins were filled with one, two, three, or no brick(s). These tins were mixed up and the children were asked to find the 'right one'. For instance, the experimenter asked them to find 'the tin with two bricks in'; or 'the tin with no bricks in'. First the children could just guess. Then they were allowed to make marks on the tins to help them to get the right answer. Thus they were encouraged to invent symbols. The marking of the 'no brick' tin varied from a 'default' response (no mark as opposed to one, two or three marks) through many different idiosyncratic responses, to the conventional sign for zero.

Games like this 'tin game' seem well suited for introducing 'zero' and guiding a child towards the idea that a sign for 'nothing' has its uses.

Using 'longhand' notation

Compared with the concept of nought as 'nothing', the second concept of nought as a 'place holder' in a place value system is not only difficult to understand but also very difficult to teach. For someone who knows the system, a written number like 204 makes sense and the function of the '0' in it is obvious. The trouble at the early stages of number work is that the child meets zero in the place value system when he does not yet know the system. Moreover, he meets it in a position where its use does not seem a compelling necessity, namely after learning '9' when the next number is labelled '10'.

Let us try to look at the problem naively. The child is introduced to the first two-digit number: 10. As far as he is concerned, this number could be represented by any other single symbol, since he is not familiar with the conventions of the written decimal system. The puzzling thing is probably not the nought, but the 1. He knows '1'. 'One what?' he may ask. Our answer will be: 'one ten' or, since one ought to have some concrete materials at hand, 'one long one' (Dienes rod, standing for 'ten'); or 'one big orange one' (Cuisenaire rod); or 'one row' on the Slavonic abacus; or 'one full column' in the Stern box (see Units 3 & 4 for a fuller discussion of the materials mentioned).

Let us presume that we are working with Dienes materials, limited for the time being to the following selection:

unit cubes (1 cm × 1 cm × 1 cm),
'longs' (10 cm × 1 cm × 1 cm), and
'flats' (10 cm × 10 cm × 1 cm).

Thus 'ten' can now be described as '1 long' and we can proceed as follows. We begin by asking: 'Do we need any little ones (1s)?' The answer would be: 'No, no little ones.' Then we write: '1 long – no little' in longhand.

The next step would be to follow the same procedure for 11: '1 long – 1 little'. Further steps could be:

21: '2 long – 1 little'
70: '7 long – no little'
99: '9 long – 9 little'.
Finally 100: '1 flat – no long – no little'.

This admittedly seems a very time-consuming way when one knows that there is a shorter way, but it seems to make sense to the naive child. If one is worried about time, this can also be seen as a good opportunity to practise handwriting and spelling of individual words like 'flat', 'long' and 'little' repeatedly and purposefully (preferably using joined-up handwriting right from the beginning; cf. Grauberg, 1985a).

Thus the idea that the 'bigger ones' are written on the left, and the 'little ones' on the right is being absorbed. After a period of recording numbers in this rather laborious 'longhand', I suggest that the teacher highlights the number figure in such combined notations by writing them in colour to make them stand out more. Thus our recording system vaguely emerges visually through the highlighted figures. This also seems the right time to change from the written word 'no' to the special sign '0' to which the child will probably have been introduced earlier as a sign for the empty set (see above). The conventional notation of numbers will thus be even more apparent.

In the end, the idea that one can do without most of the writing and shorten '2 long – 0 little' to 20, as long as one agrees that the figure representing the bigger measure is always recorded on the left, will be a welcome relief. Figure 1.7 gives a summary of the steps described.

(a)	2 long – 8 little
(b)	**2 long** – **8** little
(c)	2 —— – 8 ——
(d)	28

Figure 1.7: Summary of steps when introducing place value through 'longhand' notation

The convenience of using place to indicate a certain value will now hopefully dawn on the child. As his knowledge of the system as a whole extends through work with numbers beyond 100, he may increasingly appreciate the system. Thus it will not appear as something strange and bewildering which he knows he has to use although he cannot understand it, but as a clever invention to make things easy for him.

Superimposing multi-digit numbers

My next practical suggestions deal with recording larger numbers. How can we ensure that Eric, who wrote $1024 - 10 = 24$, develops a habit of checking his work by referring in his mind to the overall meaning of this notation? How can we avoid any loss of the full meaning which the dense mathematical notation conveys? Eric clearly had not visualized a quantity made up of a $1000 + 20 + 4$. He had thought of a 10 and a 24. I suspect that he was introduced to conventional written forms of computation much too early and that he spent too much time on them. Learning to add in the common way by writing two figures, one under the other, causes children to forget that they are dealing with thousands, hundreds and tens, because they are asked to treat them like one-digit numbers – like 'ones'.

Eric is not alone with his problem. Children with no handicap in dealing with symbols make similar mistakes, but mostly at an earlier age. Ginsburg (1989: 109), for instance, reports the case of Rebecca (7 years 3 months), who wrote 'fifty-three' as 503 (i.e. 50 and 3). Recent extensive investigations (see Nunes and Bryant, 1996: 66–75) clearly confirm that difficulties can be expected when non-impaired children of 5–7 years are asked to write multi-digit numbers. They follow the oral expression and write 1008 for 108; 10029 for 129. These are comparable mistakes to that of one of Luria's adult patients who wrote 1003 as 10003 (1969: 46).

Thus another problem becomes evident: there is a confusing discrepancy between what we say and what we write. Orally, we do not use a 'place-value' system but state the full term, for example 'fifty-three', meaning five tens and three. Mathematically, the order in this *oral* sequence does not matter. One can just as correctly say 'three and fif-ty', as was customary in former times and as is still done in German (sieben/und/zwanzig). In *writing*, however, we use sequence (or 'place') as a marker of value, which makes the '-ty' or 'ten' redundant but does not allow 53 to be substituted for 35. Again, this incongruity of symbols obviously calls for some special teaching methods that can ensure a firmer understanding of the links between 'what we mean', 'what we say' and 'what we write'.

One possible way to help pupils like Eric might be to counteract the loss of meaning right from the beginning by using an initial 'gimmick' (Grauberg, 1985). This involves the teacher writing what is said and what is meant 'over each other' and seems to work in most cases.

We might, for example, teach a child that '10' stands for 'one-ten and nothing more'; likewise '60' stands for 'six-tens (or six-ty) and nothing more', and '64' stands for 'six-ty and four'. So one writes the full 60 first and then writes the '4' into the nought – in other words one writes what one says (see Figure 1.8). After some time of writing figures in this way, the teacher suggests that the place-holding 'nought' should be written rather faintly so that the '4' can be seen more clearly. As a next step it will not be difficult to make the children agree that the two figures written one into the other look rather messy. Could one not just write an 'invisible' nought while saying 'ty'? One just goes through the *motion* of writing a nought, but leaves no mark on the paper. After all, that's what 'grown-ups' do. The last step, which is dropping the motion as well as the writing, will happen at different times with different children. Some children will drop the motion on their own accord, because they have grasped the convenient 'trick'. Some will go on for some time writing an invisible nought while saying 'ty'; at some stage they may have to be made aware of the fact that one can do without it since it leaves no visible mark anyway. But some will have to be *encouraged* to keep on writing 'invisible noughts' for their own sake for some time, as a reminder to think of '60 and 4' rather than '6 and 4'.

The same method can then be applied with relative ease when numbers with more than two digits are first encountered. For 4321 one:

- first writes 4000, perhaps checking the number of noughts by saying four-thousand, no-hundred, no-ten, no-unit;
- then one writes 300 'into the noughts' to get 4300;
- then one writes 20 into the remaining noughts to get 4320;
- and finally one writes 1 into the last nought to get 4321 (see Figure 1.8 for the different steps).

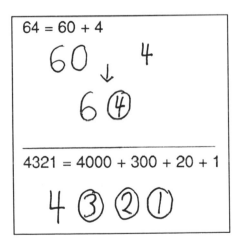

Figure 1.8: Superimposing multi-digit numbers (64; 4321)

This should be practised for some time, either in writing or with motions only, and kept fresh in the child's memory as a checking device for difficult numbers.

Using overlays for multi-digit numbers

The use of transparent overlays can reinforce the understanding of place value and is suggested as parallel work. As we have seen, special difficulties are caused by numbers such as 604, or Eric's 1024, where there is an 'empty column' which has to be marked by a space-holder – a 'nought'. I suggest making a set of small transparencies from clear acetate. Write one number on each: units, full tens, full hundreds and perhaps full thousands respectively. The numbers should be written in such a way that the same digit is in precisely the same position on all transparencies. For instance, if one had two transparencies with the numbers 400 and 40 and the first was overlaid by the second, the noughts in the unit-position would appear as one, the 4 of the 40 would cover the middle nought of the 400, and the 4 of the 400 would appear unchanged (for a detailed description of how to make such a set see Unit 4). If the writing of the numbers is done carefully, a number like 1024 can be made up by placing the relevant transparencies one over the other, as Figure 1.9 shows.

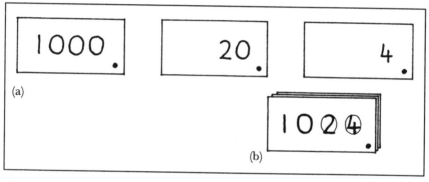

Figure 1.9: Building up the number 1024 with the use of transparencies

Any number can be built up with a full set. Conversely, a number that has been built up previously can be 'broken down' and the component parts can be identified. In the case of numbers with an 'empty column', like 1024, it is advisable to let the child say 'no-hundred' when he builds up the number, which means that he need not put down a transparency in the 100 position. For pupils with real difficulties one can make a transparency to put down with 'no hundred' which consists of an overlay with 000 (00 for tens, 0 for units).

The object of these exercises is to remind a child with a handicap in symbolic understanding that a '4' in the number 400 stands for something different from the '4' in number 4.

Writing 'sums' horizontally rather than vertically

A last suggestion concerns the application of place value in calculations. By writing two or more figures one under the other in the conventional way of 'doing sums', children may forget that they are dealing with tens or hundreds because they treat them as if they were 'units'. The problem is well addressed in Fuson and Kwon (1991: 216 ff.), where the difficulties of adding and subtracting encountered by English speaking children are compared with those who use a more regular system (e.g. the Chinese). Although in the end the way we line up numbers vertically when adding and subtracting brings out all the advantages of the place value system, there is a danger that the children lose the meaning of what a figure stands for. They can forget why they are doing what they are doing. I therefore suggest that they work for a considerable time in a semi-mental fashion by 'adding in stages' as shown in Figure 1.10 (Grauberg, 1985; cf. also Bierhoff, 1996: 23 and 34: 'two-step methods'). Working in this way will constantly remind the child of the real value of his numbers. Such a procedure should be continued for as long as feasible, and should only be changed when there is an obvious need for the child to learn more efficient computation skills with larger numbers.

$$
\begin{array}{lll}
63 + 24 & \quad \text{or} \quad & 63 + 24 \\
60 + 20 = 80 & & 63 + 20 = 83 \\
\underline{3 + 4 = 7} & & \underline{83 + 4 = 87} \\
\qquad\quad 87 & &
\end{array}
$$

Figure 1.10: Examples of horizontally arranged semi-mental sums

Checking and re-checking

Even when work with written symbols is well established, it is helpful to have sessions at regular intervals when one goes back to concrete materials. This is to ensure that the child remembers what the symbols stand for. An occasional session devoted to building up quantities with Dienes materials, for instance, will generally be seen as a treat by a child to whom the use of symbols does not come easily. Such a child can relax on 'concrete ground' when building up a quantity like 2672 out of two fine large wooden cubes (10 cm × 10 cm × 10 cm), each representing 1000 units; six flats, each representing 100 units; seven rods, each representing 10 units; and two small unit cubes. One should also check whether the child can still cope with a number like 1024 where he has to put down 'no hundreds'.

If a child would appreciate a bit of 'romance' (in the sense of A. N. Whitehead, 1949), one can pretend that the wood of the Dienes cubes, flats and rods is a pirate's treasure of 'gold', just found, which the child and teacher (or the child and the other members of the group) want to share. Such a sharing exercise will give valuable consolidation. All in all, these checking sessions should be fun and should give the teacher the opportunity to note unobtrusively any remaining weakness in a child's ability to link the concrete with the abstract.

Finally, if the teacher wishes to make a quick check to find out whether a child has really grasped the idea of place as a determiner of value, I suggest the following:

(a) Present the child with the same number written both in hieroglyphic signs and in Hindu-Arabic figures (see Figure 1.11(a)).
(b) Tell the child to write the first number (hieroglyphic representation) in a different arrangement. For example, the child may wish to put the nice curly 100 symbol as a focus in the middle (see Figure 1.11(b)). Discuss with him whether the change has made a difference to the value or not.
(c) Now ask the child to do the same with the Hindu-Arabic symbols (i.e. to rearrange the number symbols; see Figure 1.11(c)). If the child sees that one can alter the order of symbols in the first system without changing the value, but that this is not possible in the Hindu-Arabic system, he must have a reasonable understanding of the idea of place value.

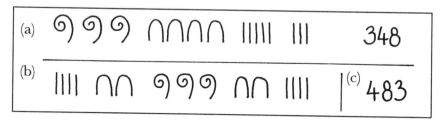

Figure 1.11 (a)–(c). The effect of changing the order of symbols in two different systems

A last remark

A teacher, reading all this, might sigh and think: 'How complicated, how time-consuming! Why should a child who finds symbolic mathematical recording difficult be bothered with these way-out methods? Can't we just teach him to add and subtract and let him get on with it?'

My answer is that all children are probably puzzled by 'place value' at some time. There may even be an initial feeling of bewilderment, but this will not normally last for very long. But for a child with asymbolic features there is the danger that the period of bewilderment, in which he has to handle a concept that does not make sense to him, will be a long one. Such a child might never feel 'at home' with numbers, unless he is introduced to the symbolic language of mathematics very carefully (Grauberg, 1986; Anghileri, 1995); hence the recourse to approaches that might fulfil the condition of 'emotional acceptability' (Buxton, 1982). Without emotional acceptance of procedures a child will enter a vicious circle. His responses to mathematical symbols will be chronically anxious and will thus hinder further learning.

Admittedly, the child's progress will be slow. He will need much more time at the beginning, and this could mean that less time will be available for 'higher' problems at the end of his mathematical school career. But our aim is to make things less complex for the child. This seems necessary in practice and is supported by Johnston's (1992) suggestion that language-impaired children are often easily stretched to the limits of their cognitive processing capacity.

If the teacher starts with a broad approach such as the one outlined above, the children should be able to work cheerfully. They should acquire the confident attitude towards mathematical problems that stems from solid basic understanding. Thus they will have a foundation on which they can build in the future and on which they can fall back securely in later times.

Relational Signs: 'Plus', 'Minus', 'Equal(s)'

What are the problems?

Plus and minus

Plus and minus signs, as young children normally experience them, are symbols for *actions*: you add something, you take something away. Symbols for actions appear to have a strange, nebulous quality when first encountered. They seem to be at one remove further from reality compared with symbols for *objects*. Symbols for objects, animals and people have a semi-concrete token character. At the pre-reading stage, an old piece of fabric wrapped around a doll might be taken as a symbol for 'grandmother', or a small battered model tractor could – for the time being – symbolize the real new tractor the child is definitely going to drive when he or she is grown up. Later, when reading starts, written word-labels can stand for real objects. These labels can be attached to objects, they can be matched with objects, and they can be exchanged for objects. But how can one put a label on 'jumping', or 'falling'? Actions have a ghostlike quality, they flit away before you can catch them. Likewise, pictures are of limited use for teaching verbs, since, as Crystal (1985: 50) states, 'it is in the nature of verbs to be undrawable.' No wonder that the first words a child learns are normally words for people and objects rather than words for actions (cf. Gleitman and Gillette, 1994). The idea that one can represent 'movement' with a static symbol like a picture or a written word, seems alien to young children.

Children with delayed speech are known to lack verbs in their active spoken vocabulary (cf. Crystal 1984: 111; Crystal, Fletcher and Garman 1976: 114). In beginning reading, words for actions also seem to prove more difficult than words for nouns; there is no one-to-one relationship between the word and the referent, since verbs have many forms (e.g. climbs/climbing/climbed – the last one with a visually distracting ending: '-bed' – or worse: go, went, gone). Such observations suggest that children have difficulties when actions are to be labelled, and it is therefore not surprising to find that symbols for 'plus' and 'minus', understood as 'adding' and 'take away', are also more difficult for children than labels for the more 'concrete' quantities.

One of the most revealing accounts of children's struggles to express actions through symbols and their reluctance to use conventional symbols for 'plus' and 'minus' is given in Hughes (1986: 72 ff.). He describes an extensive study that he undertook in co-operation with Miranda Jones. Here is one part of it which I summarize: 96 children (24 at each educational level from nursery class to class 3) took part in various experiments. In one of these the children had to find a way of representing addition and subtraction. The materials used were wooden bricks. The children had pencils and paper. During the experiment, some bricks were added or taken away from an initial quantity, and the children were asked to find a representational sign for the actions that took place. Their responses varied greatly. For instance, some simply drew the final quantity, or the quantity which was added or subtracted; others drew outstretched hands with the number of bricks added next to it; some used arrows; some wrote numerals, just recording the bricks which had been handled (e.g. '3'; '1'; '6'; '5' for, respectively, three being added, one taken away, six added, five taken away); one highly idiosyncratic response was a drawing of soldiers (number of soldiers corresponding to number of bricks been handled): British soldiers marching from left to right represented addition, while Japanese soldiers (recognizable by their head gear) marching from right to left represented subtractions. (see Figure 1.12).

Figure 1.12: An attempt to represent addition and subtraction (bricks added and taken from a pile; boy: 7 years 7 months)
Note: plus six: 6 British soldiers going from left to right; minus five: 5 Japanese soldiers going from right to left (with permission from Hughes, 1986: 75)

The most surprising result was that *not a single child* who took part in the experiment used a '+' or '−' sign. This result becomes even more revealing when one takes into account that the children were at an educational level where the majority of them must have been familiar with these signs. Some might have been using '+' and '−' almost daily in conventional exercises while 'doing sums'. What did the signs mean to them? It seems quite clear that there was no 'carry-over' from the formal class work to the less formal work with bricks, and the idea of representing actions like adding and taking away through fully abstract symbols was still alien to them. If this is so for children with no specific problems, how much more will it be true for a child with asymbolic features?

The sign for 'equal(s)'

A third symbol to which children are traditionally introduced fairly early in order to 'do sums' is the sign for 'equal(s)'. Since 'equal' cannot normally be expected to be one of the words known by a young child, the teacher is faced with the problem of having to simplify the expression; hence 'two and two *makes* four'. The teacher can be sure that 'makes' is a word in the vocabulary of young children: they make rockets out of toilet rolls, they make funny faces and they make a mess. They can also put two counters and two counters together to 'make' four. 'Makes' here really means the same as it would do when tallying. There is no need for recording and comparing the state before 'making' with the state after.

However, the moment one thinks of an equation like 2 and 2 (on one side) equals 4 (on the other side), and tries to express it in the form of something like II + II = IIII (in number primers often seen with pictures, e.g. chicks or soldiers), one creates problems. An uninitiated child will interpret such a representation of an equation as meaning '8'. He will justifiably ignore the funny little signs ('+' and '=') as irrelevant and will put 'what counts' (pictures of boxes, sticks, beads) together, to find out how many there are. He will 'make it 8'. The word 'make' to the child means an action. Children who have learned to express 'makes' with the sign '=' think of it simply as an invitation for action. In an open written equation like '2 + 2 = __?' (two and two 'makes'?) the sign '=' means 'I have to *do* something', and this rigid idea seems to prevail for a long time (cf. Behr, Erlwanger and Nichols, 1980; Kieran, 1981).

If one compares this interpretation with the mathematical meaning of '=' as a sign for 'equal', which suggests the final static condition of 'equilibrium' where everything is 'balanced', one realizes the possible source of many problems. No wonder that children who are quite competent in 'doing sums' are often puzzled when presented with a notation like '7 = 4 + 3'. In their interpretation this may mean 'seven makes four and three' – very confusing when they are familiar with sentence structures like 'Mother makes jelly and custard.' Who has ever seen a 'seven' making something? They have not learned to see 4 + 3 as just another way of expressing 7, and despite having 'done sums' for some time, they have not really understood that the value of a certain quantity can be seen as the sum of several other values (cf. Davydov, 1982: 231).

If such a notation is then met as an open sentence (7 = 4 + __?), the child will be at a loss. He may ask: 'Why isn't there a "makes" sign at the end? What I am supposed to *do*?' Or: 'You can't have the "make-sign" after the first number!' Another reaction I witnessed was for the child to change signs and happily write 7 + 4 = 11, which brought him back to familiar ground on which he could 'make' something (cf. Luria, 1969: some of his patients completely ignored relational signs; when asked 'is 10 – 8 = 2 correct?' some answered 'yes, 20'). And the harder it is for a child to understand symbols in general, the more he will cling to his first learned association of '=', which means to him: 'I have to put some numbers together or take the second number away', namely, a request for an action.

Even if the child has been carefully introduced to a wider understanding of the equal sign (preferably by the use of the two-pan balance scales – see below), and the concept of 'equal' is dawning on him, he may still have problems. He knows that '=' stands for 'equals' or 'is equal to', and in his search for understanding he may link the term 'equals' to the more familiar term 'is the same as'. He will now have to learn to restrict the term 'equal' to a more narrow mathematical meaning. He has to learn that in number work there is only one single attribute out of many possible ones to which 'sameness' applies: the abstract concept of 'numerosity'. This is a difficult step. After all, seven old battered wooden bricks are not really 'equal' to seven new clean and shiny ones for anybody who is mathematically unbiased and who has some common sense. What is easy in arithmetic, namely that $1 = 1$, will be constantly contradicted by common knowledge and non-specific use.

Historical development

Some historical knowledge about relational signs may be of use when one thinks about methods of teaching these signs to the young and learning-impaired. Such historical accounts are fascinating in themselves, but they are also instructive, since they show some of the problems that the search for representations of common mathematical operations posed for our ancestors. They are sometimes similar to the problems faced by the young child. Here are some historical details:

Plus and minus ('+', '–') – The origin of these two signs is somewhat uncertain. They seem to have been in use in various general ways. For instance in the fifteenth century German merchants used '+' for packed goods in warehouses that were 'overweight', and '–' for goods that were 'underweight'. The plus sign was used in general texts for 'and', and may have developed as a shorthand form for the Latin 'et'. 'Minus' and 'plus' were both shortened at some time to their first letters with a wavy line as a superscript; this line may have developed into the straight sign for minus. In England the first person to use these signs mathematically was Robert Recorde in a textbook with the fine name *Whetstone to Witte* in 1557 (Howson, 1982).

Equals ('=') – By contrast, the origin of the equality sign is well known. It was first used by the same Robert Recorde, who was also the first English mathematician to be a mathematics educator. He took the trouble to write the first textbook for basic arithmetic in the English language, although Latin would probably have been easier for him; the first part of this book was written for those who could work 'with the penne'; the second part for 'thyme that can not write and reade' (what a methodological task!); the third part for reckoning with fingers. With regard to the equality signs he stated quite clearly that he was irritated by the tedious repetition of writing 'is equal to' so he settled for a pair of parallel lines because 'no 2 thynges can be more equalle' (for Robert Recorde cf. Howson, 1982; for general historical information see Flegg, 1983; Menninger, 1969; or Hughes, 1986: section 6.)

Perhaps such historical knowledge can give us ideas for methods to teach the often totally alien signs to children (see below and Unit 3).

How can we help?

Delaying written sums

Firstly, one ought to remember that all symbols should be seen as 'records of things already known' (Hiebert, 1988) and that operational signs, like figures, are only needed when the time comes to record number work formally in writing. And this, as I would urge again, should be delayed for as long as the child is able to progress efficiently without writing (see above).

Using children's own inventions

Secondly, as with the introduction of any symbol, one ought to provide situations in which the need for the symbol becomes obvious. Ideally the children ought first to have a chance to invent their own ways of dealing with relations between numbers. They could happily express '3 + 3' as three crosses in one colour and three crosses in another colour; or as '3 XXX'; or even with a '33' (which will give the teacher some uncomfortable feelings). A common way of dealing with addition seems to be to write the word 'and' in full ('3 and 3'), thus following the oral convention. As stated earlier, such inventions will be clumsy, perhaps deviant, and their use time-consuming.

Only when the children have become fully familiar with the use of their own inventions – or those of their neighbours – should the teacher mention that there are actually signs used by 'grown-ups'. Most children will probably have seen the adult signs and may perhaps be ready to use them; if not, there is no need to hurry them at this stage.

Using mediating representations (icons)

The use of children's own inventions may be expanded to include other 'mediating' representations of relational signs. The terms 'mediating representations' and 'mediating methods' may best be explained by reference to Bruner's different modes of representation (1964; 1966) which are summarized below.

Bruner describes three ways in which we can 'translate experience' into a representational model.

(a) *Enactive mode:* this works through action and is based on motor responses, which are 'represented in our muscles, so to speak' (1964: 2). It is a mode that works without imagery and without words.

(b) *Iconic mode:* this works through organized images (icons), which can be seen as 'great summarizers' of perceptual events. They rely mainly on visual memory and, like a picture, can stand for the object: an abstract picture, as it were.

(c) *Symbolic mode:* this works through symbols that are mainly arbitrary. There is no need for analogy between them and 'the thing' they stand for. For instance, a word with only five letters like 'whale' can stand for a very big creature, and a much longer word with 13 letters like 'micro-organism' can stand for one that can hardly be seen (1966: 10 ff.). This gives symbols a quality of 'remoteness' but at the same time makes them a powerful means to abstract thinking.

The three modes are to some extent related to stages of development, but no mode is ever totally replaced by another: in one way or other most of us use all of them until the day we die. Figure 1.13 illustrates the modes with regard to the concept of 'equal' (an adaptation of Bruner's example of the balance beam, 1966: 45).

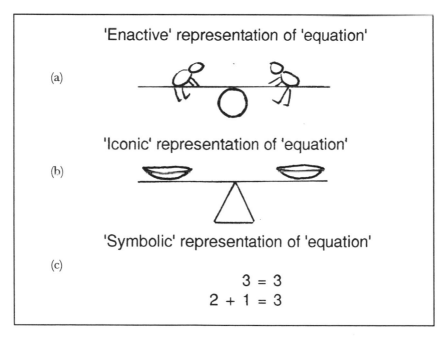

Figure 1.13 (a)–(c): Three representations of 'equation'
Note: there is some simplification in this figure; it does not account for the possibilities that 3 may balance with 4 when one uses different units (three heavier children against four lighter ones), or when the placement of the weights along the beam is not the same; see also Skemp's qualified reservations (1986: 48 and 49)

In teaching, a concept can be presented on these different levels, which means, in Bruner's brave words (1966: 44): 'any idea or problem or body of knowledge can be presented in a form simple enough so that any particular learner can understand it in a recognizable form.' For children with asymbolic features, the middle stage (the iconic representation) is of crucial importance. (Interestingly, Recorde's symbol '=' is still somewhat 'iconic'; this may help children, as long as they are made aware of it.) Unfortunately, it is also a stage which in my opinion is sometimes neglected in elementary mathematics. We all know the importance of the first stage, the 'enactive' one. The English primary school, for instance, is normally full of materials offering opportunities to learn through the 'enactive mode'. But the next step is often cut short. It is almost as if the teacher suddenly feels that it is time for the child to become familiar with more formal ways of work, and a fairly sudden jump takes place to the last stage – the symbolic one. The child is then made to use abstract symbols, and this may lead to reactions like that of Jamie reported by Martin Hughes (for a full description of the interview see Hughes, 1986: 99): Children aged 5 to 7 were given a heap of bricks. A pack of cards was lying face down on the table, each card showing either just a numeral (5), or a numeral with a '+' or '–' in front (e.g. –2), or an equation (e.g. 3 + 4 = 7). One card was turned over at a time and the child was asked to show what was on the card by using the bricks (the actual wording during this part of the experiment was 'show me what's on the card, show me what it means'). Jamie, a boy aged 6 years, faced with the numeral '5' made an arrangement like the one shown in Figure 1.14.

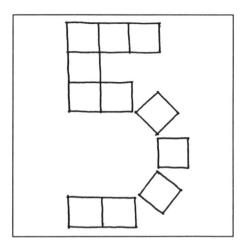

Figure 1.14: Jamie's representation of '5', using bricks (with permission from Hughes, 1986: 99)

This seems to be a case where a child lost the meaning of the symbol. He needed to be taken back to the iconic stage where there is still a visual link to the concept represented by the symbol (for example, tally-sticks or hieroglyphic numbers).

Iconic representations ought ideally to develop from the child's own inventions (see above). Their representation of relational symbols will probably turn out to be arrows of some kind, or hands stretching out for something; sometimes a child may use familiar written words (e.g. he may write in full that he 'takes away three'). Again, such inventions may be clumsy and rather impractical but they are worth using for a while. Firstly, the children are working with representations that are meaningful to them, so their understanding of symbolism is consolidated; and secondly, the more inconvenient their methods are, the readier the children will be to accept the need for a more abstract but more manageable symbol.

After a while, perhaps in the wider frame of a historical discussion, the teacher may wish to suggest a more streamlined historical symbol system, but still one with a visible link to the concept it represents. For example, I have used the hieroglyphic number system with different colours to represent plus and minus. Once the children are familiar with the symbols and are asked to add a number (e.g. 12) to a given hieroglyphic number (e.g. 24), they draw the additional symbols with a green pencil (next to the original symbols in black). When they are asked to 'take away 12', they cross out the original symbols with a red pencil. The 'equations' can then be 'read off' easily (see Figure 1.15, where colour is represented by the different strength of the lines).

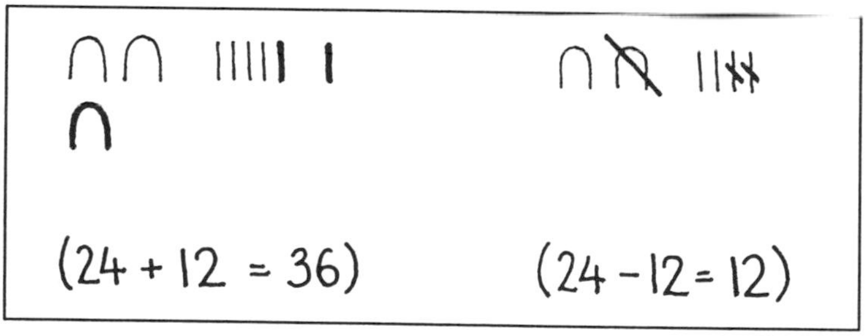

Figure 1.15: Equations with hieroglyphs
Note: plus: means adding signs in green (here shown through 'bold'); minus: means crossing out signs with red

As an alternative, one can use scales as an iconic representation of 'equal'. Instead of using conventional equal signs, one draws some scales on top of a 'division line' (see Figure 1.16). Obviously, this can

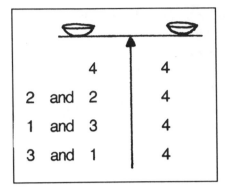

Figure 1.16: Using the picture of balance scales as a symbol for 'equals'

only take place once the children have had sufficient hands-on experience with the balance scales and Cuisenaire rods during the earlier
'enactive' stage, so that they can understand the suitability of the
scales.

Another suggestion for working on relational signs in a mediating
way is to make use of the 'warehouse theory'. As mentioned earlier,
the origins of our '+' and '−' may be found in the use of such signs to
indicate 'overweight' and 'underweight' in measured warehouse
goods.

After some 'enactive' preparatory work with balance scales and
Cuisenaire rods one can record the 'warehouse activities' in the
following way:

(a) A target measurement (number) is agreed on and put on the top
of the record sheet.
(b) On the left of the sheet is a column of numbers, representing the
quantity of 'measured goods'.
(c) The task now is to find the amount and the relational direction
('plus' and 'minus') by which the measured quantity differs from
the target quantity (see Figure 1.17). The child has to state (first in
words and only in the end with '+', '−' and '=' signs) if he is 'short'
or 'over' or 'just right'.

Again, this activity should initially be carried out in a concrete
manner (for example, with Cuisenaire rods, with or without scales)
and closely linked with oral recording. The next step would still
involve carrying out the task in a concrete way but with written
recording. Only in the end should it be tackled just as a paper-and-
pencil exercise, and even at this last stage the children should be
given the opportunity to check their results with rods or scales if they

```
┌─────────────────────────────────────┐
│         Target Number:  7           │
│       ──────────────────            │
│         4    │   short 3            │
│         6    │   short 1            │
│         9    │   over 2             │
│         7    │   just right         │
│         2    │                      │
│        10    │   etc.               │
│         8    │                      │
│        etc.  │                      │
└─────────────────────────────────────┘
```

Figure 1.17: 'Warehouse relation' of three numbers

feel the need. For a more detailed description of how to introduce and how to work with targets see Unit 3.

Introducing the signs '+', '−' and '=' in relation to each other

In the last section we have seen the three concepts and symbols of 'plus', 'minus' and 'equals' used in relation to each other. I would like to emphasize this. The three symbols ought to be introduced and connected very early. This can be done by letting early arithmetic develop from the simple relation of three numbers where one is the sum of the two others, for example numbers like 8/5/3; or 8/6/2. The flexibility of such a relation is best demonstrated with Cuisenaire rods first; and then, if the child seems ready for it (i.e. when he is confident with conventional numerals), relations are symbolized by a triangle, where the 'whole' is written on the top, and the two parts at the bottom right and left. Finally the relations are expressed as properly written equations (see Figure 1.18 (a)–(c)).

Adding thus one representational step to the other is a process that should be carried out slowly, perhaps over months. After that I suggest that activities with rods, triangles and written equations be carried out in parallel for a generous period of time.

The main aim of such work is to let the children become familiar with the sign in its widest algebraic meaning: as a symbol which stands for a *relation*. Only later should they meet the rather narrower *operational* meaning of a sign as an invitation to perform a certain action, such as 'doing sums' (or just pressing a button on the calculator). This does not mean that learning to 'do proper sums' is to be neglected; in fact, the child *is* 'doing sums' but with a different focus. The mechanics of doing sums efficiently is certainly a proper concern of the teacher,

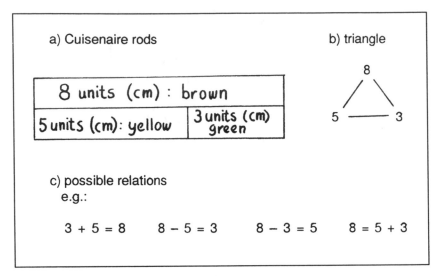

a) Cuisenaire rods

8 units (cm) : brown

5 units (cm): yellow | 3 units (cm) green

b) triangle

8

5 —— 3

c) possible relations
   e.g.:

3 + 5 = 8   8 − 5 = 3   8 − 3 = 5   8 = 5 + 3

Figure 1.18 (a)–(c): Different representations of three related numbers.
Note: at this stage the lines in the triangle are not meant to be drawn by the child;
he is just asked to show them with finger movements and express different relations
verbally, first in his own words and later with 'plus', 'minus' and 'equals'

but only as a last step: skills will be practised in the end as a specific
application of a wider, well-understood rule (cf. Skemp 1976).

A final remark: sometimes a child will be reluctant to leave the
cosy work in the enactive or iconic mode. In such cases one may
need to give him a little push in the end and tell him to 'join the club'
and use conventional signs and forms for his sums. But this should
only be done when the child is considered capable of understanding
signs: one must be sure that he has indeed realized that signs are
arbitrary constructs, and that one can change them without changing the substance they stand for.

Further practical work concerning relational understanding of
'signs and sums with three numbers' is described in Chapter 2 and
Unit 3, and suggestions are made about the order in which they may
be introduced; for the problematical task of the meaningful teaching
of 'sums' see also Hughes (1986: section 8); Haylock (1992); Haylock
and Cockburn (1989); Bierhoff (1996).

Money

What are the problems?

Teaching 'money' seems more difficult today than some decades
ago. Coins and notes keep changing in value, look and feel. Educational toy money can hardly keep up with the changes, and hours

must have been spent by teachers and their assistants covering up ha'pennies on work-cards and games, sorting out old coins and ordering new ones.

Moreover, the opportunities for many children to handle small 'cash' and to see 'cash' being handled are diminishing at a steady rate, hand-in-hand with the decreasing number of neighbourhood corner shops and the increasing use of supermarkets, checkpoints, credit cards and cheques. Despite these developments, there is probably agreement that all children ought to learn the skill of handling the money in their pockets. Some children still seem to 'absorb' the skill; others have to be carefully taught. Most language-impaired children seem to belong to the latter group, and certainly children with difficulties in symbolic understanding do so.

Money as a two-layered system

Some of the more severe problems faced by such children seem to arise from the fact that money involves a two-layered system of symbols. Firstly, *numbers* are involved, and all the difficulties presented by numbers as symbols discussed earlier will be present. Secondly, quite apart from the numbers on the coins and their value, children have to come to terms with a complicated token system which works according to rules they cannot comprehend. The metal coin or paper note stands for a potential which can be realized in many ways. Nowhere is there the one-to-one relationship that children with asymbolic features love so much. The same token can be exchanged for a brilliant red toy bus (the one the child always wanted), or for a relatively boring pair of socks, or for something as revolting as pickled olives. Thus two layers of symbolism – numbers as symbols *per se* and the rather incomprehensible token value of real money – are interlinked in the system.

Arbitrariness

There is another factor, closely connected with the difficulties outlined above, which may lead to unease and bewilderment: it is the failure to recognize the arbitrary nature of symbols in general and of money-tokens in particular. For a young child, money seems something 'given'. He has grown up with it, just as he has grown up with day and night or summer and winter. It takes some degree of sophistication in symbolic understanding to recognize that money is 'man-made' and arbitrary like all symbols.

Asymbolic children cannot be expected to learn this spontaneously. They need to be shown. Making them aware that money is a set of tokens with values that have been arbitrarily set may give them the freedom to look at money as something they can 'handle' and control. Although the ultimate aim is that the children should acquire practical competence in handling money, one would also like them to feel comfortably 'at home' when doing so. Thus, as their money skills grow, they should increasingly realize that money is nothing more than a tool, made by fellow human beings to make things easy rather than difficult for them.

How can we help?

Using Dienes and Cuisenaire materials as money tokens

Dienes and Cuisenaire materials were introduced earlier and are described in detail in Unit 3. The Dienes materials provide small cubes used as units (1 cm³), 'longs' (rods of 10 units), '100-flats' (10 longs), and large 1000-cubes (10 flats). If one adds to this a selection of Cuisenaire rods (yellow = five, red = two) as well as some 'bundles' of 'longs' (two longs = 20, five longs = 50) one has a representation of the current British money system (see Figure 1.19).

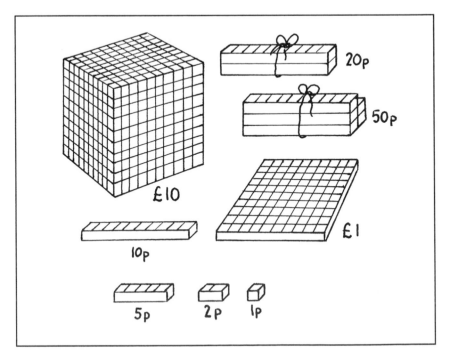

Figure 1.19: Representation of current UK money through 'cubes', 'longs' and 'flats'

The materials can be adapted to other money systems or to any changes that may occur. They can be used as a preparation for work on money in different ways. For instance, the wooden or plastic cubes, longs and flats can be declared 'desert island' money. They can be used as money tokens for buying and selling in play shops; or one particular set of money can be exchanged for a different set or for a 'cheque' in play at a 'Wendy-House'-type bank (or a desk turned into a bank counter); or a random heap can be a rich treasure found by pirates or acquired by Robin Hood, which must be shared out evenly among his Merry Men (and women). Another version that I have frequently used with severely impaired children in a one-to-one situation starts with a random heap of materials. This is then to be shared out first between the child and the teacher (i.e. divided by two) and later – more demandingly – shared between the child, the teacher and a charity of the child's choice (i.e. divided by three). Finally, such rods of different value can also be used to provide tokens for gains and losses in some games.

Advantages

The advantage of working with this kind of 'money' as a first step rather than with a toy version of real money, is threefold:

(a) The materials represent the quantitative value they stand for in an accurate and obvious way. For example, a flat of 100 times $1\,cm^3$ is worth 100 single $1\,cm^3$ cubes. Although English money uses size to indicate value to some extent, this is difficult to estimate (is a 2p piece twice as big as a 1p piece?). Furthermore, the idea of *size* as an indicator of value suffers by an interference from the *type of material* as an indicator of value (copper versus silver; metal versus paper). By contrast, the cubes mirror the value in a logical and visually perceivable way.

(b) With these relatively heavy wooden materials, the advantage of using a piece of paper instead of the large wooden cube becomes obvious: a £10 ($10\,cm^3$) cube will not fit into your pocket. Thus the way is prepared for understanding why we use paper rather than real pieces of gold for higher values of money nowadays.

(c) Since the materials use values that replicate the monetary system exactly, children are already practising the skills that they will need later in real-life situations, but they do so in many different ways. The next step will be to work with more abstract but also more 'real' toy money. In this way one avoids endless repetitions with the same materials (mostly replicas or drawings of coins).

One can save the fun of using 'real' play coins for a later stage and finally do 'real shopping' for the crowning stage. Ideally the competence of handling money should then come to the child with the same ease as a ripe apple dropping from an apple tree.

Generally, real shopping and even 'playing shop' are much too time-consuming to be used as a practice activity. The value of both lies mainly in their motivational power and the fact that they form a link between classroom activity and real life, rather than in their providing the necessary amount of practice. Both motivation and application are certainly valuable but the motivational force of playing shop or of real shopping might be blunted if repeated too often, and the link between the classroom and the outside world will be best understood if a few but highly memorable excursions are made at the right point in the child's development of understanding money.

In my experience, children are likely to enjoy the new activities with 'real money' more, and understand the principles behind them better, after they have already acquired some of the necessary number skills with different 'money-like' materials as suggested above.

Using a game to show the arbitrariness of money (Chopstick Game)

A game can be used to show the arbitrariness of money. This is another way of practising money skills without using money. It involves using different value systems for the same token. The tokens are chopsticks marked with different colours at one end. There are more sticks of some colours than of others. At the beginning of a playing session a certain value for each colour is agreed and written down for reference: perhaps red (i.e. the colour of which there are most sticks) is assigned 5p, blue 10p, etc. The sticks are put into a container in such a way that the coloured ends cannot be seen. Each player in turn then takes a stick as a 'lucky dip'. At the end of the game the value of the sticks is added up separately for each player, and the winner is the one with the highest value. This description may bring to mind a game called 'Mikado' (or 'Pick-a-Stick'), on which indeed my game is based. The essential difference is that in my variant the values are set by the children or carer and can be changed each time by agreement (for a detailed description of how to make the game set, of how to play various versions, and of the sometimes surprising values suggested by children, see Unit 3; see also Chapter 2 where the game is suggested for children with organizational problems).

Advantages

One advantage of such a game is that the degree of difficulty can be easily monitored and that money skills can be practised in yet another different way. More important, however, is the fact that, since the children have the opportunity to change and fix the value themselves, they will gain insight into the arbitrary nature of tokens. Above all, they will have the feeling of 'being in charge of the symbols', which should at all times be one of the aims in teaching mathematics to children who have difficulty with symbols.

Practising money skills

Consistent work is needed when it comes to practising money skills. Some of the children with asymbolic language problems are able to acquire mechanical skills of this kind relatively quickly initially, relying mainly on memory. They may appear competent for two or more successive sessions. If their memory fails them in subsequent sessions, however, they seem liable to make sudden gross and recurrent mistakes or to work very inefficiently. The kind of mistakes they make and their way of working will show their severe problems in understanding basic mathematical reasons and rules.

For instance, a child may have been playing 'bank' for some time, with the teacher writing 'cheques' and the child handing out the right amount in toy money. All might go well until the cheque shows a sum like £104; the child may now give out a £10 note and four £1 coins in exchange (thus he looks at the written symbol and interprets it as 10 and 4 despite all the work he has previously done correctly with tens and hundreds).

Alternatively, the teacher and a pupil might want to share evenly a random sum of toy money consisting of a mixture of notes and coins. The child might start by sharing the coins with the smallest value first (I have noticed that in such sharing exercises pupils frequently seem to go first for the tokens of which there are most). The child will thus be left with the tokens of the larger value and will have to rearrange his work in order to share these. He has not realized (or has forgotten) that starting with the higher values first and then gradually working downwards to the lower values means less work and easier work.

I have found that the best way of dealing with errors like those described is to go back to the Dienes/Cuisenaire representation, and to work in parallel with both systems (on the one hand play money which mirrors real money, and on the other materials where value is represented by size). The size of the wooden materials will remind the child of the values that the 'real' money coins and notes stand for.

A regular revision period, perhaps at the beginning of each new term, is recommended (starting with wooden cubes and made-up money systems and then going on to 'proper' money skills).

Further suggestions of how one could practise money skills are given in Unit 5.

Time

What are the problems?

'Time' is probably one of the most difficult aspects to be tackled with children who have a weakness in symbolic understanding. It is generally questionable whether the teaching of 'time' actually falls within mathematics; indeed, some quite major works about the psychology of mathematical instructions ignore time (e.g. Skemp, 1986; Resnick and Ford, 1981). The concept of time involves much more than numbers and quantities: it involves the rhythm of day and night, summer and winter, action and pauses, as well as beginnings, ends and age. In more abstract terms, it covers points in time, duration of events, sequence of events, frequency of events and intervals between events (cf. Piaget, 1969; Quirk and Greenbaum, 1973: 230).

One specific problem in early mathematics is that when dealing with 'time' it is almost impossible to work on a 'concrete' level: time is not made of the 'stuff' that can be translated into concrete materials. It is not surprising therefore that research with normal children shows that everything to do with understanding and using time concepts develops rather late (cf. Dickson, Brown and Gibson, 1984: 151).

The concept of time versus 'telling the time'

Two aspects of time have to be distinguished in teaching: firstly, one must try to develop a *concept* of time in a child; and secondly, one must teach the child to 'tell the time' (teaching *clock time*). Experience shows that the former is clearly the main problem for a child with difficulties in understanding symbols. It is easy to see why.

(a) You can't touch or see time. It 'passes', but nobody can stop it. How can we have a 'look at it'?
(b) Time is *relative*. Modern time is supposed to be measured with precision, yet this precision is often meaningless since the child's 'subjective clock' works to a varied scale: how long is the night

before Christmas, and how short is the hour you are allowed to play out before tea!

(c) 'Long' and 'short' are themselves puzzling and potentially misleading words when measuring time. Is time a line? Where does it start, and where does it end? We use the same term for space and time, thus making the distinction difficult.

(d) There are difficulties due to the *constantly changing point of reference*, so that expressions like 'late', 'early' 'in two hours', 'two hours later' can objectively relate to different points in time (for example, 'two hours later' can mean 4 o'clock or 7 o'clock depending on whether your point of reference is 2 o'clock or 5 o'clock).

These are all aspects with which a child is expected to come to terms. Naturally, a teacher of children with learning difficulties tries desperately to find ways and means to bring in some concrete representation of time for the child to latch on to, albeit with the uncomfortable conviction that fundamentally no concrete materials will fit the elusive essence of the elusive concept (compare Chapter 4).

In view of this, teaching children how to 'tell the time' seems more straightforward (although any teacher who has done so will probably be able to recall feelings of despair with regard to some children). Here the challenge for teachers of children with asymbolic features will be to make them see the relation between the skill they are learning ('what the clock time is now') and the concept of time in its wider sense. With some exceptional children one will, in the end, decide to settle for just the socially valuable skill of being able to tell the time, at least for the moment.

How can we help?

Firstly, teachers should not feel guilty if they initially decide not to spend much time on teaching 'telling the time', no matter what the curriculum (National or other) may say. Secondly, when teachers think the conditions are right for tackling the 'time problem' they should not limit its teaching to the sessions allocated for number work. There ought to be many activities designed to develop in the child a somewhat intuitive feeling for what 'time' means, and one ought to grasp any opportunity during the school day that lends itself to this purpose, rather than spending a fixed period teaching 'time'. Below I will list some activities that may help to develop knowledge of time, starting with those which can serve as preparation for more formal work on time-telling at a later stage.

Using invented 'timers'

As most teachers will know, it is helpful to set aside a small part of the school day as 'quiet time'. This is a time when talking of any kind is discouraged – even in special classes for children with language problems where the aim is normally to make children talk. Children are expected to concentrate on some kind of individual work during these periods. This could, for instance, involve solving a jigsaw puzzle, matching words and pictures, or handwriting; in short, the time is set aside to practise any skills which need practice, so long as the child is familiar enough with the task to be able to work on it alone. This period will vary in length according to the group's attention span, and one ought to have a timer which indicates the progression of time and the end of the period. The decision of how to measure the period could involve the children themselves.

This is an excellent opportunity to use 'timers' which the children have invented. Davydov (1982) advised that children should always be given the opportunity to invent their own 'units of measurement' before they are introduced to the conventional ones.

Such invented 'timers' may range from the extraordinary (such as a snail trail) to the more conventional (such as a sand timer); some will be practical, others will definitely not be so. Some examples of possible 'timers' are given in Unit 5.

Using races: time versus performance in space

Races of all kinds provide another opportunity to foster an intuitive feeling for time and duration. However, research has shown that children generally find it difficult to distinguish between space and time even up to the age of 8 and 9 (Piaget, 1969). In a study by Lovell and Slater (1960) children of 8 years thought that a taller tree must be older, no matter what the tree was. In my experience this confusion seems to remain obstinately in children with asymbolic features. They seem to take the 'output' of an action (space covered, beads strung, etc.) as determining the time it took. Peter, for instance, thought that, if he managed to put more small red Cuisenaire rods on top of each other than Jessica within the time set by 'start' and 'stop', it must have taken him longer.

In this particular case the period had not been 'visibly timed'; the teacher had just given an oral start and stop sign. This leads me to suggest that for 'races within a fixed time' like the one described above, the duration of time ought to be measured in an *obviously visible way*, perhaps with a sand clock, or later perhaps with a suitably set kitchen timer. Such a recording instrument will help the child to realize that the time factor is stable: that each child has the same time and that any difference in 'output' must have a different cause.

There seem to be two ways in which races can be used as a means to promote an understanding of duration. One can take a given period of time as a fixed point of reference and see how much of a certain activity can be completed within it (how many Cuisenaire rods can be stacked, or how many laps can be run round the play-ground). Alternatively one can take a particular activity as a fixed point of reference and see how long it takes a child to finish the task.

In my view the first approach seems preferable at the beginning. The reason for this is that the answer that the child is supposed to look for can be measured in a 'concrete' form nearer to the child's level of development (like the rods stacked or the number of laps run). This approach means that the point of focus is the perfor-mance, which is measured as output in 'space'. Unfortunately, this could possibly add to a child's confusion between time and space. For this reason I wish to emphasize the earlier suggestion that an 'obvi-ous' timer be used — one where the 'movement' of time can be also be observed as a change (which means as something that, like all changes, tends to attract children's attention).

Some examples of group activities for this first type of task (time fixed, output measured) are:

- Can we clear up within the time of a sand timer (a 5-minute timer)?
- Can we solve a certain jigsaw puzzle together in a fixed time?
- As a group, how long can we make a paper chain in a fixed time?
- As a group, how many squares can we make with a heap of rods (such as playmatches or, if a more difficult task is required, differ-ent lengths of Cuisenaire rods) in a fixed time?

For the second type of activity (task fixed, time measured) one has to alter the question, for example:

- How much time do we need for clearing up today?
- How long will it take us to make a paper chain 5 metres long?
- How long will it take us to walk a mile?
- How long will it take us to weed our flower-bed?

Again, all racing activities are best tried first with non-standard timers. The sequence in which different kinds of timers could be introduced might be:

- non-standard timer;
- sand timer with precise minutes;
- traditional clock which shows the seconds;
- and lastly, when telling the time on a clock face is fairly well established, perhaps a digital clock.

In these activities estimations should be asked for when this seems suitable. The results can then be discussed in relation to the estimate. One hopes that gradually the figures for estimation and result will become fairly close.

Using competitive races

All the activities mentioned above take place on a group basis and any competitive element is directed against 'the clock' rather than against another group or individual. If one decides to measure and record the times of an individual child's performances in the same task, a competitive element is introduced since a comparison with others will be almost inevitable. The emotional stability of the competing children has to be considered. There may be some language-impaired children for whom competition can have a motivating effect, but for others – especially for the performer who has some ambitions but who is weak at the task to be measured – it may lower motivation and performance.

Curiously, the effect of competition can be almost neutral among the special group of children with asymbolic features. They often don't seem to see the point of competing against each other. The same weakness that prevents them from entering with understanding into symbolic play also prevents them from becoming intrinsically involved in competition, although they may sometimes be seen trying to copy their peers' competitive behaviour.

One also wonders how much a child will be able to learn about 'time' during such intensive actions, where he is primarily interested in 'beating' the competitor or beating his own previous performance.

These reservations do not mean that individual children with a lack of symbolic understanding should never take part in competitive activities. They have their place in as much as they can help to clear up the kind of confusion apparent when Peter insisted that he had taken more time than Jessica because he had stacked more rods than she had done.

Competitive 'fixed-time' activities

A first introduction to competitive tasks could involve measuring the individual performances with reference to a fixed time. They could include tasks such as 'how many cubes can you stack in 10 minutes?' This can be contrasted with tasks that have a chance element ('how many sixes will you get in a fixed time?'). A clarifying discussion should follow: 'We all had the same time; why could Peter stack more cubes?' 'He is good at it'. 'Why did Lizzy get more sixes?' 'She was just lucky!'

Competitive 'fixed task' activities

Fixed-time activities can eventually be followed by activities where time is measured and the task is fixed. 'How long will it take you to complete a lap round the playground?' In the end this will lead to stopwatch measurements as in official races, but at the beginning it would seem advisable to start with fairly rough but concrete measuring instruments. One ought also to ask the child to estimate the time that a particular task will take at the outset: 'How many times do you think I will have to let the sand run through the sand timer before you have stacked a tower with bricks 25 cm high?'

One could discuss practical questions like:

- Is it a good idea to start measuring your performance with the biggest sand timer (out of a commercially available set of three or more)?
- What will happen if you finish the task before the big sand timer has had a run-through?
- Would it make sense to use all sand timers simultaneously?

Questions like these may help the child start to understand different measuring units with regard to time. The need for more precise measurements may become obvious.

One hopes that in this way a bridge is being built to the general understanding of how we try to come to terms with the constant flow of time: by breaking it up into manageable bits such as seconds, minutes, quarter-hours and, later, hours, days, years and centuries. It is important that these units should be manageable for the child at a certain stage of development. In practice this means that one introduces short stretches of time before longer ones, for example chunks of minutes before hours. Periods that are too short, like seconds, should be avoided at this stage. The aim is to establish a 'feeling for time' as the base from which telling the time can be approached at a later stage.

Working with intervals

In order to gain a fuller understanding of the continuity of time, children need to be aware of the concept of an interval, more precisely, they should become aware of the 'duration of intervals' (Piaget, 1969), the length of time between two happenings. How can we provide experience with intervals?

One suggestion is to use notes on a musical instrument that are separated by intervals of different duration and then related to time. For example, the teacher gives three bangs with short intervals, and then three bangs with longer intervals. She asks questions such as:

- How many bangs did you hear the first time?
- How many the second time?
- So, did I do the same thing twice?
- What was different? Listen again!

It seems natural to children to think that 'three bangs are three bangs are three bangs'. Only after they have noticed that there *are* intervals and that these can be somewhat different (different in length, like the morning break is from the school lunch break) can the question be asked: which of the intervals ('breaks between') took more time?

One thus tries to make the child focus on the 'blanks' – the time that is filled with 'nothing'. This is a negative aspect which the children with their developmental preoccupation with 'happenings' tend to ignore. These 'blanks of time' can now be given importance by measuring them. They will thus assume a degree of 'substance' which can be manipulated. Awareness of intervals will grow and, in the end, even the learning-disabled child should begin to understand the fundamental fact that time passes evenly, even when nothing happens.

Working with 'sequences over time'

For children to understand a temporal sequence they must already have an understanding of 'duration' and they must be able to use the concept of a 'point in time' as a reference point. Developmentally they will first learn to distinguish between 'now' and 'not-now' and then learn to differentiate the 'not-now' into 'past' and 'future' (cf. Clark and Clark, 1977: 541).

Obviously, 'a point in time' used as point of reference does not need to be an exact 'clock-time point'; it can be as vague as 'breakfast time', 'bed time', 'the time when Daddy comes home' or as specific but unrelated to the clock as 'he is just turning the ignition key to start the car; that means we are off'. It is thus possible to teach temporal sequences without the child being able to tell the time with the clock.

Most teachers of language-impaired children are familiar with the problems faced by their pupils in sorting out temporal orders of events and the use of appropriate vocabulary, since mistakes become obvious in many areas beside mathematics. For children with asymbolic features, however, the difficulties are also linked to a specific inability to understand how the symbol – perhaps words or pictures – can be used to record happenings over time.

In recent years a number of special sets of 'sequencing cards' have come on to the market, which a child has to put into an order showing the temporal sequence of the events illustrated on the cards. On one card, for instance, there might be a boy putting toothpaste on his brush; the same boy might be brushing his teeth on the next card, and the same boy again might be wiping his mouth with a flannel on the last card. Such cards can be helpful to give an insight into temporal sequences. However, one ought to be prepared to let a child with asymbolic features *act out* the sequence first and then link what has happened to the pictures. Another useful procedure might be to start with the action in the middle (brushing teeth), and let the child (a) suggest an event that must have preceded the act and (b) predict an event that may come after; only then is the full set of pictures used in comparing, checking and discussing the sequence.

In short, special methods have to be used to mediate between the symbolic picture representation on the card and the real life events. Simple questions like 'What is the boy doing now?' asked when showing a photograph of a boy, may otherwise be answered with 'How do I know?' In one case, which I experienced with surprise, the child seemed to think of the real 'now' and could not answer the question because he thought of the boy in the photo as a real person, perhaps being at school now, perhaps having his dinner now, perhaps even being grown up now.

Working on vocabulary

Pupils' lack of a vocabulary for 'time' concepts is a common problem for a teacher of children with language difficulties. For children with a deficiency in symbolic understanding the problem seems to be not so much a shortage of the actual words but rather an uncertainty about their interpretation and their appropriate use.

Firstly, problems can arise with a group of words that indicate boundaries of time in a rather vague manner (such as 'soon' and 'later') and to which a child therefore cannot attach a certain once-and-for-all meaning; and, secondly, difficulties can occur with some words which are not intended by the speaker to be precise, even though precise terms are used (such as 'just a minute', 'once or twice', 'now and again'). One thus has to teach explicitly the fact that such words and phrases tend to have a relative meaning and that the periods of time they stand for cannot be measured in a precise way.

The remedy here is not specific to mathematical work. The teacher must be alert to recognize any use of words by the child that do not carry meaning for him. It also means that there ought to be concrete materials at hand at all times to link the verbal label to a concrete situation. For instance, in the case of 'minute' the teacher should have a timer and a clock with a minute hand available, and should consciously create a situation where the phrase 'just-a-minute' can be used. Then both the precise measurement and the loose meaning should be contrasted and discussed.

In general, the teacher should not shy away from going back and spending time on absolute basics if necessary, although this may create motivational problems since the child will be sensitive to anything that looks 'babyish'. My earlier suggestions to use historical and foreign ways of dealing with simple number problems may also be of value when dealing with 'time'. An example of a fine book to use for this purpose is H. Michel's (1967) book about scientific instruments in art and history.

Working on 'telling the time'

Teaching children how to 'tell the time' is more directly related to 'number work'. But I am not sure whether it should figure in *early* number work. I would like to start with some warnings.

Firstly, isolated mechanical exercises with the clock face have their danger. They can actually hinder a child's deeper understanding of time, as Kerslake (1975) pointed out. A teacher might work with an instruction clock indicating a certain time and ask the child to 'tell what the time is now'; a second later she might change the clock's hands to an arrangement that indicates a time lapse of 3 hours and ask: 'what is the time now?' Under these circumstances the child may learn to read a dial with numbers, but he will not be able to relate this to any real feeling for time he may already have acquired.

Secondly, a static clock face printed on paper, either with a special rubber stamp or in exercise booklets, can mislead children. They might be asked to read a specific time from it, or to draw in a given time. Will they be aware that, in reality, the hands are never static but are constantly moving and that there is a specific relation between the movement of the small and the long hand (Dickson et al., 1984: 144)?

Finally, the role of the digital clock in teaching has to be questioned. Does such a clock make things easier for children? This might be the case for some children, especially those with a spatial/directional disability. For a child with a weakness in symbolic understanding, however, it can make things worse. There is no doubt that a digital watch or clock is an efficient tool. But greater efficiency seems to have been achieved at a loss: things have become harder to understand. A child sees some figures separated by dots that appear and disappear, placed on a wrist strap, perhaps next to a confusingly irrelevant popular cartoon character. Where do they come from? How many are there? Will they ever come back? On the digital clock a momentary point in the time sequence is isolated and shown, second by second, without context. On the traditional clock face there *is* a context: each moment of time is shown in the context of the 12-hour cycle. One can see the neighbouring 'times', both those before and those after. The movement can be related to the cycle of the sun with which the child is familiar and which helps us still to divide eternity into manageable parts. This means that 'telling the time' might admittedly be a more complicated task to 'figure out' than reading the numbers on a digital clock, but a task which still makes sense in itself. The relation between telling the time and the concept of time is closer, and it is therefore easier to gain insight into it.

If, in the context of 'early mathematics', the teacher thinks that a child with asymbolic features ought to be introduced in a more formal way to 'telling the time', Kerslake's general approach (1975) to work with young children could be helpful. One of her specific suggestions is not starting with neat hours and half hours but with seconds and minutes. These are units of time that are more accessible to a child than an hour, which is too long for a child's relatively short memory and concentration span. Kerslake also suggests that clock times should be related to events and activities that have some meaning for a child (such as a television programme at ten to three), even if the event in question does not take place at a 'neat' time, such as 'on the hour'.

Attention should be given to special numbers relating to time measures (5, 10, 15, 20, 30, 45) when one restricts work to activities using time periods smaller than the hour. If special exercises (simple adding, subtracting, multiplication and division) are carried out with these numbers *before* time-telling is tackled, this might make the difficult subject easier. Chinn and Ashcroft (1993: 187–194), who make suggestions for 'time-telling' with older dyslexic children, stress the importance of 12 and 24 when work is extended up to the 24-hour clock.

Summing up this section, one can perhaps say that it is generally best not to use valuable teaching time trying to get children with an asymbolic feature to tell the time, unless one has first given them opportunities to acquire a rudimentary understanding of some concept of time such as points in time, duration, frequency, intervals and order. To do otherwise runs the risk that the fundamental aspects of time and the more mechanical skills of 'telling the time' may never really be linked and a general anxiety about 'time' may become an additional handicapping feature of these children.

SUMMARY

A weakness in symbolic understanding is a feature that the language-impaired child shares with many children who do not have such a handicap. In an 'asymbolic' sub-group of children with language-impairment, however, this weakness is likely to be much more pronounced. Some problems in this area arise from our varied use of numbers. Others stem from the abstract nature of the conventional Hindu-Arabic number system – a system which was invented for sophisticated computation rather than for facilitating intuitive use and understanding, and which includes the difficult concept of 'place value'. Special measures therefore seem necessary to bridge the gap between the children's more global 'enactive' ways of working with numbers and tasks involving this abstract symbol system.

I have suggested that the children should start mathematics with extensive work on *large non-specific quantities*, followed by work on specific numbers, with emphasis on *subitizing*, and by the introduction of *numbers as entities*.

Simple, *iconic but rather inefficient ways of representing numbers* should be used for a longer period of time than is usual. This, in the end, will show the child the usefulness of abstract symbols, so that they are welcome rather than puzzling. Operational signs can be made familiar to the child by showing their development in history.

The overall aim should be to *make the arbitrary nature of symbols obvious* to young children, whether as part of the number system, or as money tokens, or as measures of time. In these early stages it is essential to give children all the time they need to feel 'at home' with symbols.

Chapter 2
Weakness in Organizational Skills

INTRODUCING THE FEATURE

Hans Freudenthal (1905–90), a mathematician and mathematical educator whose influence is still on the increase in the Netherlands and elsewhere (Van Est, 1993; Goffree, 1993; Dickey, 1994), considered mathematics 'an activity of organising fields of experience' (1973: 123). It follows that any child with a weakness in organizational skills can be expected to have problems learning elementary mathematics. A child with added language difficulties will have even greater problems because the strategy of 'talking a problem through' while solving it – essential for most of us when organizing a problem-solving situation – will not come naturally to him.

Such a child will probably have first come to the notice of a language specialist rather than a specialist in learning difficulties because of his slow, disorganized way of expressing himself. But, like the child with a weakness in symbolic understanding, he will be learning-impaired in a wider sense. Although his work shows good understanding in some fields, it seems poor overall and shows general inefficiency.

It is normally easy to identify children with a deficiency in organizational skills when faced with a group of language-impaired children: their weaknesses are very striking. For example, Dick, a boy of nine, thoughtful, friendly, obedient, started his work on the left-hand page of his exercise book like everybody else, day in, day out; but one day he started on the right and did not even notice that something was different.

And there is Sammy, 11 years old, who seems to know everything about beans and bees, and who reacts with mature sensitivity to the fact that even a teacher can be tired. He is a child who normally gets all his 'sums' right on paper – slowly but correctly; however, in one situation which called for mental rather than written arithmetic, it became obvious that he could not think of a better way of adding 11 to 60 than by counting on, one by one.

More generally, a lack of organizational skills includes one or more of the following sub-features:

Impulsiveness

Such children will often start a task without thinking about it first, testing their parent's or teacher's patience to its limit. They will jump to conclusions without trying to stand back and look at the information available; and if they are made to stop and look, they will find it hard to sort out the relevant details from the irrelevant. This will become especially obvious with numerical word problems.

Lack of concentration

There may be a genuine lack of concentration (whatever that really means), but a child may often be concentrating quite hard on a simpler aspect of the task that was set. For instance, when asked to make 'patterns of six', he may have to concentrate on counting each pattern carefully and therefore not realize that three out of his six patterns are the same; in the meantime, his more fortunate classmates who 'know and see' without effort that there are '3 and 3' or '2 and 4' may have produced eight different patterns of six. Telling the child to 'concentrate' will certainly not be the best way to improve his concentration (cf. Anderson, 1990: 47 ff. for 'perception and attention').

Clumsiness

Children with an organizational weakness often suffer from quite obvious problems of physical co-ordination; their movements seem slow, and they seem to lack any sense of rhythm (Cromer 1991: 264). Thus they account heavily for the high proportion of 'clumsy children' often found among language-impaired children. In written work this results in untidiness and a lack of clarity, and more problems therefore appear when the children have to read and interpret their own work.

Lack of spatial ability

A weakness in spatial ability, as shown in the case of Dick above, can make life bewildering for a child: the pet shop which he discovered yesterday will not be there today because the child turned right instead of left. It is not easy to imagine exactly how the world may appear with weak visual perception, with a lack of visual memory and without stable spatial grids in one's mind. The relatively few cases I know where a language impairment was combined with a very severe spatial disability suggest to me that it leads to a resigned timidity, to a vagueness in almost all responses, and a sad, almost melancholic insecurity.

Lack of grouping strategies

This will cause difficulties when common sequences must be learned. At times it may become almost nightmarish. Imagine having to learn to count by remembering a sequence of 100 nonsense syllables with the vague feeling that there are more to come: a threatening 'number line' is stretched out before you, endless, unstructured, with no pattern to cheer you up, no rhythm to keep you going. The lack of grouping strategies will make this task and others (e.g. classification or hierarchical ordering, cf. Cromer, 1991) unimaginably difficult for the child, both in school and outside.

In general, problems arise from a primary weakness in *perceiving* structures, and thus a disabling weakness in *using* structures as a means of organizing thought, experience and work.

CRITICAL POINTS IN THE ELEMENTARY MATHEMATICAL SYLLABUS

The children with such difficulties will obviously require help in very different areas. I will discuss four critical points in the syllabus:

understanding the decimal system as a useful structure;
organizing quantities;
organizing mathematical word problems;
spatial organization.

Understanding the Decimal System as a Useful Structure

What are the problems?

Daniel's case: counting up to 78

The problems can be shown through an example. Daniel is a boy of 10 who has severe expressive language problems and attends a special school for children with language disorders. His speech and his movements are extremely slow. His drawings, though immature, have character. He comments on yesterday's beautiful sunset, is a fairly competent reader and a great friend of 'Winnie-the-Pooh' with whom he seems readily to identify. All in all, although sometimes silly, he has considerable strengths.

Besides his speech handicap, his low achievement in number work is a real problem at school and at home. In my first individual

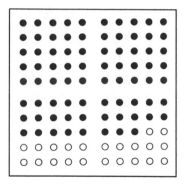

Figure 2.1: Quantity picture of 78

session with him he was presented with a quantity picture of 78, grouped for easy recognition into fives and tens (see Figure 2.1; for quantity pictures generally see Unit 4).

I asked him if he could tell me how many dots there were. He smiled pleasantly and said he would probably get into a muddle, but he would try.

The lesson proceeded as follows. He started to count one by one. I stopped him and drew his attention to the fact that there were always ten in a row, and that there was a gap after five rows. We established the fact that there would be 50 dots up to the middle of the sheet. He then started to count from 50 onwards, one by one. With his slow speech and inaccurate pointing he was already wrong by the time he reached 57. He had no hope of arriving at the right answer. If asked to count again, he probably would have come up with a different answer in every count.

I stopped him and asked if he remembered how many dots there were in a row.

'Yes, ten.'

Could he not count in tens then?

'Yes, ten, twenty, thirty . . .'

I stopped him again and reminded him that we knew where 50 was. Could he start counting in tens from the fifty-gap onwards?

'Yes, sixty, seventy . . .'

I stopped him and suggested that he wrote 70 down so that he would not forget. Then he could look at the rest. He did so while I covered the 70 on the quantity picture with a transparent overlay to make quite sure he could visualize what his written number meant. I said:

'Here is your 70, now let's look at the rest.'

He started to count:

'71, 72 . . .'

I stopped him and said:

'Don't bother about the 70 for the moment. You have written it

down and I have covered it up. So we can't forget it. Look at the rest. Is it more than five?' 'Yes'. 'Can you see the five, the gap?' 'Yes'. 'Right. Now start counting from the five-gap then.'
He counted correctly:
'Six, seven, eight.'
'So. How many altogether? Here is our seventy and there are your eight'
'Seventy-eight.'
'Good, write the figure "8" into your 70, into the nought.'

I explained to him that one could think of the figure 78 as being made up of the two figures 70 and 8 (compare Chapter 1 and also Unit 4). He smiled and did so.

I made him look at the quantity picture again and say the number. I showed him my 'express-way' of counting by saying (and pointing to) '50/70/75/78'. We went through more examples and he grasped the idea of grouping by 5/10/50 surprisingly well in this first session.

With this description of a remedial session we are already halfway into the next question, 'How can we help?' But it is worth considering first what persistent unchecked false counting can mean for children and how it can affect their ideas about numbers.

Let us assume one counts a quantity and ends up with 57 in a first attempt; then, in a recount, one arrives at 55; next time it may be 56, and then 57 again. Which is the correct number? As far as someone like Daniel is concerned, only the teacher seems to know, and Heaven knows how she knows. It would confirm his general suspicion that numbers are not to be trusted; they behave in an erratic fashion. One important quality of numbers, the quality of invariance, of constancy, is obscured for the child at an early critical stage – a learning handicap from which he might find it hard to recover.

It seems obvious that Daniel was not able to use the advantages of decimal groupings. He surely must have been introduced to the system somehow during his five years of schooling. If he had some knowledge, he failed to see its relevance to the task before him. Clearly, the use of a visual approach – tackling the problem through grouping as suggested by the quantity picture – did not occur to him.

How can we help?

Using the Slavonic abacus

In order to limit sequential demands and to prevent such inefficiency as shown above, one ought at a very early stage to provide children with a working model that can illustrate the underlying structure of the decimal system clearly and memorably. They need a tool at their fingertips, a picture in their minds, ready for use. In my opinion there is no better way to do this than through the representation of the decimal system in the arrangement of beads on the 'Slavonic abacus'.

This apparatus has already been mentioned in Chapter 1, where it is pictured (Figure 1.3). It presents the child with a clearly structured image of the 'field of 100', a visual whole that is sub-structured with breaks at five and ten. These breaks make it possible to recognize any quantity at a glance without counting. Seven, for instance, is seen as five-and-two and is instantly recognized as such; 70 is recognized as five-rows-of-ten-and-two-rows-more. Numbers are thus seen as two-dimensional geometrical shapes, as 'quantity pictures' rather than as points on a number line.

Moreover, quantities are never seen in isolation but always in the context of five, ten, or hundred. For instance, seven is not only learned visually as 'five-and-two', but is recognized at the same time as 'three-missing-from-ten'. All complementary numbers to 100 can simultaneously be seen in the field of 100 and can be easily read off: if 75 is shown by pushing 70 + 5 beads of the abacus on to one side, the complementary number can be seen as 20 + 5 beads on the other side. A detailed description of how to make such an abacus and how to work with it is given in Unit 4.

In my view, such an abacus is one of the essentials for a young child's intuitive mathematical development through play; it helps to bring about the familiarity with the decimal system which is needed later. If I had my way, every child, perhaps on his third birthday, would be provided with such a bead frame, by law, and in his favourite colour!

Using a paper abacus

A paper abacus is an adaptation of the Slavonic abacus. It has the same structured field of 100, arranged in rows of 10 with a break after 5, but the beads are drawn on paper as dots, and the 5-break in both directions is indicated by a small gap between the dots. It can be home-made and consists of two parts:

- a base card showing 100 dots arranged like the beads on the Slavonic abacus; and
- a coloured transparent overlay, cut in such a way that every number from 1 to 100 can be exposed by sliding it along horizontally and vertically.

For an illustration see Figure 2.2.

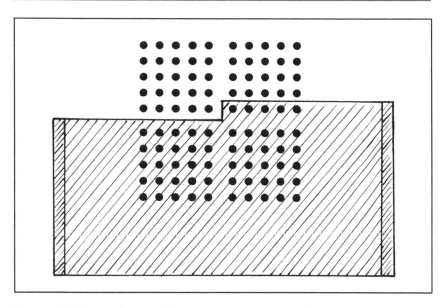

Figure 2.2: Paper abacus with transparent overlay (showing 45/55)

The apparatus shares most features with the Slavonic abacus: again there is no need for counting, and the complementary numbers can be seen simultaneously through the overlay. Although it lacks the tactile appeal of the bead movement, it has some advantages. It is easy to make, fairly large and colourful for the younger child, and more sophisticated for the older child by using for example, a small card holder of clear plastic, with computer symbols representing the 100 beads. Also, storage is no problem; the paper abacus does not take much more space than a bookmark and each child can keep a personal paper abacus in his exercise book. Mathematically it has advantages, too. These are shown in Unit 4, where detailed descriptions of how to make a paper abacus and how to use it are given.

At this stage it is mainly used for introducing the child to the structure of the decimal system by letting him find his way around 'the field'. Later it can be used for arithmetic proper. It is possible to work with both the Slavonic and the paper abacus in parallel – another example of trying to turn the necessary 'same old thing to learn' into something new for the child through different materials.

Using quantity pictures

An example of a quantity picture was shown above (Figure 2.1). Earlier in Chapter 1 it was suggested as one way of recording a quantity on paper. It provides yet another way of working with the same image – the structured 'field of 100'. The blank 'field' is identical to the base card of the paper abacus; blocks of dots representing a number can then be filled in with black or in colour to show a particular quantity, with its complementary number still blank. An easy way to make sets of quantity picture cards is described in Unit 4, together with detailed suggestions for use.

With Daniel, in the example above, I needed a few more introductory sessions with quantity pictures where he could work at his own speed. Later I used full sets of such materials aiming at speed recognition until he could 'read off' quantities and their complementaries to 100 with ease. Such familiarity will obviously be helpful, for example when giving and receiving change in a decimal money system.

Using a selection of Cuisenaire or similar rods for building up quantities from 1 to 100

Another way to consolidate knowledge of the structure of the 'field of 100' is to use a special selection of Cuisenaire rods (1-, 5-, and 10-rods only) to build up quantities according to the abacus schema (for a description of such rods, how to make them, and how to organize the materials see Unit 3).

Work with the rods can be carried out in parallel with any of the exercises suggested so far. The advantage is the fact that the child physically handles materials. The disadvantage is the clatter and the fact that the quantity is not seen in the frame of the whole 100 field. If one feels strongly about the lack of a 'frame', one could use an appropriate box, similar to the 10 × 10 cm Stern materials box (Stern and Stern, 1971), or work on a squared base card of 10 × 10 units.

In order to be able to build up quantities from 1 to 100, each child should have a box with a selection of 15 rods:

— five 10-rods bundled together flat to make one '50-flat' (use elastic band, masking tape or Sellotape);
— four single 10-rods;
— one 5-rod;
— five single unit cubes.

With this 15-piece set, any number up to 100 can be built up quickly, using the abacus grouping of 1/5/10/50. It pays to have a few spare pieces on hand, although it is good practice to let the child check his set regularly before he puts it away (it should make one complete 10 × 10 square).

Exercises can be carried out in group or individual sessions. In the latter case the instructor should also have a set and should work in parallel with the child. Although such a set can be used in more than one way, here, where we are concerned with strengthening the understanding of structure in the decimal system, the main exercise will be the building up of named quantities. It will involve tasks such as 'let's make a 77' and 'let's make a 28'. (For an illustration of a 28 built up with rods see Figure 1.2 in Chapter 1.)

Drawing quantities

It is good practice at all levels of number work to let children with organizational difficulties make drawings of number problems if they show uncertainty. However, the drawings of such children are often so disorganized that they become useless. One way to help them is to teach them to draw quantities in a standardized fashion. Such drawings can depict quantities as they appear when they are built up with the rods. It is advisable to start with quite a long period where work with rods and with drawings go hand in hand: the child builds up a quantity and then copies it with pencil and paper. Drawing can be practised on its own at a later stage. The use of squared paper or blank 'field of 100' sheets can be helpful at the beginning for children with severe difficulties. However, as the aim is to give them a quick-and-ready means to make a representation of a number they should in the end be able to make such a fast drawing on any scrap of paper. Figure 2.3(a) shows a fairly carefully drawn practice example of 64; Figure 2.3(b) shows the same number represented through a quick sketch.

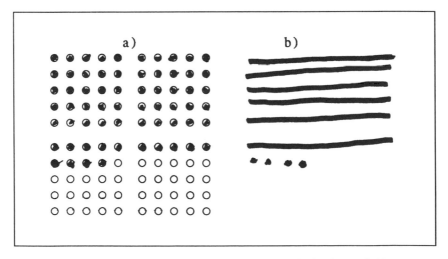

Figure 2.3 (a) and (b): Drawing a picture of a quantity in abacus fashion

Using a blank 100-square (linking the ordinal and cardinal aspect of numbers)

Most teachers will be familiar with commercially produced number squares on which the numbers 1 to100 are arranged in the familiar 10 rows of 10 numbers. These squares may have their place at later stages but in my experience they are often misused in elementary mathematics. A *blank* 100-square is similar but, as the name suggests, it has 100 small blank squares instead of 100 numbers. Such squares, expendable and easy to make at home (see Unit 4), can be used in more than one way.

Initially they can be employed as an aid to drawing quantities in a clear and structured way as suggested above. Their main usefulness becomes clear, however, when one tries to make a child familiar with the position of a number inside the structured field of 100.

The following suggestions assume that the child knows what figures up to 100 look like and knows how to write them. Minor uncertainties in this respect can be resolved on the way. There are two main ways to organize this activity:

- the teacher gives a certain number and the child finds its place on the square; or
- the teacher indicates the place on the square and the child finds the number.

Some children will find the first easier, others the latter. Both seem of equal importance and children should become competent in both. Here are two examples, one of each kind:

(a) A list of random numbers is given (e.g. 5, 19, 23, 40, 56, 63, 76, 81, 82, 99); the child has to write the numbers into the appropriate places on a blank square.
(b) A blank square is prepared by the teacher by indicating certain positions on it (i.e. by drawing a circle or square around them with felt tip) and the child has to write the appropriate figure into the marked places.

Once the child has gained some skills in such tasks, the squares can be used as 'test-squares'; these 'tests' can be fun as well as enhance confidence, for instance by 'going backwards' or 'round in circles'. The real test at the end is to see whether the child is able to fill in a full 100-square correctly. This should be checked regularly in later years. More examples and illustrations of (a) and (b) and of 'tests' are given in Unit 4.

To conclude this section: one would hope that by this stage the children not only feel 'at home' in the 'field of 100' when they see it, but also that they have built up a firm image of the structured field. Ideally the beginning of the decimal system should now be fixed in their minds as a 'good *gestalt*' – something they have learned to see as useful, which they can bring forth at will and use as a tool for the rest of their lives whenever a number problem calls for it.

For work with numbers over 100 and the continuation of the place value system see Chapter 1 and Unit 4.

Organizing Quantities

What are the problems?

In the last section quantities were presented to children in a stable and orderly frame, so that they could grasp the structure of our number system globally. Now we shall be looking at children faced with numbers outside the frame, with unordered quantities, or groups with varied and changeable relations to each other. Whereas in the previous section the aim was to make children *perceive* a given order, now we are asking them to *create* order. They are faced with problems of sequencing, classifying, halving, sharing, and seeing the same quantities, sometimes as wholes, sometimes as parts of different wholes. Grouping and re-grouping are required. Children have to learn to explore various possibilities of grouping; to make decisions about the most efficient ways of dealing with quantities in problem solving; to do the organizing themselves.

This will lead us to the heart of the problems confronting a child with a weakness in organizational skills. Such a step may prove very difficult for some, and often it seems advisable to introduce such activities while continuing the work with pre-structured quantities as discussed in the previous section.

Where to start?

Nine year old Dick, with an unordered heap of Cuisenaire rods in front of him, is asked to guess and then to find out how many '9s' he could make with this heap. His reaction is an instant wild guess of '100' – no thought is given to the size of the heap and the size of the rods; there is no tentative sorting with eyes or hands. The actual number of '9s' that could be made was only 18. When it came to 'finding out' he started building up '9s' with the smallest rods (putting together all the unit-pieces), which left him with the problem of what to do with the larger 8- and 7-rods at the end.

Something similar might occur when children like Dick have to deal with money. If they are given a handful of coins and asked to find out how much money the heap comes to, they will probably start by adding up the coins as they lie randomly before them; no attempt will be made to sort them into groups (50s, 20s, 10s etc.) or to get the higher values 'out of the way' first.

Another example of children failing to use grouping as an efficient way of dealing with quantities is described in detail in Chapter 5. Four boys, aged 11 and 12, were faced with a task like Dick's. They had to work as a team, which complicated matters. The account is an example of striking inefficiency in organizing quantities. All four members of the group showed later that they possessed the mathematical 'tools' to sort out the problem, but they did not see how to apply their knowledge to the situation. This missing link between knowing procedures and knowing when to apply them seems to be a major feature of a child with weak organizational ability.

Part–whole schema

This is a somewhat different problem. A child might know how to add $5 + 3$ but might find it more difficult to add $3 + 5$. The same child might come to a halt when confronted with $5 + ? = 8$.

One can assume that such a child hardly sees more than one relation between a triple group like 3/5/8. Perhaps he has been working extensively with the number line and is limited to seeing numbers fixed in a line, where the only relation between them is perceived as a linear one. He may perhaps be able to see numbers in terms of 'before and after', 'right and left' and 'larger/ smaller', but not recognize that these three numbers have more to do with each other than, let's say, 3, 5 and 6. If he had learned to see 8 as 'the whole' and 3 and 5 as components, the number problems shown above should have been of equal difficulty.

Such uncertainty suggests that there may be an inability to see numbers inside a part–whole schema, a schema which most children seem to grasp more or less intuitively at an early age. Although they may not be able to express the principles, their work shows that they can act on them. They seem to have understood that when dealing with numbers, 'the whole' remains, no matter what order the parts are in; or that the sum of the parts cannot be more and cannot be less than the whole. This will have to be taught explicitly to a child with a specific organizational deficiency, together with general skills in handling, switching, swapping, sharing, and grouping quantities in such a way that they give the most convenient start to the task at hand. It means painstaking effort for both teacher and child.

How can we help?

Starting with counters

This suggestion, applicable to all children at infant school level, will be particularly appropriate for young children with organizational difficulties. The work might also be helpful to older pupils who need help in organizing quantities. Some children may have missed out on such activities at an early stage, or they have not had enough of them, or they could not benefit from such activities when they were offered because of general immaturity.

The following suggestions often require a break in a child's current written number work with 'sums'; they sometimes mean asking the child to forget all about counting and figure-writing skills and have fun with counters. For some children the activities suggested may have to be altered in style so that the tasks do not appear too infantile. This can be achieved in different ways: by using appropriate counters, by turning the activity into a race against the clock or, if the pupil has learned to lose fairly gracefully, by turning it into a more competitive game.

My suggestions are based in part on the work done by Johannes Wittmann (1885–1960), a German mathematician and psychologist who became interested in teaching methods and applied the principles of gestalt psychology to educational situations, mainly early reading and early mathematics (Wittmann, 1967). Some of his suggestions will be familiar to any infant teacher (cf. Bednarz and Janvier, 1988).

To start with, one will need a fairly large heap of counters, about 100 per child. In fact one should ideally have several sets of 100 made from different materials such as bottle tops, play matches, beans and melon pips. As we have seen, an activity for a young child is normally 'new' if the material is new. The initial stages presuppose no formal number knowledge; figures are not used at all and the skill of naming quantities of different sizes can be developed at the same time. For example, the child might learn to name a pair of two as 'two' or a group of four as 'four'. The aim is to let the child create order out of a mass of unordered unit counters. In doing so he will gain 'hands on' experience with quantities.

The starting point will be work with a single line. The child is asked to line up the counters in a single line, which can be straight, curved (like a snake), in a ring, with the counters close together, or with the counters spaced out. Figure 2.4 gives an illustration of such lines, which may help to show how such work can also offer good

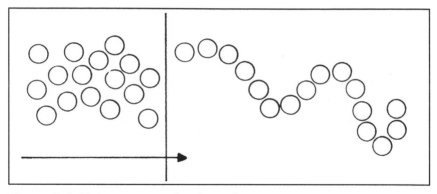

Figure 2.4: Lining up an unordered quantity

opportunities to learn essential concepts of space such as beginning, end, middle, first, last, spaced-out, close together, lined-up, in a muddle.

The next step to follow will be work with double and multiple lines. Lines of pairs (twos) can be developed out of a single line by bending it in half, or they can be arranged directly from the heap. Other lines might include:

- lines of double pairs (fours);
- lines (blocks) of twice double pairs (eights);
- lines of threes;
- lines of double threes (sixes);
- lines (blocks) of three threes (nines);
- combining lines of ones and twos (threes);
- combining lines of twos and threes (fives).

Further steps are outlined in Unit 2. They are concerned with:

- dividing the heap into parts (two parts, four parts etc., approximately as well as exactly);
- making groups by 'rounding up' various quantities 'in one go'; and
- tallying (which offers the first opportunities to apply the decimal system tentatively).

Using full sets of Cuisenaire or similar rods for learning to organize unordered quantities

Such rods were mentioned before and are described and discussed in detail in Unit 3. The original idea behind these long-established materials was to represent numbers by rods in various colours and lengths. The number 'one', the unit of the system, is represented by a white cube of 1 cm × 1 cm × 1 cm; 'two' is represented by a red rod of 2 cm × 1 cm × 1 cm, 'three' by a green rod 3 cm × 1 cm × 1 cm, and so forth. Each number (from 1 to 10 and an optional 12) is allocated a specific colour and the length of the rod corresponds to that number. See Figure 2.5 for the 'staircase of rods'.

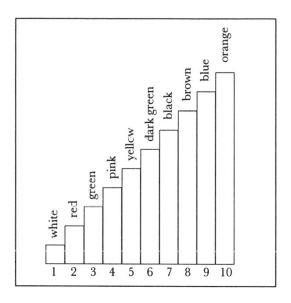

Figure 2.5: Staircase of rods (colours according to the Cuisenaire system)

It is best to start the activities with a period of 'free ordering'. Only after that should the child's attempts be channelled into the order that will be of greatest use to him – the decimal system. This means that some counting/subitizing skills are assumed. If the child has not yet had a chance to work with the rods, some practice sessions are advisable so that the child learns which colour represents which number and becomes familiar with the rods. It may be helpful to have a reference sheet on hand, showing the 'staircase' in colour (see Figure 2.5) – with or without numerals.

The procedures are as follows: the child is presented with a random heap of rods. The number of rods can be varied, starting with a handful and going up to tipping out a whole box (the standard set contains 291 pieces if complete). First it has to be established that the 1 cm cube is the unit that counts as 'one'. Then the task is to find out how many such units are contained in the heap.

In my experience, even after preparatory sessions, children's first attempts at the task can vary considerably and are often incorrect or inefficient. The children might count each rod as one; there is often no pre-ordering: they try to add up the rods 'as they come'; or they may start with the smallest rods.

Thus at the beginning the children will have to be told to stand back and think before they start. They will have to be guided towards the most convenient organization for the task (here: building up tens). Even if they seem to have understood the advantages of pre-organizing, it is not certain that they will use their experience at the next trial. They will need ample repetition, so that starting a task with efficient organization will become 'second nature' to them.

Repetition can be varied:

(a) by increasing the size of the heap;
(b) by using only certain rods (e.g. only 10s, 5s, 1s; or only 4s); or
(c) by letting the children 'swap' rods so that 10s can be made up (e.g. one 4-rod against two 2-rods).

Partner work can also be a useful variation that will add complexity to the task (see description of a group of session in Chapter 5).

Thus one hopes that the children will in the end leave such a series of work with the feeling that life is easier when one organizes matters first.

Using the chopstick game for ordering quantities

This game has already been introduced as a means of making children understand the arbitrariness of money (see Chapter 1). It is described in detail in Unit 3. When using this game, the possibilities of teaching different ways of 'pre-organizing' seem unlimited, since the value of the colour-marked sticks can be altered for each session according to the purpose of the exercise; also the number of sticks can be monitored, which allows for many degrees of difficulty in number and organizational tasks.

The idea is for the child to be given a suitable number of sticks (e.g. 3 or 5; a handful; all sticks), or to pick them out of a container without the colour markings being seen. He then has to establish the total value of the sticks. The task is similar to the one dealt with in relation to Cuisenaire rods in that it requires the child to organize the sticks before starting to sum up the total value. However, there are some important differences. Firstly, the possible variety of sticks is greater; also, there is a chance element when picking the sticks that will make the task more of a game. Most importantly, it is a step into the abstract, because, unlike the work with Cuisenaire type rods, there is now no visible relation between the symbol (colour) and the quantity it represents. Thus the game can serve as a playful introduction to the way we express values with abstract symbols when we use number figures. I have used such sets of sticks extensively and in various ways. They provided the necessary repetition, yet never failed to interest the child.

Organizing money before counting it

Here one will need a fair amount of up-to-date play money. The task is basically the same as above: the child is presented with a heap of coins – or a heap of coins and notes – and is asked to establish the value of the heap. Again, sensible grouping is called for to make the work efficient (see the section on practising money skills in Chapter 1). The difficulty of the task can be varied by using heaps of different sizes, or by a special selection of coins and notes. For more playful work (coins only) one could use a 'money machine', as suggested in Unit 5, which will turn the exercise into a game.

Working with number triplets

These suggestions start from a different angle. Whereas so far work has started with an unspecified quantity, the child is now given precisely quantified numbers to organize or reorganize. As mentioned before, structuring in elementary mathematics means, in most cases, grouping numbers in such a way as to make working with them convenient. The child has to learn to see possibilities of changing quantities around, of chunking groups together, and of dividing other groups. 'Wholes' must be split into parts, and parts become new wholes. This means that numbers have to be seen as more than figures sitting forever in a fixed position on the number line. Instead of emphasizing number line and counting-on procedures, I suggest that it might be helpful to concentrate on three numbers at a time which can be turned into simple equations (e.g. 3/5/8 into $3 + 5 = 8$, or $3 = 8 - 5$). I will call such groups of three numbers 'number triplets' (for want of a better term). Number triplets can be described as any three numbers where one number is the sum of the other two. Such triplets can be presented in written form with the numbers set out in the form of a triangle rather than as the horizontally fixed equation or vertical sum. If this is done at an early stage, one will perhaps avoid the danger of children with organizational difficulties becoming rigid in their understanding and handling of numbers. They are made to see the three numbers 'from all sides'. The numbers are to be treated as movable pieces in a game, taking this and that position, while their different relationships are explored.

I suggest that Cuisenaire rods could once again form the starting points of such explorations. The 'triangle' of the triplet 8/5/3 can be represented by an 8-rod on top, with a 5-rod and a 3-rod underneath (cf. Figure 1.18(a)). With the help of the rods one can work as follows.

Introducing a triplet

Take (or let the child take) an 8-rod; 'break up' the rod into 5 and the rest; put a 5-rod under the 8-rod and ask the child what is missing (3-rod). Ask the child 'What can we see?' 'What can we say?' The answer should be: 8 (as our 'whole') can be broken up into the two parts 3 and 5 (8 = 3 + 5).

For the next task, start with a 3-rod; put an 8-rod under the 3-rod and ask the child to find what is missing in the top row (5-rod). Ask the child 'What can we see?' 'What can we say?' The answer should go something like this: we have got a 3-rod; we want something that will make the whole as long as an 8-rod; so we need a 5-rod (3 + 5 = 8).

Comparison of members

The next task should be to explore relations between the whole ('top number') and the two parts:

8 is more (or is bigger, longer, heavier) than 5 (by 3);

8 is more (or is bigger, longer, heavier) than 3 (by 5);

Changing one part of the triplet

The child must realize that if he changes one number in the triplet, another number must be changed accordingly to keep a true relational triplet (example: 8/3/5):

if we change 5 to 6, then we must change 3 to 2; or 8 to 9;

if we change 3 to 1, then we must change 5 to 7; or 8 to 6.

These changes are best made with rods first, and only later with figures on paper.

Making chains of number triplets

Finally, the child should become aware of the fact that what acts as 'the whole' in one relation can become 'a part' in another relation and vice versa. So, the number '8' which has been 'the whole' in the previous tasks can be used as 'a part' in another triplet:

make '8' a part in a new triplet (possible solution: 10/8/2);

make '5' the biggest number ('the whole') in a new triplet (possible solution: 5/2/3).

A good way of practising this is to make 'chains' (either with rods, drawings, or figures) as Figure 2.6 illustrates. These chains can be read from the top down or from the bottom up.

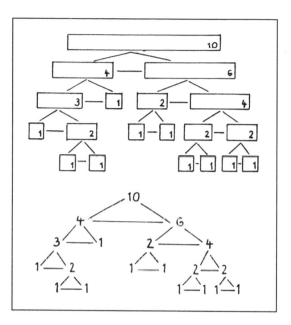

Figure 2.6: Chains of number triplets

More extensive work with number triplets is described in detail in Unit 3.

Concluding remarks about organizing quantities

The suggestions made above are all intended to help children see the advantages of efficient organization or reorganization *before* starting to solve number problems. They also aim to give them some skills in doing this. Beyond helping in the solution of mathematical problems, the suggestions may serve a wider purpose, particularly appropriate for children with organizational difficulties. If one succeeds in making such children aware of similarities, this may actually help them to 'stop and think' in solving 'real-life' problems such as, perhaps, where to start clearing up the kitchen or, later, how to set about buying a house.

Organizing Mathematical Word Problems

What are the problems?

Word problems in mathematics are normally seen as number problems which come as part of a story. They deal with quantities which stand in various specific relations to each other; these relations are described by the text and have to be understood before the problem can be solved.

From childhood days one may remember mathematical questions like *Peter has 7 marbles and loses 2 to Paul. How many marbles has Peter got left?* Such word problems have a long tradition, going back to the early days of printing. Before that they were apparently found on 4000-year-old Egyptian papyri (De Corte and Verschaffel, 1991). As a child I liked such stories. They seemed a welcome oasis in the dry desert of bare sums. However, as a teacher I have learned to view number stories with diffidence: some children are able to do them but don't really seem to know how; and others never seem to learn. In both cases teaching is difficult. This led De Corte and Verschaffel to talk of a 'word problem depression' among teachers, in this case among Flemish primary school teachers (i.e. teachers who deal mainly with children who have no specific learning difficulties).

Indeed, the literature is full of examples of 'normal' children who find word problems hard and often do not solve them the teacher's way. Some examples are extremely frustrating; others may amuse you. For instance, Clements (1980) reports (my summary): Australian 6th graders (age between 11 and 12) were given a drawing with twelve jolly children lined up in a row. The text, slightly ambiguous, was: 'Here are some children. I have 24 lollies and I want each child to have the same number of lollies. How many lollies will I give each child?' One boy answered: 'There are 12 children, and 24 lollies; 12 into 24 goes 2, so we have two twelves; you multiply these two twelves; 12 times 12 is 144.' Another boy answered: 'I would give each child one lolly and keep 12 for myself.' This was marked as wrong.

A second example is 'the captain's age', a number story that has appeared in various forms. The first and most sophisticated version I know was told by Freudenthal (1973: 94). A simpler version is the following:

There are 26 sheep and 10 goats on a boat. How old is the captain?

It was given, in this form, to 97 children from Grenoble (age seven to nine). The result was that 76 of them managed to work out the captain's age on the basis of the data given (Freudenthal 1982; Goffree, 1993).

One can take this simply as a striking example of 'what's going on in school' (Karmiloff-Smith, 1992: 91) but Freudenthal tries to understand what might have happened from the child's perspective. For him the key to the matter is one of context, more precisely of the 'magic context' the child might give to the story. He realizes that children live in a world of their own where dandelions can tell you the time; and where the dots on a ladybird can tell you how old it is (note: Freudenthal uses different examples, but these are the nearest I could think of in English). So, why not find the age of the captain by counting the animals on his boat?

There is a further matter of context: a child normally believes in and acts upon (thank goodness) what Grice (1967) called the 'co-operative principle', whereby a speaker's contribution to a conversation should be informative, true and relevant. The questioner in the 'captain's age' problem clearly misused the child's trust.

If the context has such an effect on children with no particular difficulties, how much more will it affect a child with language difficulties. It is sometimes very hard to enter into the inner world of such a child. Has he any inkling of the fact that communication relies on trust? Is there a 'magic world' or just confusion? Does he know how age is determined? (I remember a boy of about 13 years with pragmatic language problems who frankly and truthfully asked a school visitor with rather striking white hair whether he was going to die soon. 'I hope not', said the visitor, surprised. 'Why do you think so?' 'Because your hair is white.')

When thinking more specifically of the child with a combination of language and organizational problems, one can expect that the general difficulties with word problems (logic, language and the complexity of the task) are aggravated by both kinds of handicap.

Logic, language and the complexity of the task

Mathematical word problems, even at a low level, are complex problems. Firstly, some knowledge is needed in at least three different areas:

(a) the specific aspect of 'life' in which the story takes place;
(b) the mathematical procedures that can be applied to the problem;
(c) the logic and language of the story.

Secondly, these areas have to be integrated. For children who lack organizational ability this is a task that proves especially difficult with regard to the last area (logic and language). Here one has to organize data, plan procedures, relate x to y, and all without losing track of the story and of the question asked.

For instance, in the problem concerning Peter's and Paul's marbles, mentioned at the beginning of the section, children will need a general knowledge of what playing marbles is about. They will also need some procedural knowledge of how to deal with the numbers involved: they will have to map the story about marbles onto something like '7 − 2 = ?'. And they must be able to understand the text. Although these aspects may not be very demanding in themselves, it is the logical *interaction* between procedure and context knowledge that makes the problem complex and difficult. Perhaps a teacher can take comfort from the experience that 'world knowledge' as well as 'procedural knowledge' will slowly increase with age, but the fact that the two have to be combined under ever new conditions makes learning and teaching so difficult. If one also takes into account the highly *personal* frames of experience, outlook and motivation of each individual, it becomes obvious that it will not be easy to find relevant research evidence in this field (cf. Riley, Greeno and Heller, 1983). Some findings, however, now seem so well supported that the teacher might feel confident in using them with both impaired and non-impaired children.

There is substantial research into problem-solving in general and into children's difficulties with mathematical word problems in particular. Most of the latter relates to 'normal' children (see, for instance, the research summaries in Dickson et al., 1984; also, Lester, 1983; and Riley et al., 1983). Such research into mathematical problem-solving is still proceeding (for a fairly recent overview see De Corte and Verschaffel, 1991; cf. also Teubal and Nesher, 1991).

To my knowledge there have not been any group studies dealing with the question of mathematical problem-solving ability in *children with language difficulties*. It is easy to see why not: with such a diverse and fairly small population and such a complex issue, reliable results indicating general trends cannot be expected. There are some studies from neighbouring fields of linguistic difficulties that may be relevant, such as studies of children from linguistic minorities, of deaf children, and of dyslexic children (see, for instance: Stone, 1988; Miles and Miles, 1992). In general, the way forward will probably be through a corpus of case studies (see Miles and Miles, 1992, for some case studies of dyslexic children). One has to realize that teaching word problems to language-impaired children, especially children with additional organizational difficulties, will always call for the adaptation of any research findings.

'Real problems'

The pupil's reaction to numerical word problems is often one of panic and an understandable desire to get out of the situation, come what may. This might result in 'crunching' the numbers found in the story in any way that comes to mind, no matter whether it makes sense or not (see, for instance, the first answer to the lolly-pop example above). Also, there often seems to be a lack of any learning-transfer from previous experience with word problems, a failure to recognize similarities. Teacher and child often seem to have to tackle each problem as if the child had never met anything like it before. This may be caused by the fact that no problem is quite like another: even if the mathematical procedure that is called for is the same, the situational conceptual knowledge needed for a particular number problem, or just the linguistic structure of the text may be different. To perceive similarity under so many variables needs some ability to organize experience, which of course is the very ability the child lacks.

Before turning to the question of 'how can we help', it seems worth asking: why do we pose word problems in mathematics? Why do we clutter up a straightforward mathematical problem like '7 − 5 = ?' with a story about marbles? The main answer must be that for most people mathematics is only useful when it is applied. Word problems in textbooks are meant to bridge the gap between 'pure' and 'applied' mathematics. They seek to prepare children for real life problems with numbers. But how real are those problems? How real are adult problems for a child (cf. Freudenthal, 1982)? This is where Freudenthal's classic formulation of 'mathematics fraught with relations' comes to mind. When he talks about 'relations' in mathematics, he is not simply thinking about the interrelation between different aspects of mathematics, but above all about 'the relation with a lived through reality rather than with a dead mock reality that has been invented with the only purpose of serving as an example of application' (Freudenthal, 1973: 78).

This leaves us with the question: how does one find enough mathematical word problems for a child that are related to what he has personally 'lived through'? Furthermore, how does one find problems that need solving for the child's own satisfaction?

In practice, teacher and child together probably will not find enough 'real problems' for the child's need of skill practice, even in the most open school system. One should, however, keep this ideal constantly in mind. One ought to be on the look-out, so that the few fine occasions that meet our ideal are not missed. The rest of the teacher-initiated problems should be as near to the child's 'lived through' experience as possible. This means that one may actually have to provide certain experiences first, like a session of playing marbles for the example above. Such experiences, deliberately introduced, can then be used as a basis for the number problems which one wants to set.

The 'fishing story'

At the end of these introductory paragraphs I want to relate a true story. It will lead us into deep waters and certainly show the difficulties we can expect. It grew out of a child's 'lived through' experience and it is so beautifully embedded in an almost 'magical context' that it may keep the balance of worries right for us and remind us that there is more to life than logic.

The class (of a special school for language-impaired children) had been working on number stories of the following kind:

> A farmer has 4 fields with 16 cows in each field; how many cows has he got altogether?

The pupils were then asked to write a story on the same pattern themselves. One of the class was Jason, 14 years of age, more or less still at the stage of 'elementary mathematics'. He had been at that school for over six years, due to educational problems which were linked to widespread language problems as well as a lack of organizational abilities. This boy, besides being keen on fishing, had many qualities: he could nurse any ill pot-plant back to health, he was sweet with younger children, he was a good swimmer, he could sing quite well, keep a rhythm (which is unusual for a child with organizational problems), and play 'Amazing Grace' with genuine feeling on the tin-whistle. He was no fool, but certain things didn't make sense to him. Jason wrote:

> There are 5 lakes for fishing teams; 8 men in a team; how many fish does that make?

I will come back to this story.

How can we help?

I will limit my suggestions to the application of two strands of research on mathematical problem-solving. Firstly, there is the 'heuristic' approach as shown in the work of George Polya (1887–1985), offering general strategies for problem-solving; secondly, there is a more data-based approach which has established a kind of 'hierarchy of difficulties' for mathematical word problems (for example, through the work of Riley et al., 1983). The first approach is particularly suitable for 'real' problems where and when they arise; the second is more useful for the pre-planned systematic teaching of word problems.

Solving problems with Polya's guidelines

George Polya published his book *How to Solve It* in 1945; it has been republished in a new paperback edition (Penguin, 1990) and seems to be easily available in most English-speaking countries (and is, in my opinion, worth possessing). The book gives general guidelines that could be used by any person for any problem, although they were developed on the basis of mathematical problem-solving (cf. also Polya, 1981). The following is an attempt to modify the guidelines so that a child with a combination of language and organizational difficulties could learn to use them.

Polya's approach is based on the observation of four phases in mathematical problem-solving. These are formulated as guidelines with suggestions to think about and questions to answer oneself, both of which are meant to lead to an organized approach when faced with problems. However, the language is such that a teacher of language-impaired children will have the task of 'translating' the guidelines into a form understood by the child.

Polya's phases

I will not cover all sections of the guidelines in detail, but I will try to provide enough examples to give a taste of the method. The phases are:

I.   Understanding the problem
II. Devising a plan
III. Carrying out the plan
IV. Looking back.

These phases are broken down into sub-sections. For instance, 'Understanding the problem' (Phase I) has two parts:

Getting acquainted, and

Working for better understanding (1990: 33 ff.).

Polya suggests that each of these two parts should be approached separately and he proposes detailed questions. These are shown below for both parts of Phase I (Table 2.1 and Table 2.2) together with an adapted simpler version of the questions which I hope a pupil like Jason, the boy who wrote the fishing story, might understand. Such simpler language often means *more* language; and perhaps it will become obvious when looking at the tables that the word and concept 'condition' used by Polya seems to be the one causing most difficulties (for the pupil and for the 'translator').

Table 2.1: Some of Polya's suggestions translated into simpler language

---

Phase One: Understanding the problem

---

1. Getting acquainted

In Polya's words	**In simpler words**
(a) *Where should I start?* Start from the statement	Start by reading the text carefully; what does it mean?
(b) *What can I do?* Visualize the problem as a whole as clearly and as vividly as you can. Do not concern yourself with details at the moment	Close your eyes and think of what you have read. Forget about the numbers for the moment. Can you see what is going on in the story?
(c) *What can I gain by doing so?* You should understand the problem, familiarize yourself with it, impress its purpose on your mind. The attention bestowed on the problem may also stimulate your memory and prepare for the recollection of relevant points	You should really get to know the story. Your should remember what is going on – what we know, what we need to know, what we don't know.

When using the guidelines, I suggest that the teacher provide the pupil with a written list of the questions – at the beginning perhaps only a selection – geared to a particular problem. The teacher then helps the child to work through a problem along the questions of the guidelines. Later, a standardized fuller list can be given and the pupil can select and apply the questions to a particular problem. Through frequent use, the guidelines should be memorized in a very global way; and in the end they should become part of the pupil's strategies. It is hoped that thereby one can counteract one of the most prevailing weaknesses in a pupil with organizational problems: his tendency to rush into action without planning.

Applying Polya's guidelines to 'the fishing story'

As an example, the following is a possible way of dealing with Jason's fishing story. It is the first part of an 'imaginary dialogue'. At the time I was not involved with his mathematical education any more and therefore did not have a chance to deal with this problem myself. Thus such a 'made-up' description is the best I can offer here. However, such an imaginary solution has its joys: it can follow the ideal course a teacher always hopes for.

Table 2.2: More of Polya's suggestions translated into simpler language

Phase One: Understanding the problem

2. Working for better understanding

In Polya's words	In simpler words
(a) *What is the unknown?*	What do we want to find out? What do we want to know and don't know?
(b) *What are the data?*	What do we know? (What are the facts – the data?)
(c) *What is the condition?*	Let's look again at what we know and what we don't know. How do the two go together? Can we connect the two?
(d) *Is it possible to satisfy the condition?*	Can we actually connect the two in a way that makes sense?
Is the condition sufficient to determine the unknown?	Do we know enough to find out all we need to find out? Would we get a sensible answer?
Or is it insufficient?	Or is there something missing?
Or redundant?	Or is there something we don't really need? Do we know more than we need to know? Can we cross out something because it does not help?
Or contradictory?	Or is there something that does not fit together, that does not make sense?
(e) *Draw a figure*	Can you make a picture of the story?
(f) *Introduce suitable notation*	Can you turn the picture into a sort of shorthand sketch, something easy to work with?
(g) *Separate the various parts of the condition*	What are the different parts of the story that matter to us?
(h) *Can you write them down?*	Can you write them down in separate sentences?

In the dialogue below, the leading questions are asked in a flexible way with Polya's suggestions in mind. Jason's expected answers are reflected in the teacher's comments (signalled by a dash that is followed by sentences beginning with 'Yes', 'No', 'OK' or 'Right'); they are based on my knowledge of the pupil through extensive previous contact, both in individual sessions and when I was his class teacher.

Perhaps one should bear in mind that the 'fishing story' is not a typical textbook story; whereas in textbook problems the 'condition' is normally sufficient to determine the unknown, here it is clearly not. This can perhaps show the flexibility of the guidelines.

When starting, the first comment to Jason should certainly be: 'You have got an interesting problem here!' rather than 'It can't be done!' This is a general point that seems worth repeating. One ought to take false questions or solutions absolutely seriously, almost as a gift to teaching. They can be taken as hypothetical solutions of a kind. This is a legitimate way of problem-solving, and one should convey to the pupil the value of such 'trial-solutions' with utter conviction (cf. Whitburn, 1995, who observed such an attitude as an established part of mathematics teaching in Japan).

The dialogue

(a) 'Getting acquainted' (see Table 2.1)

> Let's have a go at your story.
>
> Let's start from what you have written.
>
> Read it aloud and then close your eyes and think of it.
>
> Can you see the men sitting and fishing?
>
> Forget about the numbers for the time being.
>
> Can you see the lakes? Can you see the fishermen?
>
> – Right. What do we actually want to find out? What is our 'problem'?
>
> – Yes, to find out how many fish they caught.

(b) 'Working for better understanding' (see Table 2.2)

> What do we know? What are the 'data'?
>
> – Yes, we know two things: we know there are five lakes and we know there are eight fishermen sitting around each lake with their fishing gear. Perhaps it will help us if we make a drawing. (Note: this is an alteration in the order of the guidelines.)

The drawing is done (see Figure 2.7). After the drawing:

> Right. We certainly know the story well now.

(c) A question from Phase II

In this particular case I would deal here with a specific question, moved up the list from Phase II: Devising a plan. The question is: 'Do you know a related problem?' This should remind the pupil of the model story (the farmer with four fields, where each field has 16 cows), and comparison would probably make the special problem of

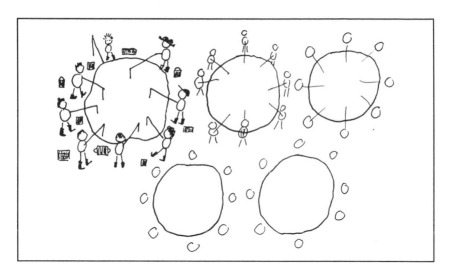

Figure 2.7: Drawing for the 'fishing story': five lakes, each with eight fishermen
Note: the figure shows progressive simplification; it is up to the teacher to decide
how much time should be spent on the drawing; for some pupils full drawings may
be good slow reinforcement, for others only a rough outline is necessary

the fishing story clearer. Perhaps a sketch could also be made of the
model story and the answer could be worked out (4 × 16). Questions
like the following could be asked:

What did we want to know in the 'cow story'? What is the 'unknown' there?

– Yes, how many cows the farmer has.

What do we know? What are the 'data'?

– Yes, we know two things: the number of fields and the number of cows in
each field.

Do we need both?

– Yes.

Do we need more?

– No.

Can we link the two numbers? How?

The conversation continues in a similar way.

(d) Back to Phase I (Working for better understanding: see Table 2.2)

Right. Let's go back to your fishing story.

Can we do the same here?

– Yes? No?

Let's see. What do we want to know?

– Yes, how many fish they caught.

What do we know?

–Yes, 5 lakes, and 8 fishermen each.

Do we need both?

–Yes. Do we need to know more?

–No? Yes?

Jason, this is the point where your story gets interesting.

I am sorry I will have to end the example here. It would take several more pages to finish it. For my own satisfaction I wrote the dialogue right through to Phase IV ('Looking back'). As can be imagined, this led to difficult problems: insufficient data; methods of data collection; uncertainties posed by 'natural' data versus 'people-made' data; averages, good ones and bad ones (i.e. with too low numbers). In the end, with the help of cutting up paper fish and comparing 'catching fish' with 'passengers in a bus' in a 'bus story', 'we' arrived at the final qualified answer which was:

In three hours' fishing in these particular five lakes and in 'normal' weather a medium-skilled fisherman can be expected to catch on average '1.2 fish'.

All this seemed necessary to make him realize the difference between the 'cows in the field' situation and the fishing situation in respect of the nature of the data that were given.

I hope the shortened form of the example is enough to give an incentive to try Polya's guidelines with the kind of child we are talking about.

Starting from what has been found easy

The above example was an attempt to show how one could deal with a word problem that arose from a pupil's writing. In that respect it was a 'real' problem. As was said earlier, real problems may not come up frequently enough for sufficient practice, and they will certainly not turn up just 'at the right level'. Thus for more systematic work on word problems one will have to use textbook problems. Unlike rich 'lived through' problems, in which the child is often thrown in at the deep end, textbook problems can be monitored and chosen according to difficulty and according to the need to practise particular aspects of the problems. Fortunately, there is some helpful research to show what is, on the whole, easy or difficult, at least in regard to simple addition and subtraction problems (see below under 'Logic').

Some aspects to consider when teaching word problems

As was mentioned earlier in this section, children have to deal with at least three interacting forces when called upon to solve word problems:

life experience
logic and language, and
mathematical procedures.

Which aspect should one concentrate on first? There is no easy answer to this question since one aspect will *interact* with the others and can – as research has shown (e.g. De Corte and Verschaffel, 1991: 119) – alter the gradation of difficulty otherwise found in one aspect. Thus it is not possible to give one single list on which to rely for grades of difficulty, and it seems therefore best to consider the three aspects separately first. However, there is a reference list at the end of this section which gives an overview of all aspects.

1. Life experience

It is easy to see that the first textbook problems should have some connection to the 'lived through' experience of the child. If that is not so, the whole undertaking would be meaningless and would be better not done at all. Any teacher who knows the pupil well will probably be able to judge whether the experience of the child is sufficient for a particular problem. If it is not, it might be possible to provide the missing experience first (so, for example, the experience of playing marbles might prepare a child for a problem involving marbles). Later, when one can assume that the child has accepted that school and 'life' are not the same, such problems can perhaps be less linked to personal experience.

2. Logic (semantic categories)

I will list four categories of semantic structures commonly found in addition and subtraction problems. Such categories were established in the late 1970s and early 1980s and were used extensively in word problem research (Carpenter and Moser, 1982; Nesher, 1982; Vergnaud, 1982; Riley, Greeno and Heller, 1983). They have been discussed again from various points of view in more recent publications (see, for instance, De Corte and Verschaffel, 1991; Teubal and Nesher, 1991; Bryant, 1995; Nunes and Bryant, 1996). The following is mainly based on Riley et al., 1983. For fuller information it is advisable to study the original writings on the topic. In summary, the categories are:

(a) *Change problems*, for example:
Mary has 8 marbles; she plays with her brother and wins 2 more; now she has . . .?
Simple change problems of this kind have been found easy, presumably because the arithmetic is straightforward addition; there is only one starting set; the answer is the result of a change due to a child's action and, as we know, children like and can understand change and action.

(b) *Combine problems*, for example:
Mary has 8 marbles, her brother has 2; together they have . . .?
This calls for the same simple procedure; two static starting sets have to be combined, i.e. there is no active play involved.

(c) *Compare problems*, for example:
Mary has 8 marbles, her brother has 2. Who has more? How many more?
Again, this is a static affair, a description with two unchanging starter sets. The child is asked to supply a third. The procedure is not as obvious as in the two examples above (either 'counting on' or subtraction) and such problems have been found to be difficult. Even more difficulties are posed by compare problems of the following type, where the second starter set has to be worked out:
Mary has 8 marbles. She has 6 more than her brother. How many marbles has her brother?
For a discussion of compare problems and implications for teaching see Nunes and Bryant (1996: 135–40).

(d) *Equalizing*, for example:
Mary has 8 marbles, her brother has 2; they want to share their marbles so that each has the same.
This involves either
comparing and then sharing: Mary has (?) more; so if Mary gives her brother (?) they both have . . . ? or
combining and sharing: together they have (?); each gets half, which is . . . ?

In both cases the structure of the problem is more complex than in those of the previous categories; however, it was found that if the child was allowed to use concrete materials, equalizing ('even sharing' as the children would call it) would cause fewer problems than combining and comparing.

To sum up: in general, 'combine' and 'compare' problems seem more difficult than simple 'change' problems. But, as was suggested in the last paragraph, there are certain conditions under which any of the four categories can become relatively easy or difficult. Thus gradations can be found within each category. Riley et al. (1983), for instance, grade change problems from 1 to 6. An example of a more complex change problem (grade 4) would be the following:

Mary's brother has 2 marbles; Mary gives him some of hers; now he has 8; how many marbles did Mary give him?

Here the answer is not the *result* of the happenings but the *change* ($2 + ? = 8$). It thus is a case where 'the position of the unknown' adds difficulties to the problem.

The following is therefore a summary of identifiable circumstances under which grades of difficulty can be altered. It is hoped that such a list of conditions will assist the teacher in judging the possible difficulty of a problem before using it, in order to make a rather daunting task easier for a child who is weak in language and organizational skills.

Conditions under which a simple word problem may be altered in its degree of difficulty

(a) *Use of concrete objects*

For young children all problems normally become easier with concrete materials. Certain problems seem to become disproportionately easier with objects to be handled. For instance, when using counters, 'equalizing' problems can become easier than certain types of 'change' problem (for example, the 'grade 4' problem above) because they can often be solved by the simple infant method of 'one for you and one for me . . .'.

(b) *The position of the unknown*

One case has already been mentioned in the example above (*Mary's brother has 2 marbles...*). There the end result of the change (8 marbles) was known, and the unknown was 'hidden in the middle'. Such problems are understandably harder for a young child than problems where the result is the unknown (where the 'normal' sum pattern of $1 + 1 = 2$ is obvious).

Problems that *start* with the unknown seem to be just as difficult or perhaps even more so. These would constitute a 'grade 6' change problem according to the study by Riley et al.:

Mary had some marbles; she gave 6 to her brother; now Mary has 2 left. How many did she have to start with? (? − 6 = 2).

Here only the change and the result of the change are given. Again, what is described in the text cannot be mapped directly onto the more familiar 'canonical' arithmetical procedure. The problem has to be rearranged so that it leads to a solution and gives the child a line of action (6 + 2 = ?). The question is: how can one try to make such organizing tasks easier for the child who finds organizing difficult?

Nesher in her study with normal children (1982: 26) used an approach where the relevant operations with numbers were taught *before* the children were asked to apply them in 'real world' situations. Likewise, with regard to normal children, Nunes and Bryant (1996: 135–40) emphasize the importance of consciously connecting strategies already known to the child in order to facilitate the development of new understanding.

With a child who is weak in language and organizational skills it certainly makes sense to try to ensure that *non-verbal* problems have been understood and practised well previously, which means one first works concretely with plain number sentences where the unknown number takes different positions (e.g. 2 + ? = 8; ? − 2 = 6). This can be done fairly well through the use of 'number triplets' and Cuisenaire rods as suggested earlier. In general the aim will be to develop the relevant arithmetical models first and to see that they are stocked in the child's mind, ready for use. Only then is the child asked to tackle problems that are embedded in language and represent familiar life situations.

(c) *Discrepancy between the 'real' order of events and the order in which the events are mentioned in the text (see Teubal and Nesher, 1991)*

This is another difficult situation where the child has to understand and rearrange a story pattern that is perhaps unfamiliar. It frequently occurs in connection with conditions mentioned under point (b) above. An example is the following:

Mary and her brother have a game of marbles; at the end of the game Mary has 8 marbles. She was lucky; she won 6 marbles from her brother. How many did she have to start with?

Teubal and Nesher (1991) found that younger children tend to reorganize the problems in a way that minimizes any discrepancy between real time sequence and the sequence mentioned, regardless of the arithmetical usefulness of the resulting number sentence.

What are the implications of the difficulties posed by such discordance for teaching?

– Easy 'combine and compare' problems, which by their static nature do not involve time, may be useful as a start, although the naturally motivating appeal of 'action' in the story-line may be lost.
– These can then be followed by the easier kind of change problems.
– Later, however, problems that need reorganization should be introduced to allow the children to practise organizational skills.
– It seems best to start with problems that only need reorganization of time sequences.
– Word problems needing reorganization in both time sequence *and* data should only be practised at the end.

(d) *The given order of numbers and the size of numbers*

In some word problems, the larger number is the first to be mentioned; in other problems it is the smaller one. This can have an effect on the strategies a child employs to solve the problem. With regard to addition problems there is evidence that word problems are easier when the first number mentioned is the larger one (6 + 2 rather than 2 + 6). The reason is obvious: there is less 'to do' when a smaller change takes place, especially if the child is still employing counting-on methods. If a problem starts with the smaller number, children often spontaneously reverse the numbers (i.e. they correctly use the property of commutativity) in additions; if they do not do so, this is probably a good time to make them aware of the property.

(e) *Direction of procedure*

Finally, one would expect that the direction of the arithmetical procedure required (increase–decrease; more–less) would have some bearing on the relative difficulty of 'change' and 'compare' problems that are otherwise similar. Experience gives the impression that children prefer to do additions rather than subtractions. This, however, does not mean that additions are always the easier problems, as the following may show.

– Word problems involving 'change' that ask for a *decrease* generally seem easier. This is presumably because a young child with a

limited knowledge of higher numbers is working from the largest
number over the lower 'change number' towards the lowest
number; the child is going 'home' as it were, towards familiar
ground (e.g. $9 - 2 = 7$) whereas additions may lead the child into
the realm of the less familiar.
– In 'compare' problems, however, the positive direction (expressed
through the familiar 'more') seems to be generally easier, presumably because the negative direction involves the difficult concept
of 'less'.

3. Language

The next area to look at is the language used in a word problem. We
know from experience that texts conveying the same message can be
very different in regard to comprehensibility. But what makes a text
easily understood? This is an almost impossibly wide-ranging question. In early mathematics it could lead us into the detailed discussion of Piaget's work and the language used there (for this, see
perhaps Freudenthal, 1973; Donaldson, 1978; Hughes, 1986; Wood,
1988). I will narrow myself to the discussion of two specific language
factors, assuming that the teacher is aware of a child's general stage
of language development and thus uses appropriate vocabulary and
syntax when posing word problems.

The two areas which have been researched and found to be relevant to word problems are: *density of text* and *cue words*. Both seem to
influence the ease with which a mathematical word problem is read,
understood, and organized, and both can to some extent be
controlled to make things less difficult for the child.

(a) *Length and density*

A word problem, especially if it requires more than one mathematical procedure, will often result in a long text. This will burden the
child's memory, and demand more understanding and more organization than a shorter one. However, it is not length in itself that
makes for difficulty. There are fairly long narrative texts that are easy
to understand because they offer more than one contextual clue,
paint vivid pictures, and involve the child. Unfortunately, mathematical word problems are mostly not like that. Like riddles and jokes,
they have by tradition a peculiar discourse structure which differs
from normal narrative structure. This often results in a rather dense
text which is difficult to understand (cf. Nesher and Katriel, 1977).

One of the best examples to illustrate this is probably Hudson's
(1983) beautiful 'bird and worm' problem, widely discussed (Riley et

al., 1983; Fuson and Hall, 1983; De Corte and Verschaffel, 1991. See also Nunes and Bryant, 1996, where the parallel form of 'children and balloons' is used and discussed).

Hudson recorded young children's answers to two pairs of texts, dealing with the same word problem but differing in length and density. He worked with three age groups: nursery school, kindergarten, first grade. The children were given a picture to introduce each word problem. For instance, for one such problem they were given a picture where a group of five birds look eagerly at four worms crawling away, presumably similar to Figure 2.8.

The text of the shorter version was a typically dense 'compare' question:

How many more birds than worms are there?

The text of the longer version was:

Here are some birds and here are some worms. Suppose all the birds race over, and each one tries to get a worm. Will every bird get a worm? . . . How many birds won't get a worm?

Figure 2.8: Example of Hudson's picture cards (drawn from information in Hudson, 1983: 85)

The results showed that in all three age groups a higher proportion of children gave consistently correct answers to the longer versions. For instance, only 25% of the kindergarten children gave consistently correct answers to the short versions, but 96% gave consistently correct answers to the longer versions.

It follows that, with regard to length and density of text, the teacher will have to perform a fine balancing act. The problem and question should be phrased in such a way that the text is long enough and lively enough to engage the child in story fashion. At first it should be given in a straight temporal sequence where redundancies give the child time for on-line processing. On the other hand, too much redundancy could obscure the relevant elements and burden the child's memory and reading skills unduly.

To give a common example, a rather dense problem story like:

Mary has 8 marbles. She loses 2 to Tom. How many has she got now?

could be changed into:

Mary and her little brother are having a game of marbles. Mary starts with 8 marbles. She loses 2 to her brother. How many has she got left now?

This example illustrates two additional suggestions I would like to make:

- start each problem with at least one introductory sentence ('setting the scene' as it were), and
- do not just use two names (e.g. Mary and Tom, or worse, Peter and Paul as in the introductory example), but have one person described in a more memorable special relation (e.g. Mary and her little brother). This will make the text livelier and it will also help the child to differentiate the two protagonists, visually as well as verbally. It thus lessens the danger of mixing them up while trying to organize the problem.

(b) '*Cue words*'

Children solving word problems often seem to rely on certain cue words to decide on the arithmetical procedure required (for example 'altogether' and 'less'). This is a fairly common observation and has been confirmed in research (e.g. Nesher and Teubal, 1975; Nesher and Katriel, 1977; cf. Anghileri, 1991: 99 ff. for 'each').

Reliance on cue words seems a special temptation for children with organizational problems who have a tendency to rush into action without much preparatory thinking. For instance, the moment they recognize the word 'altogether' somewhere, they will probably say 'I know' (no need to consider the rest of the text) and start adding any numbers they can find; in the same way 'less' or 'away' may signal subtraction. Although a tendency towards such stereotyped action may be the result of experience, it can lead to false solutions. For example, a word problem like:

Mary plays 4 games of marbles; she wins 2 marbles each time. How many marbles has she won altogether?

may receive the answer 'six'. Here the word 'altogether' – which happens to be stressed and easily recognized by its end-position – might lead the child to a quick decision about the procedure: the two numbers can be added (4 + 2); thus the phrase 'each time' in the middle of the text will be ignored.

How can one help the children to avoid such mistakes? Perhaps the only way is to provide them with a sufficient variety of problems to make them realize that such cues may be helpful in some cases, but that they are not always reliable. More specifically, it might help if one rigorously teaches the following strategy, in which the children must *always* asks themselves:

Are there any helpful verbal cues?

If the answer is 'yes', the next question should follow as a matter of course:

Are they really helpful here? Let's look carefully at the whole text!

4. Procedures

Lastly, there is the question of mathematical procedures in word problems. One of the most important issues for teaching is perhaps whether a child should have learned the necessary skills to carry out a mathematical procedure before being asked to apply them in word problems; or should the two (i.e. 'application' and skill-training in the mathematical procedure) go hand in hand? The answer is probably that both approaches are valuable, and that one should not exclude the other.

If the aim is *practice and efficiency*, the word problems should be of the kind for which the child has a stock of arithmetical solution patterns firmly in his mind, ready for use. For instance, in the word problem used above, the number sentence '$4 \times 2 = 8$' should be well-known, come to mind and be chosen as the appropriate one from a stock of other well-known but rejected patterns like '$4 + 2 = 6$' or '$4 \div 2 = 2$'. This selection should happen fast and fairly effortlessly so that the problem content is not lost from memory. The main focus can then be on 'looking back' in order to check the appropriateness and correctness of the procedure selected by judging the result in terms of 'common sense'.

If, on the other hand, one aims at developing or consolidating the *understanding of a certain procedure in context*, then it makes sense to use word problems to this end. One could start with the child's informal solutions based on concrete materials and drawings and work gradually towards more formal arithmetic (cf. De Corte and Verschaffel, 1991). In that case the numbers used should not necessarily be very easy, otherwise a kind of sleep-walking intuitive response might lead to the right answer without the child consciously realizing the general principle behind the solution (cf. Ginsburg, 1989: 177, 'smaller numbers can be harder than big ones'). One hopes that such intensive slow work with close supervision will result in a balanced growth of general problem-solving strategies, organizational skills, and specific procedural skills. Most of all, however, it should enable child and teacher to tackle rare numerical 'real life' problems as they arise. Arithmetic can then really become 'fraught with relations' (Freudenthal, 1973).

A reference list (word problems)

The following summary may be helpful for quick reference in teaching. It lists the factors discussed above that can affect the difficulty of mathematical word problems:

- *The underlying logical structure.* For instance, 'change' and 'combine' problems are generally easier than 'compare' and 'equalizing' problems.
- *The use of concrete materials.* This will make all types of the problems discussed easier. In general, the younger, the less able or less experienced the child, the more such materials will improve performance.
- *The position of the unknown.* Word problems are normally easiest when the arrangement of numbers follows the 'canonical' sequence of equations ('2 + 4 = ?' rather than '? = 2 + 4').
- *The time sequence.* Word problems are normally easier when the 'real' time sequence of events is the same as that in the text.
- *The position of the largest number.* Addition problems are normally easier when the first number mentioned is the larger one.
- *The direction of a 'change' and a 'compare' problem.* 'Change' problems with a decrease, like 6 − 4, often seem easier than change problems with an 'increase', like 6 + 4; 'compare' problems seem easier when the direction goes towards an increase, using 'more' rather than 'less'.
- *The length and density of the text.* A long text may be difficult to organize and may burden the memory. However, opening up a very dense word problem through additional text within the child's experience can often make it easier to understand.
- *The use of cue words.* Although such words can improve speed in solving the problem, they may lead to incorrect solutions when used without due consideration of the whole text; children with a deficit in organizational skills seem especially prone to the misuse of cue words and have to be made aware of this by being encouraged always to ask: 'Are there cue words? Are they helpful here?'
- *Previous knowledge of mathematical procedures.* Well-established mathematical procedures will normally help in finding the most effi-

cient solutions to word problems. This applies particularly to children with an organizational weakness.

Spatial Organization

What are the problems?

Spatial organization seems one of the most difficult areas to teach with confidence. This is despite a wealth of educational materials on the market aiming to develop specific spatial skills. It has to do with several fundamental uncertainties in the field. Firstly, there is the question of definition: what do we mean when we use the term 'spatial ability'? Then there is the question of importance: how much does a spatial disability really matter? There are also serious doubts about methods and transfer of training and there seems to be very little information about the frequency and severity with which spatial disability occurs, in general and among children with language difficulties. Consequently my suggestions will be tentative and limited, concentrating on two extremes: one very general and the other very specific. I will start with a description of children who seem to have a weakness in spatial organization.

Signs of difficulties

A child with spatial difficulties may be noticed in his very early years because he will not be good at putting one wooden brick fairly straight on top of the other; he will not be good at finding the right opening for a shape to put into the toy 'posting box'. Often a more than age-related general clumsiness becomes obvious. At school, such a child may find beautiful materials for early tessellation work a cause of anxiety rather than fun because he knows that he cannot work well with them. Or there is Seamus aged between eight and nine who cannot build a wall with toy bricks in a simple 'bond' pattern: he just does not see that there *is* a pattern and simply puts one row of bricks on top of the other.

Such children produce poor paper-and-pencil work: what has to be straight is not straight; proportions are neglected; any free drawing may be oddly set in one corner of a large sheet of paper. When writing, they may not know where to start on the page or, like Dick who was mentioned earlier, they might not discriminate between the left-hand page and the right-hand page of an exercise book.

Later, children like this will have problems in interpreting and producing graphs, or, in woodwork, they may be seen turning a try-square five times round before being able to mark a piece of wood for squareness.

Are spatial skills important?

As early as 1905 Alfred Binet produced an intelligence test in which a normal seven-year-old child was expected to copy a rhombus with pen and ink (cf. Binet, Simon and Terman, 1980; Jäger, 1988: 19). Thus spatial ability was and still is regarded as a factor that can add to a person's 'intelligence' (see, for instance, Gardner and Clark, 1992). And if the seven-year-old cannot copy a rhombus? Does this matter?

Looking at life both inside and outside school, the answer must probably be 'yes'. Although the connection between mathematical thinking and spatial thinking still seems somewhat elusive (Battista, 1994) one can expect a child with a weakness in spatial ability to fail almost certainly at school requirements that lead to learning geometry. But what about the rest of his life? Is there a more general dimension to such an impairment? It is probably safe to assume that spatial organizing skills, which link visual perception with co-ordinated activity, must be helpful in many ordinary daily tasks and that, without such skills, the order, stability and security of a person's visual world will be lacking.

Defining 'spatial ability'

Before asking the difficult questions of 'can spatial ability be trained and if yes, how?', it is perhaps of value to look at the apparently unresolved question of defining it. A common sense definition of spatial ability in simple English can be found in *Collins Cobuild English Language Dictionary*, 1987:

> Spatial ability is the ability to see and understand the relationships between shapes, spaces, or areas.

A more educationally oriented search for a definition emphasizes the importance of *spatial memory*. Smith's research-based conclusion in the NFER 'Spatial Ability Project' is relevant:

> it is a blanket term for a whole array of distinct skills, linked by a common reliance upon spatial memory processes. (Smith, 1991: 6)

On the whole one has to agree with Bishop (1983: 181) when he states:

> it is clear (to a mathematical educator at least) that there can never be a 'true' definition of spatial ability; we must seek definitions and descriptions of abilities and processes that help us to solve our own particular problems.

It is thought today that 'visualization' as a process of understanding and organizing one's perception of the world is of a highly individual nature. We all seem to have our own personal way of creating and using images (for a review of research that emphasizes the personal nature of visual processing – in children learning as well as in teachers teaching – see Bishop, 1989).

Can spatial ability be trained?

Obviously Froebel (1782–1852) and others after him (e.g. C.M. Crandall, 1833–1905, in the USA; Maria Montessori, 1870–1952, in Italy) believed that spatial training was not only possible, but that it should be a normal and important part of education, particularly early education. Generations of teachers and parents have continued to believe this. I too believe that a child ought to have building bricks to play with as soon as he can sit up, and more structured materials in solid and plane shapes soon after, to see, feel and handle. Educational catalogues are full of such materials and schools and parents buy them. But does this mean that spatial ability can be developed in all children? Does it include children who seem to have very little natural spatial ability, who may suffer from a kind of 'spatial-blindness' which seems as difficult to treat as tone-deafness is in others?

Research

Research has been often inconclusive (cf. Lean and Clements, 1981; Bishop 1983; Dickson et al., 1984). Bruner's words from the 1960s still seem to ring true: we have not 'begun to scratch the surface of training in visualization' (1966: 34). More recently, Giaquinto (1992) concluded that 'the nature and functions of visualization are far from well understood'. An NFER research project is currently taking place in the UK, building on the work of MacFarlane Smith (1964). This research aims at producing a 'spatial ability handbook' for educators (c.f. Smith, 1992).

Some earlier studies suggested that training in spatial skills might produce better test results but might not lead to long-range improvement (for example, with respect to the Frostig training programme, see Koppitz 1975: 124). Such results have been attributed to the general narrowness of training programmes. Studies into the treatment for dyslexic children led Benton (1978: 474) to conclude that 'remediation via visuo-perceptual and visuo-motor training has not been effective'. With regard to language-impaired children a study by Wyke and Asso (1979) suggested that low attainment shown in some spatial ability tasks may be due to a general short-term memory weakness rather than to specific problems with spatial relations. This might explain some disappointing results in training.

However, there have also been studies that suggest more positive results (cf. Bishop, 1989). Training at the right time, with well-structured manipulative materials and accompanied by attention to appropriate language and individual differences in visualization, have all yielded some success. Some details of research into the conditions under which improvement can be expected are listed below.

Under what conditions can improvement be expected?

- *'Optimal time'*. There might be an 'optimal time' for spatial training (Bishop, 1983: 186). In general, the younger the child, the higher the possibility of improvement.
- *Experience with manipulative (structural) apparatus.* A study by Bishop (1973) showed that experience with Dienes, Cuisenaire and Stern materials can relate positively to later performance in tasks requiring spatial ability (for a description of such materials see Unit 3).
- *Previous 'disadvantage' and 'low attainment'.* A case study by Choat (1974) showed positive results when specific work (finger-tracing of shapes) was undertaken with a six-year-old boy from an Educational Priority Area school. Another case study by Wheatley and Wheatley (1979) showed similar good results in spatial training with a low attainer. In both studies the work on spatial aspects was combined with encouragement to the child to use appropriate language while working on the task.
- *Work with emphasis on language.* As the two case studies listed above showed, work which emphasizes the use of appropriate language in spatial activities may lead to improvement on spatial tasks.
- *Width of the training programme.* Bishop (1983) suggests, after a study of first year students in Papua New Guinea, that training programmes need to be be wider than the term 'spatial training' implies, and that cultural contexts ought to be considered. This confirms to some extent the findings of Koppitz mentioned earlier. Kerslake (1979) shows the importance of working with more than one example in a field (e.g. work with triangles of different kinds and in different positions).

All this research is concerned with children who have no specific language impairment. The difficult question is: how can we help the child with a combination of language deficits and spatial problems?

How can we help?

It is obvious that children who suffer both from language impairment and lack of spatial ability cause special methodological problems, and any uncertainty about the effectiveness of training will be aggravated. As mentioned before, my suggestions will be far from comprehensive.

I will start with a very general suggestion that can be applied to many situations: 'making lists'.

This will be followed by suggestions for a series of narrowly defined tasks. The particular tasks were chosen because they appeal to most children and combine work aiming at the improvement of spatial skills with some aspects of language work. Thus the choice is purely pragmatic: one certainly hopes that the tasks will develop spatial ability, although this may be difficult to prove. But there should be a strong likelihood that the activities will benefit the child in at least one or two other aspects: language and motivation. One thus ensures that the child's time and energy are not wasted, even if improvement in spatial ability is uncertain.

A short general section about the advantages of geometric materials for language work completes this section.

Making lists

Lists – one of the oldest forms of writing – were and are used to get complex matter and situations under control. Whenever there is uncertainty about the next step in dealing with an issue, I have found it helpful to make a list. This applies to life and education in general, as well as to particular didactic questions where no suitable 'set course' is available. Therefore, if one is concerned about a child's lack of a specific ability, if one wants to intervene but does not know where to start, compiling a personal, relevant, running list (or two), may be helpful. The following describes how such lists can be drawn up, in this case relating specifically to spatial ability. This is a subject that lacks clear definitions, and I know that not only I but other teachers too find it frustratingly complex when an obvious weakness in a child calls for action. Lists will not help directly in teaching, but they can clarify the issues, provide working definitions, give confidence and offer starting points.

Below are two different lists presented as tables:

(a) Table 2.3 contains information about what other people mean when they think of spatial ability; it shows almost randomly relevant items found in books and catalogues.

(b) Table 2.4 is a summary of what I have found out about the subject and what I want to remember when teaching.

Such lists can deliberately be left sketchy and incomplete; they need only include items that 'make sense' when the teacher has a particular child or a particular teaching situation in mind.

Table 2.3: What does 'spatial ability' include?

Found in Anderson (1985)
spatial imagery
visual memory
geometry
area measure
real space versus model space (pictures, maps)
visual perception
mental rotation of objects
mental folding
spatial development:
    from the qualitative to the quantitative
    from globality to differentiation

Found in Bishop (1983)
spatial visualization:
    e.g. ability to rotate or fold an appropriate visual stimulus in one's mind
spatial orientation:
    e.g. comprehending pattern arrangements, being able to cope with changes in the
    arrangement of visual patterns
memory for design
IFI: the ability to 'Interpret Figural Information'
    e.g. geometric work, graphs, charts, diagrams
VP: the capacity for 'Visual Processing'
    e.g. visualization; translation of abstract relationships on non-figural information
    into visual terms; manipulation and transformation of visual representations and
    visual imagery.

***Looking through parts of Dickson et al. (1984)* (partly my formulation)**
spatial appreciation (pictures, diagrams)
spatial thinking
shape recognition
shape copying
shape labelling
awareness of properties of shapes:
    e.g. right angle, parallel sides;
perceiving relationships of shapes; what new shapes can be made out of different shapes
(as in tangrams and pentominoes) e.g.:
    square from triangles;
    larger triangle from smaller ones
    rectangle from squares;
discriminating and relating 2-dimensional and 3-dimensional shapes
    e.g. coping with 2-dimensional representation of 3-dimensional shapes
paying attention to orientation of shapes

Found in catalogues

(a) DIME Mathematics 1993:	(b) Galt, Play and Learn 1992:
shape recognition	pattern making
spatial reasoning	grading by size
3-dimensional thinking	spatial awareness
area	spatial skills
being able to work with:	shape sorting
line symmetry	being able to work with:
reflection	tessellation shapes
isometric diagrams	pin (geo) board
building 3-dimensional forms from	
2-dimensional drawings	

Table 2.4: A personal summary of what seems to be known about spatial development and what seems relevant for teaching

- Start early.

- Provide lots of manipulative materials for free 'play'.

- Look for 'optimal time': watch carefully and see what the child can do; then provide materials or instruction which may lead him just one step further.

- Emphazise the use of language (integrated with the activity) – your language and the child's.

- Don't follow a narrow training programme, go with an observant open mind for width and be aware of individual differences.

- Generally, go from the simple task to the more complex.

- Remember general rules of transfer (e.g. link two tasks which have some similar components; make sure that the child either detects the similarity between them or has it pointed out; use language to ensure awareness of similarity).

- Go for fun and games in order to make transfer of positive attitudes possible.

How to use the lists

It is good to remember that these lists are meant to be 'working lists', and that new information can be added at all times. Sometimes it may be helpful to go back to the original source where an item was found.

In practice, if one is faced with a child's problem and no appropriate teaching aid is available, one can turn to lists with new confidence. As an example, how could the two lists help in the case of Seamus, who could not build a bond-patterned wall? Looking down Table 2.3 one may perhaps write notes like 'visual memory rather than perception (with a question mark) – memory for design – spatial thinking – perceiving relationships of shapes – tessellation'. From Table 2.4 one may note: 'do something *now* – start with a simpler (related) task – remember fun – language (of course)'. The next next step would be to translate these abstract items into something practical, perhaps:

(a) *Simple task:* Start (tomorrow!) with three single bricks, two at the base, one on top; let the child make lots of those triplets until he runs out of bricks (motivate him by saying: guess how many you will be able to make, find out if you are right).

(b) *Memory:* Let him do each task from memory a day or two later.

(c) *Fun:* Use different materials for the task (e.g. empty soap-powder boxes, real bricks in the sandpit).

(d) *Spatial thinking / language:* Ask, why is it good to have one brick in the middle on top of the other two (in contrast, make a high wall with bricks neatly one on top of the other); question: how do we cope with 'end bits'?

(e) *And so forth.*

Although such lists are not related to a particular theory, work should nevertheless be systematic, based on a sequence of consistent observation, recording and review. The actual steps might be:

- decide on starting point – select activity and materials – record;
- start work – observe – record;
- continue work – record; or
- review – change – record; or
- plan next step ahead – record.

In the following sections I will suggest some specific activities, based on points from Tables 2.3 and 2.4. The activities are meant to integrate the development of spatial ability with two other aspects: language development and motivation to learn.

Starting early with building blocks

Bishop (1983) suggests that the optimal age for systematic training of visual processing may be around 7–12 years. This must presuppose some visuo-spatial experiences in infancy, experiences which ought to be consciously fostered from the early years onwards. Just as we now realize that children's babbling activity in their early years and the responding noises by carers play an important part in language development, so shared play with simple well-shaped objects ought to be seen as crucial for the development of spatial ability and it is no coincidence that the first piece in the sequence of Froebel's materials is meant for a child aged two months. Luckily, such play will often happen naturally, but its importance is worth emphasizing. Every parent should be aware of its value in itself and of the added benefit that comes when an adult shares it with the child and perhaps structures it to some extent.

The advantages of such an early start are obvious: never again will children so willingly explore simple three-dimensional objects with intensity, through their mouths, with their fingers, with their eyes. Such free exploration should lead on to simple construction play with wooden and plastic blocks, perhaps at around the age of two. One hopes that such play will lessen any innate weakness or promote any innate talent right from the beginning, as it perhaps did in the case of the architect Frank Lloyd Wright, who is said to have played intensively with Froebel blocks at an early age (cf. Lupton and Abbot Miller, 1993: 18). For an adult, sharing such play means good opportunities for the simultaneous fostering of language development. These opportunities should not be missed, especially if some problems are suspected.

Good and attractive materials for early spatial development are not difficult to find. (The 300 page catalogue by GALT, one of the leading British firms in educational toys and primary teaching mat-erials, offers, for instance, more than 200 items intended to develop spatial ability in one form or other – such as awareness, perception, recall, production skills; cf. Table 2.3.) However, because of this, perhaps a word of caution is necessary to over-enthusiastic parents or grandparents: avoid overstimulation; give the child a chance to concentrate on one item at a time. For instance, let him first explore the cube itself fully, and only then add diagonally halved cubes which will make 'roofs' for his cube-houses. In respect one ought to remember Froebel, who called his set of materials for early spatial learning 'gifts'. His gifts gently increase in complexity and are given to the child one at a time (cf. Lupton and Abbott Miller, 1993).

Young children are normally happy to do the same activity or play the same game again and again until they are totally familiar with it; then they drop it and look for something else (the so-called *Montessori phenomenon*). One should not unnecessarily interrupt this intensive first play. It may create an attitude that will help the child to concentrate with the same intensity and endurance on other tasks later.

Deciding when it is a good time for a new 'educational toy' is not easy and calls for good observation; the rule of thumb is: wait until the child himself stops, ready for something new, which will not necessarily be the day before Christmas.

Despite the variety of materials available, play with simple building blocks should in my opinion be the centre of such early activity. Such play will provide the basic three-dimensional experience of handling solid shapes (stroking their faces, following their edges, pointing at their vertices, predicting what fits together). This will cover a wide range of spatial learning, of the kind outlined in Table

2.3 above (i.e. in skill terms: shape recognition, shape discrimination, shape sorting, shape labelling, recognition of shape properties, attention to shape orientation, grading by size, tessellation). Detailed suggestions about the kind of materials one could use and the sequence of introduction can be found in Unit 6.

Playing with building blocks at a later age

Before moving on to discuss other forms of activities for younger children, it is worth considering what can be done with older children, perhaps aged 10 or more, who have somehow missed out on play with building blocks in their early years and who show a worrying degree of spatial disorganization. There is certainly a need for the same basic three-dimensional experience of handling solid shapes but it will be much harder to find enough time and motivation for such essential play. On no account does one want the child to become embarrassed over it or to turn silly.

My first suggestion is to use blocks on a theme appropriate to the children's age and interest. For instance, one could show them a picture of the Manhattan skyline or of Hong Kong harbour and ask them to build a similar scene; or one could work from a picture of an Italian walled hill town; or ask them to use a heap of bricks to make a plan of their school building, or the one they would like to have. Language can flow freely into the activities and motivation seems normally high.

My second suggestion is to use a more sophisticated selection of blocks with a greater variety of shapes, including smaller ones unsuitable for young children. A box of Poleidoblocs A-Set (where the pieces are related in size and volume to larger pieces of the G-Set) may be useful (for a description of Poleidoblocs sets and some work with them see Unit 6); or a selection of materials from the expensive but beautiful range made by the Swiss firm Naef ('Cubicus', 'Cella', 'Scala', 'Diamant', 'Palladio' and others). In active play, all these materials can also be mixed with chess pieces as 'actors'.

Such work at a later age will probably only be 'second best' and not have the impact that continuous repetitive infant play might have had, but it seems an efficient remedial action to take, especially if it is consciously linked with language learning and if the children continue to regard it as fun.

Working with paper and pencil

Building blocks, influential as they may be, are perhaps surpassed in importance for spatial development by pencil-and-paper work.

Drawing is a symbolic act with which we can select chunks of our environment at will and represent them in a two-dimensional plane. It is one of the universal human ways of controlling the environment.

Although infants are astonishingly competent at recognizing two-dimensional representations of three-dimensional objects in pictures, the other way round (i.e. the active change of objects from three dimensions to two) does not seem to be so easy. One is not always aware that there is a lot to learn. I remember when I watched with amazement our eldest child's reaction to her first pencil line at the age of about 18 months: she carefully tried to pick up the line between two fingers, the same way she had previously picked up odd threads left on the floor. Her face showed utter puzzlement at the fact that the line would not come off.

Later, at school and in life, working from a drawing on paper into the third dimension, or drawing a three-dimensional object flat on paper, is frequently necessary. Such a 'translating' task needs experience, and early drawing in all its forms can perhaps ease the way.

Scribbles

It seems good practice to start relatively early with paper-and-pencil work, as long as work with the 'real' world (i.e. with three-dimensional materials) still continues at times.

The first drawings are best made with a carer in close attendance to supply language and respond to the child's utterances. Language intervention can become so natural here that it may cease to be interventional. The starting point will normally be the scribbles interpreted by the child, or a suggestion by the adult taken up by the child. Such scribbles can show what the child knows about an object. What is missing can be discussed and a more complete concept can be developed. Figure 2.9 gives an example of such a scribble.

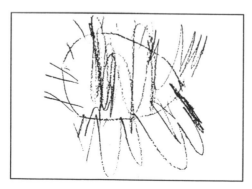

Figure 2.9: A 'hedgehog', drawn by a three-year-old child

Like the person who cannot sing in tune but nevertheless sings happily in the bath, so even young children with spatial difficulties will happily draw pictures that look good to them (and, one hopes, to their carers). Only later, when the results of their scribbles are seen in terms of developmental measurements will they perhaps be judged as 'worrying'.

Shared concept drawing

Later, shared 'concept drawing' is one way to foster spatial development in connection with language work on concepts. The aim is to establish a concept by simultaneously talking about it and drawing what can be drawn; it is not meant to provide a lesson in 'drawing' and almost all drawing efforts are acceptable. Normally the teacher or any other carer suggests a topic; child and carer then work together, thinking, talking and drawing. The following is an example where the concept is 'tree'.

Setting. The carer and a small group of children (or an individual child) sit around a table, all with a sheet of paper and a pencil in front of them (in an ideal world this could be a family affair, including grandparents).

Starting point. Initial statement by the carer, for example: 'Let's draw a tree today. Where shall we start?'
Discussion. 'Shall we start with the branches . . .? With the trunk . . .? With the ground . . .? Right, let's start at the bottom and draw upwards, the way a tree grows. Is there something underground? The roots . . .'

Drawing. 'Let's start drawing the ground line (not too near the bottom!) and the roots underground.' The carer draws a line and some roots for all to see and to copy if necessary. Anything in roughly the right position and resembling roots is acceptable, no matter how 'abstract' it turns out to be. This is not an art lesson. Depending on the situation, a discussion of the question 'Are all roots underground?' may develop and lead to the drawing of some roots above the ground.

What next? When each child has drawn some roots, the carer takes the lead again with the question: 'What's next, going upwards?' 'The trunk.' Perhaps a discussion could follow: 'Do we need straight lines?' 'No, better not.' 'Why not?'
The carer draws a trunk for all to see and to copy if necessary. The children do the same, more or less simultaneously.
'Next?' 'Big branches, growing out of the top of the tree.' Discussion and drawing follow. 'Next?' 'Smaller branches, growing off the

thick branches.' 'Next?' 'Twigs.' 'Next?' 'Leaves, as many as we can draw, there will never be enough.' 'Anything else?' 'Yes let's make an apple tree' (see Figure 2.10).

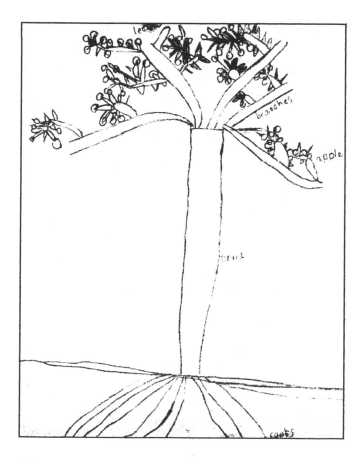

Figure 2.10: An apple tree (result of 'concept drawing')

The example illustrates the first basic session. More suggestions (follow-up work, other topics) are given in Unit 6.

It seems vital for the group spirit and results that the carers join in the drawing with infectious enthusiasm, whether they can draw or not. Most concepts that would normally only be talked about can thus be enhanced and consolidated. Paper-and-pencil skills are practised in a way that challenges thinking. In my opinion this is definitely better than any 'colouring-in' exercises.

Comprehension drawing

'Comprehension drawing' is related to concept drawing, but differing from it in the complexity of language. The language goes beyond single words, phrases and sentences to form a story. It also puts more emphasis on listening skills and requires:

(a) listening on the discourse level;
(b) making sense of what is heard;
(c) reacting to it by drawing.

The situation can be described as follows: a carer and a child (or better still, a pair or group of children) draw a cartoon-like sequence of fast sketches while listening to a story; the story is interrupted at fixed points to give time for the drawing to take place. Again, the activity allows for combining language and drawing in a situation likely to keep the child motivated. The result will often be a well-organized visual record of a story.

The ideal situation can be exemplified by a session of comprehension drawing with the help of a musical masterpiece such as Prokofiev's *Peter and the Wolf*, where word and music combine to make for good comprehension, and where the music provides the natural interval for each drawing. Unit 6 gives a description of such a lesson, which includes details of organization as well as suggestions for further work. I have used this exceptionally suitable musical story with quite different groups of children and always thought it a success. Figure 2.11 gives examples of some of the resulting sketches.

Summing up

The benefits of such paper-and-pencil work can be manifold:

spatial skills are fostered;
visuo/motor co-ordination is practised;
concepts are developed;
oral comprehension is practised;
the child learns to visualize situations given in words;
story sequences are made obvious;
the child realizes that drawing can be used for purposes other than making fine pictures;
the child will have had fun.

In general, it seems good practice when working with language-impaired children to have paper and pencil ready at all times. We know that these children often cannot concentrate for long on verbal matters, and so, at times, we can encourage them to draw what is talked about while listening, if only in doodles or sketches. This may help to keep their attention on the subject.

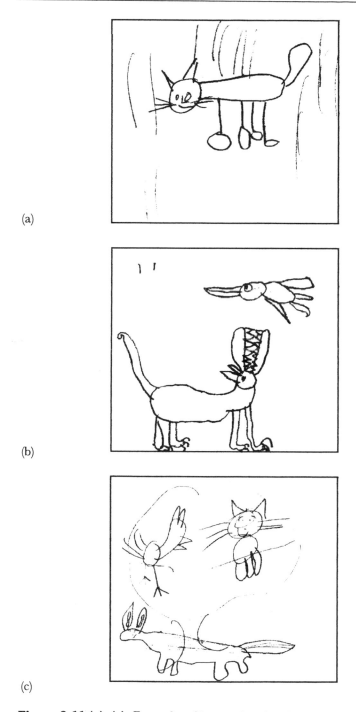

(a)

(b)

(c)

Figure 2.11 (a)–(c): Examples of 'comprehension drawing' (Peter and the Wolf)
(a) 'Suddenly, Peter saw a cat, crawling through the grass on her velvet paws.'
(b) 'How that bird worried the wolf!'
(c) 'The cat was sitting on one branch of the tree, the bird on another, not too close
     to the cat. And the wolf walked round and round the tree, looking at them both.'

Paper-and-pencil work has an additional value for children with organizational problems. When one puts down on paper situations that need mental organizing, the elements of the situation become visible objects. The children can recognize the whole as well as its parts simultaneously in their sketches; they can notice what is missing; they can emphasize what is relevant and cross out what is not; and they can change the position of parts. In other words, with the help of visual means they can learn to organize a situation on paper and in their own minds.

Using geometric pattern blocks (or pattern tiles)

This is an activity which can combine the manipulation of geometric shapes (based on the square) with the practice of following verbal instructions, either oral or written. Sets of tiles or cubes for making patterns are on the market in various forms, in plastic and wood. An example is a set of 4 × 4 cubes in two colours with the six faces of each cube as shown in Figure 2.12.

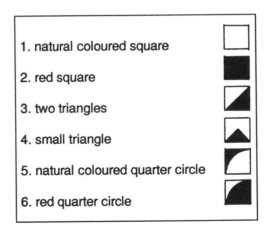

1. natural coloured square

2. red square

3. two triangles

4. small triangle

5. natural coloured quarter circle

6. red quarter circle

Figure 2.12: Distribution of patterns on geometric pattern blocks (example with 'standard' shapes)

Such sets are available commercially. For instance, high quality wooden sets with shapes as outlined above were produced by the Swedish company Permanum under the name 'Bobby's Box'; similar ones are now available from the Swiss company Naef under the name 'Ornabo'. Slightly different patterned plastic 'tiles', with patterns only on one side, are produced by Lego as 'Lego Dacta Mosaic Sets'.

Making patterns with such shapes is an old geometric art form, applied, for instance, in Roman tile-patterns and in patchwork. An amazing example is the work on permutation for design-making by

P.D. Douat, a Carmelite priest, published in Paris 1722. He worked with a grid of 5×5 square tiles, where each tile is divided by a diagonal into two equal triangles, one light, one dark. His claim was that just by rotating the tiles by 90 degrees as many as 1,057,145,886,720 designs could be obtained (cf. Durant and Darling, 1993; Gombrich 1984: 70). If one adds further colours or shades of colour to a set of cubes with such simple shapes one can arrive at the most amazing designs.

A child handling such tiles or cubes is involved not only in the ancient and universal tradition of pattern-making but also in a variety of spatial activities. These activities can cover almost every aspect of spatial skills mentioned in Table 2.3. Most children seem to like working with pattern blocks or flat pattern tiles, and I have certainly witnessed their obvious delight many times when familiar shapes combined to form new shapes under their eyes.

Such pattern-making activities have been formalized by providing work cards with models of patterns which have to be copied (for example, Lego Dacta activity cards). I have linked such spatial training with language comprehension/reading work by supplying precise written instructions to be followed with various sets of pattern blocks. For instance, I made a set of 20 instruction sheets for a 4×4 cube set (with shapes as shown in Figure 2.12 and with the colours red and natural). The instructions can be given orally or in writing. Each sheet when followed correctly ends with a picture or pattern. A sheet may start like this:

Work across in rows (start at the top left-hand corner)
Row 1:
– One block with a natural coloured square.
– One block with a small triangle (red edge must be at the bottom).
– Two blocks with natural coloured squares.

After the completion of all four rows of the sheet, a picture of a 'flying fish' should have appeared (see Figure 2.13).

Figure 2.13: Pattern block picture: 'flying fish'

Looking at the text one may feel that the task is made difficult by the wordiness of the instructions. However, anybody who has tried to formulate unambiguous written instructions of any kind will know that in order to make them 'foolproof' a lot of words have to be used. A closer look at the words shows that they are mostly 'adult' words, useful for general purposes as well as for mathematics (left/right, column/row, top/bottom, circle/square, etc.), and that they are repeated over and over again. Any new words will only have to be learned for the first sheet. Work with pattern blocks is described in more detail and with different examples in Unit 6.

Working with Tangrams

This is another example where practising the skill of 'following instructions' can be linked with practising spatial skills.

A 'Tangram' is one of many different two-dimensional geometric dissection puzzles, perhaps one of the oldest forms of recreational mathematics. Such puzzles are sets of geometric shapes which, when put together in different ways, can form a variety of other shapes and pictures: rectangles, triangles, letters, people, animals and many more. The 'Tangram' set is probably the best-known of all dissection puzzles and perhaps also the most subtle. It consists of seven pieces in three basic shapes: one square, one parallelogram and five triangles (triangles in three different sizes, all with angles of 45/45/90 degrees). One strict rule of the game is that whatever is built with the pieces must include all seven pieces. Figure 2.14 shows (a) the seven pieces as a square; (b) a picture of a boy running built up with the seven pieces and (c) the same boy showing the lines of the pieces, normally shown as the 'solution' in books with models of Tangram pictures to follow.

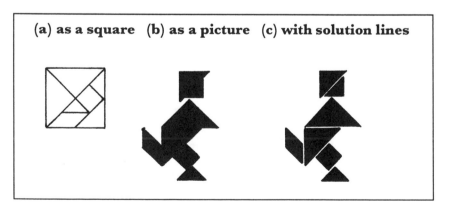

(a) as a square   (b) as a picture   (c) with solution lines

Figure 2.14 (a)–(c): The seven pieces of a Tangram

There are conflicting claims concerning the origin of this puzzle. It is generally thought to have come from China, and the earliest known reference is said to be a Chinese woodcut from 1780 (Slocum and Botermans, 1987: 23). Famous players include Napoleon, Edgar Allan Poe and Lewis Carroll (Thiele, 1988: 98). In China there were even highly decorated sets of tables made in the seven shapes (cf. example from 1840 in Slocum and Botermans, 1986: 23); more recently the Italian furniture designer Massimo Morozzi has made a modern version of Tangram tables – coloured and beautiful (Börnson-Holtman, 1994: 119).

Although it is a special pleasure to play with a Tangram set made from fine wood, a simple set can quickly be made out of card or cardboard by following the lines of Figure 2.14(a) and pictures to be formed can likewise be invented. (For suppliers and special books about Tangrams see Unit 6.) Most books with mathematical games include activities with Tangrams, and it is now generally appreciated that such work seems to help the development of 'spatial ability'. To quote Wheatley and Wheatley (1979): 'working with Tangrams provides practice in gestalt thinking and may help children to develop an important dimension of thought'.

I have used Tangrams in connection with language work in two different ways: as a 'following-instruction task' and as an opportunity to develop 'speech for self'.

Following instructions for Tangram pictures

The activity itself and the benefits from it for the development of spatial and language skills are similar to those with pattern blocks described above. The child is provided with a Tangram set and an instruction sheet and builds up a picture by following the instructions. Some new and perhaps more abstract concepts are used. This, together with pictures which are not constrained by a grid and which therefore result in more open forms, makes the activity slightly more difficult than pattern block work. As with the pattern blocks, the language used in the instructions seems tediously complicated, but again the advantage is that with a relatively small but useful vocabulary and with a limited set of phrases, one can produce almost unlimited numbers of exercises in various grades of difficulty, leading to new and unexpected end results. Here is an example of the language involved; it describes how the first two pieces are to be placed in making 'a goose':

- Take the two large triangles.
- Make a large parallelogram with them.
- Place the parallelogram so that the shorter sides are horizontal.
- Place it so that the top leading corner is on your left.

Such work is especially valuable with older children where a lack in organizational skills is linked with a lack in language or reading skill. A more detailed description of how and when to use Tangrams in this way, together with an example of a complete instruction sheet, is given in Unit 6.

Developing 'speech for self' with Tangram work

'Speech for self' is a term used by Wells (1985) to describe language directed to oneself rather than to someone else. It can be 'inner speech' as well as audible speech. It is 'an instrument of thought', often used by an individual to organize difficult situations such as the solution of a problem in mathematics (for a short informative paragraph about speech as an instrument of thought see Crystal 1987: 13). It is obvious that, for a child with language difficulties and organizational problems, such a use of language ought to be encouraged. The idea of using Tangram pictures for encouraging 'speech for self' came to me after watching a young Cambridge graduate as well as our 92-year-old great-aunt starting spontaneously to talk to themselves while trying to solve such a Tangram puzzle.

The procedure is as follows: the child is given a model of a Tangram picture to build. At the same time he is encouraged to talk aloud to himself while working at the puzzle. At the beginning, and certainly with children with a weakness in spatial ability, it is generally advisable to use pictures of Tangram models which show the lines of the individual pieces ('solutions lines'). A model of unlined pictures might often prove too difficult to follow and might inhibit speech.

The language used in such an activity will obviously vary considerably, not only because of children's differences in language and spatial ability but also because not all children are equally motivated to talk aloud to themselves. As an example, some children will produce little more than:

    and that –
    there –
    that there –
    that there – ...

Other samples reflect the child's thoughts more openly and one may hear:

    and – get this – the diamond sort of shape
    and put it – un-der two
    the two squ – triangle – ...

Some more details of how to encourage such 'speech for self' with the help of Tangrams, together with two transcriptions of Tangram sessions, are given in Unit 6.

Some general advantages of using geometric materials for language work

Working with geometric materials (of all kinds, i.e. not only those mentioned here) offers at least three advantages for language work that are listed below.

1. Monitoring the degree of difficulty in a task

Language teachers or therapists take great trouble when deciding what the next stage in a child's language therapy should be. They are also careful to make the level of their own language suit the child's understanding. But language difficulties can sometimes arise not because children do not possess the right structures or the right vocabulary, but because the conceptual situation in which we want them to talk is too difficult. If this is the case, language will not be forthcoming. It is no use telling a child to try harder, instead one has to simplify matters. One has to look for a means of grading the complexity of the situation, and it is one of the advantages of working with geometrical materials that the level of difficulty can be graded fairly successfully.

Some criteria for what influences the complexity of a task are offered by Gillian Brown (1986), a specialist in second and foreign-language teaching, a field where task-related practice of language is as important as it is for work with language-impaired children. She observed that there are at least three variables that help to determine whether a task is easy or difficult:

- the total number of objects involved – the smaller the number, the easier the task;
- the identity of the objects – if they are all the same, the task will be easy; if they are different, the fewer the differences, the easier the task; and
- the relationship between the objects – the simpler the relationship, the easier the task.

If, for instance, one wanted to make a task like a Tangram picture easier, one could ignore the classical rules of the puzzle and

- use fewer pieces;
- use the same number of pieces but restrict the shapes to triangles;

- eliminate the parallelogram, which relates in less obvious ways to the rest of the shapes.

2. The almost unlimited potentials of geometric shapes
'Following instructions' can certainly be practised with other materials besides geometric shapes. I have done it with small toys (for example in 'Making a farm', 'Making a village', 'Making a Western High Street'), where spatial concepts like 'in front', 'behind', 'to the right' and others were practised. However, the tree, sheep, and pump in the toy village refer to one concrete unchangeable entity, whereas one and the same abstract geometric shape can help to create pictures of an almost unlimited variety and degree of difficulty.

3. Working with 'content-free' materials
The third advantage is closely linked to the one above: not only are geometric materials attractive, adaptable and easy to manipulate, but they are also intrinsically 'content-free'. Contextual 'clutter' can be avoided, and this makes them suitable for children of all backgrounds. A child might not be familiar with a village pump, or might not be interested in cowboy scenes, but pattern-making and Tangram shapes seem to be universals.

SUMMARY

A weakness in organizational skills is one that the language-impaired child shares with many children who do not have language problems. But it seems more pronounced among language-impaired children, and one can perhaps assume a causal relationship: when faced with a situation that calls for organizing, the ability of these children to 'talk a problem through', either verbally or in the mind, must be limited. Moreover, among children with language problems, there seems to be a fairly substantial sub-group with difficulties in visuospatial organization and co-ordination. Given that mathematics has to do with organizing experiences of numbers and space, difficulties in elementary mathematics can be expected, and special help will be needed.

One readily available aid for the organization of numbers is *the decimal system*. One ought to make its character, organization and usefulness apparent to the child as soon as possible. This can be facilitated by offering a clear, easily remembered image of the system right from the start. The image I suggest for early mathematics is the 'field of 100' as shown on the *Slavonic abacus*. Later, or perhaps overlapping with this, the pupils can be asked to organize more freely arranged quantities into the system or into different groups and sub-groups. This will lead to the exploration of new whole–part relations.

The treatment of *mathematical word problems* will need special attention. Work can be on two lines: with 'real life' problems (by way of illustration), and with ample practice of carefully graded 'textbook problems'.

I also suggest some practical work to train some aspects of *spatial ability*. This is an uncertain enterprise, but one can make it more fruitful by combining it with specific language work.

Finally, one has to realize that a weakness in organizational skills will be a handicap in many areas besides mathematics. In mathematics, however, it is at least possible to control the scale and difficulty of situations, especially given the advantage of the rich supply of geometrical materials available for elementary work. Thus, through consistent work on mathematical/spatial aspects, one may actually be able to alleviate some more general signs of weak organizational skills.

Chapter 3
Memory Weakness

INTRODUCING THE FEATURE
The Complex Question of Memory

According to modern research on cognition, memory is organized and structured, and the more efficiently it is organized, the more successfully it will function (e.g. Tulving, 1983: 5; Resnick and Ford, 1984: 198; Byers and Erlwanger, 1985; Baddeley, 1990: 175 ff.). Thus, to some extent, talking about a memory weakness in children with language-impairment may be considered an extension of talking about their organizational problems. What may happen, in simple terms, is that, because these children cannot easily perceive structure, they may fail to anchor knowledge in a well-organized way into their memory, and this in turn may lead to them failing to 'find' what they know when they need it.

But nothing that concerns human memory seems to be simple. I will try to give a short summary of the complex and partly unresolved issues regarding human memory, but for a fuller overview one would need to turn to experts (perhaps Tulving, 1983; Anderson, 1990; Baddeley, 1990; or Parkin, 1993).

More than one memory

Clinical studies with brain-damaged patients have shown that what is commonly and globally referred to as 'memory' has quite distinct parts. Some parts of memory can be lost while others are preserved, depending on where damage has occurred in the brain. It seems generally accepted that there are at least two main parts to memory and each has a different function.

In 1890, William James made the distinction between 'primary' and 'secondary' memory. Whereas secondary memory is seen by him as the sum of knowledge acquired over the past, primary memory is described as memory which does not really deal with the 'genuine past' but which 'comes to us as belonging to the rearward portion of the present space of time' (1890: 647). Today one tends to call these two parts 'long-term memory' (also 'long-term store' or 'permanent store') and 'short-term memory' (also 'working memory' or 'short-term store'). It is said that, whereas items in long-term memory are possibly never really forgotten, items in short-term memory are there only for as long as they are needed for present mental activities. Thus short-term memory seems to have a threshold function in that it receives outside information; with the aid of such information mental activities can take place there and then as required; in the end selected items can be sent into permanent store and redundant information can be discarded. I will discuss long-term and short-term memory separately.

Long-term memory

Long-term memory seems to have an unlimited storage capacity, but it does not always retain securely all the items we want to keep in it ('storage failure'). Items have to be 'encoded' properly, and it seems that the deeper and wider the encoding, involving as many senses as possible and aiming at meaningful associations, the stronger the stored 'memory traces' will be. But not all that is stored can be remembered and brought forth at will in the same way and at the right time ('retrieval failure').

Components of long-term memory

What has been said so far about long-term memory may give the impression that it is a unitary system. This is not so: most psychologists who have studied memory agree that there are at least two parts: one part stores 'knowing that' memories and another stores 'knowing how' memories (Ryle, 1973: 44 ff.). For example, we remember *that* the fifth of November was the day of 'gunpowder, treason and plot'; and we remember *how* to make toffee apples. The second part of memory (remembering *how*) is commonly called 'procedural memory'; the first part (remembering *that*), however, has been given various labels (semantic, declarative, propositional memory), indicating that it has been looked at from different angles. At present the most common terms seem to be 'declarative' or 'semantic' although, as Tulving points out, the strong linguistic connotations of 'semantic' may be a drawback (1983: 28). Tulving also suggests a third part: the 'episodic' memory. I will look at the three components separately.

1. Semantic memory

Semantic memory has been defined as 'the system whereby we store knowledge of the world' (Baddeley, 1990: 354), or 'a person's abstract, timeless knowledge of the world that he shares with others' (Tulving, 1983: v). It lies at the centre of school learning but one ought to remember that it includes more than just the knowledge of meanings and language as the term might suggest. Some knowledge can be acquired without language. For instance, we know 'in our bones' that the sun can warm us but that the moon cannot; and our non-verbal cat obviously knows that too.

3. Episodic memory

Episodic memory is nearer to semantic memory than to procedural memory, I will therefore discuss it now before turning to procedural memory. Tulving defines episodic memory as a memory 'that is concerned with unique concrete personal experience dated in the rememberer's past' (1983: v) – the store of knowledge gained by auto-biographical events which are not necessarily shared with others. Although there is some controversy about this kind of memory, it makes good sense to me, and my experience suggests that it has its value for teaching children with memory difficulties as it may help to anchor factual knowledge and make retrieval easier. Also, through its very personal nature it plays a role in developing 'self-awareness' and in keeping track of the temporal order of events. It is thus particularly useful to children with language and memory difficulties.

3. Procedural memory

This is the 'knowing how' part of long-term memory. Touch-typing is a frequently used example of procedural knowledge. Skilled typists will not find it easy to name the positions of all the letter keys, although they will demonstrate such implicit knowledge day after day by working correctly and speedily. According to Anderson there are three steps that must be completed successfully before procedural knowledge is achieved (1990: 256 ff.), in summary:

(a) first one has to understand what is involved and remember what is relevant (cognitive stage);
(b) then one has to find the right methods to perform the skill by trial and error (associative stage);
(c) and only after that can one reach the last stage (autonomous stage) where, through continuous practice, the 'know how' can settle into long-term memory as more or less unconscious procedural knowledge.

Although the first examples of learned procedures that come to mind are normally drawn from physical activities, it should not be forgotten that mental activities – such as elementary arithmetic – can also be proceduralized.

Organization of knowledge in long-term store

Various spatial models, from 'warehouses' with 'shelves of knowledge' to 'networks' with 'nodes', have been suggested to illustrate the organization of single items in long-term store, and new ones will undoubtedly be developed (for a short overview see Parkin, 1993: 70 ff.). Nevertheless there does seem to be agreement among scholars that there *is* organization.

What makes a teacher's task so difficult, however, is the fact that all organization of remembered knowledge is carried out in a highly personal way and may often result in 'distortion' (Byers and Erlwanger, 1985). Learning matter can be offered in a way that the teacher considers well-organized and therefore likely to be remembered and easily produced, but it is by no means certain that all children will accept the organization and store it accordingly in their long-term memory. For instance, the operational sign 'plus', which the teacher has tried to establish in the children's store of knowledge as a symbol for the linking of numerical sets, may go down very different 'pathways' with different children, perhaps as:

'It looks like a half-finished star.'
'We use half of it for take-aways.'
'I can press that on my calculator and it adds up numbers for me.'
'I must remember that it is a posh way of saying what I call "add".'
'If my big sister gets it with a B in front she is pleased, and I have not yet figured out why'; etc.

Luckily, memories can be 'recoded', and in the end the relevant knowledge may be stored in the 'right place', with the 'correct' or commonly shared meaning and with organizational 'nodes' which facilitate efficient access thus making easy retrieval possible.

Short-term memory (working memory)

'Primary' or 'short-term' memory holds what we need for the present. Its content, supported by consciousness, can be easily accessed, altered and worked with; but, as the name suggests, any information stored in it is liable to fade away quickly. There is thus always room for new content and enough flexibility for reorganization so that new tasks can be tackled. All in all, short-term memory can be seen as a centre of mental activity, a place for learning, a workplace as it were, and as such it is often called the 'working memory'. A common example of short-term working memory is when one looks up a telephone number. Perhaps one mutters it to oneself, stores it quickly, uses it almost effortlessly, and then forgets it.

How much information can normally be held in short-term memory? This is a complex matter. As Anderson (1990: 152) points out, 'the momentary capacity in our working memories is very high – we can be aware of a great many things in our environment'. However, the drawback is that only a limited number of items can be retained in a state of *activation* that is high enough for efficient work.

It is thought that information enters our short-term store through our senses, and that some short-lived visual ('iconic') or oral ('echoic') memories are selected for activation above the rest. These are the ones we want to work with. To use them, we need to take special measures. Such measures for activation are described in the 'working memory' model of Baddeley and his collaborators (Baddeley, 1990; Gathercole and Baddeley, 1993). They suggest three devices (of which more will be said in the next section dealing with the implications for language-impaired children):

(a) *The articulatory loop* – This relies on phonological skills and the ability to use an 'inner voice' for keeping the information activated.

(b) *The visuo-spatial sketchpad* – This is described as a 'work space' or system where old and new images can be temporarily stored and manipulated.

(c) *The central executive* – This is a linking device which uses the other two services as supporting 'slave systems'; its role is to plan and execute all work in short-term memory and its capacity seems to be limited by memory span and attention span.

Rehearsal

Rehearsal is a term that is often used in discussing memory; it can almost be seen as a synonym for 'practising'. In short-term memory it is an important strategy for 'activation' and seems to take place continuously by verbal and visual means (for example, muttering words, or imagining objects – in other words, by using the 'slave systems' of the central executive). The term is also used for activities in short-term memory that are specifically aimed at anchoring and strengthening knowledge selected for permanent storage in long-term memory. As such, 'rehearsal' covers what is often described in teaching as consolidation, repetition or revision: rehearsal is the daily bread of learning and teaching. Every time an item is brought forth ('retrieved') from long-term memory, some kind of rehearsal takes place and there is a 'freshening-up' of the memory.

Retrieval

Retrieval is a term used with both long-term and short-term memory; it deals with *access* to the information stored in memory. Whereas processing of information and anchoring of knowledge in memory can be seen as the 'incoming' dimension of memory work, retrieval can be seen as the 'outgoing' dimension. As such it can take place in two forms: as *recognition* and as *recall*. Suppose we were to show a child a pentagon. A question that would try to elicit recognition might be: 'Is this a pentagon?' A question that would try to elicit recall might be: 'What would you call this figure?'

Recognition is normally easier than recall but under certain conditions the opposite seems to be true – mostly when it is a case of 'cued recall' instead of 'free recall'. For instance, if the term 'pentagon' was learned in connection with a picture of the famous 'Pentagon' in Washington, and if, in a later session, a plan-drawing of the building is shown together with the recall question given above ('What would you call this figure?'), retrieval is facilitated by the link of a cue (the pentagonal 'Pentagon'). In more general terms, if the environmental context in which the initial learning took place is in some way similar to the situation in which retrieval is required, with fairly strong memory cues at retrieval time, recall can be easier than recognition.

Failure to retrieve is a common occurrence and can have various causes: poor initial encoding, perhaps due to unclear first perception; insufficient 'elaboration' (narrow information with no links to previous knowledge); or inefficient organization leading to one item interfering with another. The conditions at the time of retrieval might also have an influence (moods, motivation, distractions). Finally, a lack of rehearsal can be the cause for retrieval failure.

Memory weakness as a feature of language-impaired children

So far I have discussed theoretical aspects of memory. I will now look at the implications for language-impaired children with memory problems. A weak memory is not a feature that is peculiar to children with language difficulties. Firstly, I have not met any teachers who do not complain about the memory of their pupils, from teachers in prestigious secondary schools to those in infant schools. Such a complaint seems to be an occupational trap, probably due to a persistent wishful over-estimation of general memory capacity. Secondly, 'hard' evidence for a memory weakness in children with language difficulties is rare, and apparently does not exist with regard to long-term memory.

Anecdotal evidence, however, seems very strong. One does not need to have been teaching a long time in a school with language-impaired children to find that anchoring facts in long-term memory takes a lot of targeted effort; that the number of items which can be held in working memory is low, and that word-finding problems among the children are widespread and severe.

One moving example is the statement of a parent with two language-impaired boys (Da Costa, 1989: 87 ff.):

> Many are the times that my wife and I have suggested something simple to the boys, like going for a walk, and by the time we have explained three times over, in words of one syllable or less, where we are going, with whom, why, and so on, we are both too exhausted to set foot out of the door.

He compares his children's memory with a self-cleaning cassette: 'it doesn't matter how many times you record the message, it wipes itself clean as you go along.'

In school, the most revealing experience in this respect is probably the attempt to teach the alphabet. This is a task that relies on sequential auditory memory – one of the weakest points in many children with language difficulties (see, for instance, Haynes and Naidoo, 1991: 146).

Research

Long-term memory: As far as I know, there is no specific research suggesting that weak long-term memory is a feature of children with language difficulties. However, there is evidence that they have great difficulties with vocabulary learning – a task which obviously relies on securely anchoring items in long-term memory. Standard vocabulary scores show an increasing lag with age in spite of special language teaching and therapy. This contrasts with the production of grammatical and coherent language, which is initially often the weakest feature on language profiles but which improves with age (Haynes and Naidoo, 1991; Haynes, 1992). Also if one accepts that verbal knowledge entering long-term memory depends on work done in short-term memory, any weakness in the latter will have repercussions on the former.

Short-term working memory: Auditory short-term memory tests have resulted in very low scores by children in special schools for language-impairment or in language units. It is not rare to find an age-lag in this respect of around four years or more in a 10-year-old child (Haynes and Naidoo 1991; Haynes, 1992). Some studies suggest poor rehearsal facilities of the *phonological loop* in working memory, with consequences for long-term storage as well as for the retrieval of vocabulary (Gathercole, 1993; Gathercole and Baddeley, 1993). A study by Kirchner and Klatzky (1985) showed a lower capacity for maintaining and manipulating items in working memory in 12 language-impaired children when compared with 12 non-impaired children, which suggests a weakness in the functioning of the *'central executive'*. Such a weakness may be a crucial factor in causing the 'limited processing capacity' in language-impaired children that was suggested by Johnston (1992). Finally, one can assume that a failure of the *'visuo-spatial sketchpad'* can also aggravate the problems displayed in children with language difficulties, although I know of no research on this specific question. The 'sketchpad' certainly seems to be of special importance for compensatory measures in reading and mathematics.

All this may lead to the conclusion that a low capacity of working memory lies at the heart of low vocabulary knowledge stored in long-term memory, and this in turn might contribute heavily to more general language problems.

Retrieval problems: Word-finding problems have been found to be a common feature among language-impaired children (cf. Hyde-Wright, Gorrie, Haynes and Shipman, 1993 for an overview).

Consequences for learning early mathematics

Long-term memory: Children with poor long-term memory will find it hard to learn to count. Difficulties with counting might persist for a long time. This, in turn, can severely affect all further number work. Also, children with a poor long-term memory will suffer from a lack of known number facts. Most children soon know that 6 and 6 makes 12 without having to think. A child with a poor long-term memory will have to figure it out again and again.

Short-term memory: All mental arithmetic will be difficult for children with short-term memory weaknesses. They will not be able to keep a number question in mind while they hear it, let alone while they think about it. Numerical word problems in oral and even in written form will prove difficult because they may have forgotten the beginning of the story by the time they come to the end. Following instructions might also be difficult. Finally, the use of simultaneous compensatory methods may be beyond the children's processing capacity.

Retrieval weakness: This is in my experience one of the most frustrating problems – for teacher and child alike – in number work and generally. What is the use of knowing number facts if they are not available when you need them?

Consequences for teaching

It is easy to see that such memory handicaps will influence almost all learning and that teaching has to be adjusted accordingly. The studies by Kirchner and Klatzky (1985) and Hyde-Wright et al. (1993) are of interest here because they also suggest that remedial measures might be more successful if they are based on meaning rather than on rote learning.

Perhaps the consequences for teaching can best be summed up by taking to heart what Skemp (1976) writes about instrumental understanding and relational understanding of mathematics. Instrumental understanding is where one knows when and how to apply a rule but not really why. Relational understanding goes deeper and means that there is 'more to learn' but that what has been learned is 'easier to remember'.

In the end, instrumental understanding will certainly have to be fostered because it is necessary for daily functioning, but this should only be done after a kind of security backcloth of good relational understanding has been established, no matter how long that takes.

CRITICAL POINTS IN THE ELEMENTARY MATHEMATICAL SYLLABUS

Considering the importance of memory in all learning, it is difficult to focus on critical points in the syllabus of early mathematics. Where I do choose topics to focus on, they must be taken as samples only: I selected them because difficulties became especially obvious, and I thought that I might be able to make suggestions at least on these points. They are:

learning the first numbers (mainly 1–10);
learning to count (up to 100 and beyond); and
learning number facts (early mental arithmetic and the beginning of 'times tables').

I will also discuss retrieval problems, which seem to occur at all stages of learning.

The Introduction of First Numbers (Mainly Up to 10)

What are the problems?

Some of the difficulties faced by children with a weakness in symbolic understanding when they are introduced to the first numbers have been discussed in Chapter 1. Children with memory deficits may experience the same problems, but they are made worse because the children find it hard to remember the names of first numbers and, more importantly, they find it hard to remember the names in the right sequence.

Learning a sequence of nonsense syllables

'First numbers', as I call them here, are numbers with names that cannot be arrived at through the number system. This certainly means the numbers from 1 to 11, and to some extent the numbers from 12 to 19 (plus a few with minor distortions in higher numbers, like 'thir-ty' or 'fif-ty'). Unfortunately, when learning the number sequence, one has to start with these very numbers – the numbers that make most demands on memory. The established order and the individual names of these numbers are totally arbitrary – a sequence of nonsense syllables, as it were. Only after 11 can some system be seen to emerge, although somewhat haphazardly. The further one goes up the number sequence, the more systematic it becomes and the lighter the memory load. The young child, however, has not reached that stage yet and does not know that there is help to come. As far as memory load is concerned, he is thrown in at the deep end of learning.

Numbers, together with the days of the week, the months of the year, and the alphabet, are memory items that have to remembered in a stable sequence if they are to be useful. If the child goes shopping, he need not ask for apples, bananas and potatoes in the order his mother told him: he can start with the 'boring potatoes' in case he forgets. One can live without remembering other sequences, funny ones or serious ones (e.g. tick-tack-toe; I-am-the-lord-of-the-dance-says-he), but certain basic sequences are so essential for everyday life that a child must be able to recite them without effort. Time, therefore, has to be spent on these sequences – a lot of time for the child with a verbal sequential memory deficit. He has to learn them against all the odds, and the question is how we can help him.

How can we help?

The most important general advice is probably to overlearn; and overlearn; and overlearn. More specifically: learning should be spaced out over time; each item that is taught should be widely elaborated; the teacher should take care not to overload the short-term working memory, otherwise mistakes in the initial 'encoding process' could lead to interference at the later recall and result in 'fixed' mistakes; and finally, while new numbers are learned, there must be ongoing, supervised rehearsal of what has been learned already – supervision is essential during rehearsal, otherwise mistakes in retrieval will be reinforced.

This means, in practical terms, good teaching, a little at a time, well learned, in different contexts, with sensible intervals in learning and revising, and close supervision. Learning by trial and error and subsequent correction is certainly called for at times, but it has no place in rote learning; here the aim is to 'get it right' into storage the first time. And, last but not least, child and teacher ought to try to keep cheerful during this overlearning process, both being conscious of the difficulties that the task entails, and fighting the battle courageously as allies.

The following specific suggestions for which support can be found on theoretical grounds and which also seem to work in practice (at least with certain children), form part of an approach which proceeds on two lines:

(a) Individual members of the sequence to be learned are first filled with as much meaning as possible, and only later put into a sequence.
(b) Episodic memory is used consciously as 'back-up' memory.

The following is a description of such an approach, applied to numbers and the number sequence.

Teaching numbers as 'friends'

To a logical adult it would make sense to teach the numbers from 1 to 10 one after the other, starting with the lowest number and proceeding incrementally one by one from 5 to 6, from 6 to 7, and so forth. In doing so, one concentrates on one single aspect of a number, which is its magnitude. Moreover, one discriminates between numbers by the smallest possible difference in magnitude, which is 'one'. As was pointed out in Chapter 1, this may not make much sense from a child's point of view. Minimum differences in general are not what the young child is after, and a difference of 'one' may hardly be worth much attention. I suggest going for bigger and more interesting differences at the start and teaching each number as a unique entity, regardless of its place in the counting sequence. This can mean that 6 is taught before 4, and 8 after 9.

By treating numbers as single entities that have 'character' one goes to some extent back into history or past folklore, where individual numbers were seen as having special properties. Perhaps one ought to try to regain some of the personal feelings our ancestors had for numbers (cf. Newman and Boles, 1992; Stewart, 1995). The Pythagoreans, for instance, talked of 'perfect' and 'friendly' numbers. Likewise, special numbers have played a part in almost all religions. The most extreme example is probably Saint Augustine's belief that 6, a 'perfect' number, would have been perfect even if God's world created in six days did not exist. (A perfect number, as defined by the Pythagoreans, is a number which is the sum of its divisors, including 1 but excluding itself, i.e. 6 can be divided by 1, 2 and 3; 1 + 2 + 3 = 6; the next perfect number would be 28; cf. Flegg, 1983 – a valuable source of information about numbers in several respects.)

Work with the 'perfect' number 6 as a memorable entity may be an excellent starting point for work with memory-impaired children. Starting with 6 rather than a lower number has its advantages, mainly because possibilities of pattern-making abound. Through patterns of 6 one can arrive, in an obvious top-down way, at the development of 3 and 2 as entities (see Figure 3.1). In general, pattern-making can serve for the 'friendly' introduction of any number.

Another way of getting children to 'make friends' with individual numbers is to introduce them as memorable 'events'. For instance, the number 3 could be introduced by a three-legged race on the playground; or the number 9 could be introduced by nine-pin bowling with soap-boxes and balls in the hall.

Thus before children are asked to learn the first members of the counting sequence, they are given the opportunity to meet each member in pleasurable circumstances first and thus to anchor the concept and the label for it in their 'episodic memory'. Consolidation can later take place through a game where the selection of numbers can be monitored and where almost unlimited opportunities are available to practise the numbers that a child has found difficult (see the 'ruler' or 'racing' game in Unit 3). Work described in Chapter 1 may also be helpful at this stage.

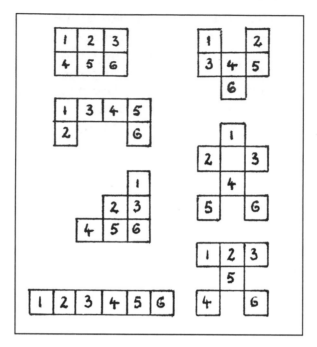

Figure 3.1: Patterns of 6 made by one child

Teaching various number sequences

Number sequences other than the 'plus-one' sequence

A decision to postpone working with the 'plus-one' counting sequence does not mean that no sequential learning can take place at this stage. There are other sequences suitable for early work where the differences and relations between steps are more obvious to the child than the 'plus-one' counting sequence. For example, there is the *'pyramid sequence'*, which, in mathematical terms, is the sequence of triangular numbers (1, 3, 6, 10, etc.) and which children often seem to build up spontaneously with cube sets (see Figure 3.2).

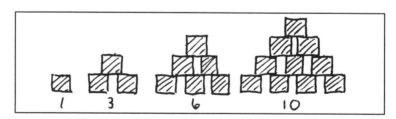

Figure 3.2: The 'pyramid sequence'

More examples of number sequences are given in Unit 2 (the doubling sequence, the sequence of square numbers, the sequence of even numbers, and the sequence of odd numbers).

The 'plus-one' sequence

In the end, numbers will have to be put into the proper counting ('plus-one') sequence, which will lead to the number line and to the ordinal meaning of numbers. It is hoped that by this time children will have become familiar with the names and contents of the first numbers of the sequence and that the concept of cardinality will have dawned on them; they may have developed lasting personal images of each quantity. Thus, when they start to chant the counting sequence – the order of magnitude with an increment of one – it will be more meaningful and therefore easier to remember.

My suggestion is to start with 'staircase work'. This means using rods of different lengths that represent different quantities in a concrete way (e.g. Cuisenaire or Stern rods; see Unit 3). They can be used as counters to which the cardinal meaning is still visually attached, but which at the same time can be sorted with the ordinal 'plus-one' principle in mind, thereby building the 'staircase of cardinality' (cf. Chapter 2 and Figure 2.5). This can lead to 'staircases' with bigger steps later (for example, the plus-2 or plus-3 sequence).

From the 'staircase of cardinality' to the number line: first counting

Counting along the steps of a staircase already leads to the number line. More formal ways of doing this are:

(a) using the first line of a horizontal abacus (e.g. Slavonic abacus, see Chapter 1 and Unit 4);
(b) using 10 beads on a string, preferably 5 in one colour and the next 5 in another colour (the colour break at five mirrors the abacus and prepares the child for later work in the decimal system, where five is used as a visual anchor point).

In both cases the beads are pushed from one side to the other while the counting sequence is chanted, with or without the teacher; the advantage of such counting is that there is still a visible link between the growing quantities and the individual number labels.

The next step could be the use of a ruler (or ruler-like strip) and a pointer. Counting now takes place along the sections with figures on the ruler (the number line). At the beginning children should be encouraged to let their finger (if the ruler is an inch ruler) or the pointer (if it is a centimetre ruler) circle round the named numbers in increasingly long movements, including the positions of all previously named numbers with the last one. Later the pointer can be used to divide the numbers counted (the numbers on the left-hand side of the ruler) from the rest. A warning here: the child should not be counting and at the same time putting a finger directly on the named number, thereby covering it; this would give a visual impression of 'n − 1' and would mean that the child names 7, covers the position of 7 and perceives 6 on the left (see Chapter 1).

Such work takes the first steps towards proper counting. The cardinal and ordinal aspects have been related and thus the 'cardinal principle' – which states that the final count term of any counting trial determines the numerosity of the full set – will dawn on the child. He should now be able to answer the question 'how many?' with understanding.

Learning to Count (Up to 100 and Beyond)

What are the problems?

Counting, as it is normally understood, is a task which involves verbal memory skills. Countable items have to be tagged with special oral labels to be applied in a fixed order; each label can only be used once in the counting sequence and only at its particular place in the sequence (cf. Gelman and Gallistel, 1978: 77ff.). All this means that one has to learn a large number of labels (in theory, an infinite amount) and, worse still, one must learn to apply them in the right sequence. This would be an impossible memory task but for the fact that the labels have been chosen in accordance with a system, in our case the decimal system. The more systematic the system, and the better its use, the smaller the memory load.

It follows that when teaching the counting sequence to children, but especially when teaching it to children with a verbal memory weakness, one ought to concentrate on the system as much and as early as possible.

Difficulties in the English counting system

The early counting words in English, as in many other languages, developed 'naturally' rather than according to one efficient, overriding system. They were geared to limited practical use in early farming or small-scale trading communities, rather than to world-wide trade, sophisticated navigation or science. This means that English-speaking children of today have to cope with an uneven blend of two oral counting systems, of which the one normally learnt first is rather unsystematic (e.g. 'eleven' instead of 'onety-one' and 'thirteen' instead of onety-three'). As was already pointed out (Chapter 1), children in other cultures are luckier. For instance, the Chinese in learning to count from 1 to 100 have to learn just 11 words (1 to 10 plus a word for 100) from which all the rest are built up consistently. The oral system is regular in a 'big-to-small' fashion (e.g. 11 is 'ten one', 21 is 'two ten one' etc.) so that a child can perceive the system easily (cf. Fuson and Kwon, 1991; Nunes and Bryant, 1996: 45 ff.; compare also Unit 2).

Despite the difficulties of the English counting system, most children gradually learn to count reliably with good motivation, fun, and ease. Some, however, stay unreliable counters for a considerable time, and these are often children whose auditory memory cannot cope with the vocabulary load of the sequence. Their 'count efficiency' is low (cf. Conti-Ramsden, Donlan and Grove, 1992) and they therefore find it hard to acquire an overall view of the sequence and to discover the 'system' which would be their best help.

Consequences of unreliable counting

An unreliable counter with weak auditory memory will have similar difficulties to those encountered by a child with organizational problems: a child might count a set of 12 bottle tops and make it '13'; the teacher will say 'count again'; the child would do so and end up with '14'; the teacher and child would then count together and arrive at 12.

As far as the child was concerned he did exactly the same thing three times. Something must have happened to the set 'while he wasn't looking'. One of the most reliable facts to aid numerical reasoning, the invariance of quantities, is lost to him.

How can we help?

Using the system as an aid for memory (from 10 to 100)

I have earlier defined 'first numbers' as the numbers which cannot be arrived at through the system. These are mainly the numbers 1–10. From 10 onwards however, the system becomes apparent; in its written form it is completely regular, in its spoken form it is less so at the beginning, but later it shows increasing regularity.

This regularity ought to be made clear to the child as early as possible, since it is the most efficient aid for a child with a weak memory who is learning to count. It has always struck me that it is a bad idea to expect children to master all the numbers up to 20 (and even to do 'sums' in this area) and not allow them to go further until they have done so. It means that weaker children, considered more or less incapable of making progress, have to struggle with the most difficult, unrepresentative part of the number system, while their abler peers move on to take advantage of the system. There is no way to discover and use the system if one's knowledge is limited to the numbers 1 to 20. Therefore, in my view, what the language- and memory-impaired child should learn after 10 is not 11 but 100. First there should be work with 100, where one explores it top-down with focus on full tens (starting with the 'regular' ones, e.g. 60, 70); and only after this exploration is satifactorily completed should units be filled in between the tens (e.g. 60 and 3 more are 63; 80 and 6, 80 and 7, 80 and 8...; cf. Bierhoff, 1996: 17). Thus right from the start one emphasizes the decimal system in which the tens give the structure.

What is the best way to make such an analytic approach work? I will have to repeat myself here, because I think that one of the best ways is to use the 'field of 100' as represented in the Slavonic abacus, in the paper abacus, and in quantity pictures (see the descriptions in Chapter 1, in Chapter 2, and in Unit 4). The 'field of 100' arrangement has the advantage of showing the decimal system in a structured 'gestalt'. It is *visually memorable* and in that respect it seems superior to the number line. Although the number line can also show the regularity of the decimal system, compared with the 'field', it does so in a way whereby it is not easy to perceive the system in all its parts simultaneously; the number line is therefore visually rather unmemorable.

Obviously it would be wrong to assume that a child with a verbal memory deficit will automatically be able to remember visual materials better. Nevertheless there is a chance that some children will do so; and in any case, two weak strands of memory can assist each other and function better together than on their own. I will not elaborate here on the practical aspects of how to work with the abacus, but refer instead to the sections mentioned above, where full descriptions are given.

If one stresses the system after 10 as an aid to memory, one will have to solve the problem of the 'half unsystematic' number words, mainly those between 10 and 20. As pointed out earlier, these obscure our system in their spoken form and therefore have to receive special treatment. I suggest using what I like to call 'system-words' ('onety-four' as in sixty-four; see Unit 2 for a full list), at least for an intermediate period of time, while introducing the field of 100 with all its numbers.

When the children are first taught to 'find their way around the field', it is advisable to ignore numbers which have irregular names and to work from the typical towards the untypical (cf. Hatano, 1982). After they have learned to find and name numbers like 61, 72, 83, 94, they will probably be able to find a number 'onety-three' or 'threety-five'. In the unlikely case of never having met the proper number words, they may find this easy and natural. In fact, they probably know that there is no number called 'onety-four' but they will see the 'joke'. It is then the teacher's task to make them understand the relevance of the 'system words'. After that, both 'proper' number words and system words can be used in parallel, until it is time to practise the verbal skill of reciting the counting sequence with its conventional names.

To sum up, children with a memory handicap need to grasp the system as early and as clearly as possible because it relieves their memory load. The aim is that they should get to know each number in the visually memorable field of 100. They should know its name, its value, and its place in the system. As an example, in the case of 48 it means that the child realizes the following and shows his understanding in one way or another:

- 'forty-eight' is the name;
- it means four tens and eight more;
- I will find this number on the abacus by going 'four tens down' and then 'five and three across';
- it comes after 47, and if I go along the line I come to 49;
- on the other hand, if I go down from 48 I come to 58, 68, 78, etc.;
- the counting sequence for the unit row is 48, 49, 50, etc.;
- the counting sequence for the ten-column is 48, 58, 68, etc.;
- if I go backwards in the unit row it will be 48, 47, 46, etc.;
- if I go upwards in the ten-column it will be 48, 38, 28, etc.;
- 48 is an 'easy' number; other numbers like 'onety-eight' are normally not called what they should be, they have strange names like 'eighteen' or 'thirty' instead of 'threety'.

Only when such 'field knowledge' has been acquired and the counting sequence has been well practised should arithmetical operations and the learning of arithmetical number facts begin.

Practising the verbal counting sequence

This is the last step in learning to count. The aim is to familiarize children thoroughly with the verbal number sequence up to a point where it becomes automatized without any overtly visible reference to quantities. Children with memory difficulties will need special help to learn the correct and automatic recital of the counting sequence.

If number words have been introduced as outlined in the previous sections the children will be fairly familiar with the vocabulary for the numbers 1 to 10. They will also have some conceptual knowledge of the quantity labelled with each number word up to 100 and some understanding of the system. Thus, when they start to establish the full counting order, each step in the number sequence should evoke lively images and radiate comfortable familiarity, backed up by episodic memories.

The task now is to memorize the sequence. It cannot be stressed strongly enough that children who find it hard to learn any sequence will need a lot of encouragement, repetition, time and care. The following gives some suggestions of how this might be done.

Practising with parallel activities ('induced distractors')

To suggest the use of 'distractors' as a teaching aid may seem strange when one is aiming at concentrated learning. It must be clear that I only suggest it for the process of automatization. 'Distractors' should be used when the child has reached the stage when he is normally able to count correctly while concentrating hard. Any distraction will send him 'off course' at this stage; he will stop, stammer and stumble through the rest and probably end up making mistakes (cf. Johnston, 1992). Common sequences, however, must be instantly retrievable and reliable under all conditions in order to be useful. Therefore the idea is slowly to stiffen the conditions of learning and gradually introduce 'distractors' to test and improve the robustness of the child's learning and ensure that there is indeed immediate retrieval, even under somewhat distracting circumstances.

Moreover, reliable counting skills can only be achieved through a great number of 'rehearsals' and the teacher's task is to find about 1001 different and interesting ways to practise the 'boring old thing'. But, by the nature of any standardized sequence, what has to be learned in these cases has always to stay strictly the same. How can one teach the same unchangeable sequence in different ways?

Since the task of memorizing a sequence cannot be altered, one thinks of a task that *can* be altered: a task which can be performed alongside the memorizing task, at the same time pleasing the child and bringing variety into an otherwise monotonous affair.

Two activities suitable for being done simultaneously while learning the counting sequence are:

(a) ordering number rods (e.g. Cuisenaire rods) by size into the 'staircase' (see Chapter 2 and this chapter above) while counting from one to ten; or

(b) throwing a small rice bag (or a small soft ball which is easy to
catch) while reciting the sequence; the bag or ball is thrown rhythmically backwards and forwards, or in a round from one child to
the next; for instance the person in charge says 'one' and throws
the bag to the child who catches it (with luck) and throws it back
while saying 'two', and so forth – in a kind of ping-pong play with
number words.

A list of various parallel activities is given in Unit 7. These seem suitable for mild distraction and for bringing variety to the task. The
activities are only meant as examples and it is hoped that teachers
and other carers will add to the list according to individual circumstances and imagination.

In the beginning the parallel activities can be related to the
concepts of quantity, as in the first example (rods). Later they should
become increasingly unrelated, as in the second example. One must
be careful, however, to make the activity fit the child or the group of
children; the 'distractor' should at no stage be so difficult as to seriously hinder the even and correct recitation of the sequence. Likewise, close supervision must be available at all times since early
mistakes in the main counting task should be avoided and, if they
occur, they should be corrected right from the beginning to minimize later interference.

Regular practice

Regular counting practice is especially important. It is a good habit
to start the day with a short counting session, preferably with a
different 'distractor' each day. This may have to be continued for
some time, perhaps for years. Even when the sequence seems firmly
established and can be used quite comfortably in other activities, it
seems advisable to ensure that there is some regular rehearsal in
order to guarantee continued easy retrieval. Later this could perhaps
take place not daily but once a week, or once a month, or after each
holiday, depending on the need of the child or group of children. For
older children this can be likened to a regular 'car maintenance test'.

Equal practice

Some thought ought to be given to how the higher numbers can be
given as much practice as the lower ones. The lower numbers in the
sequence are, by the nature of counting, constantly rehearsed. Thus
for children with memory difficulties some organized activity should
focus on the slightly higher and less-used numbers, at the early stage

perhaps the numbers 5–12. This can be done by playing the games suggested with 'distractors', but starting with higher and always differing numbers. For instance, the carer starts throwing the ball by saying 'five' and then the child continues with 'six'; thus 6-7-8-9 is practised rather than 1-2-3-4. In the end the memory link from 6 to 7 should be as strong as that from 2 to 3.

How many 'first numbers' at a time?

It is difficult to give a rule about how many numbers of the sequence should be practised at a time. As was said before, for children with memory difficulties it is especially important to get the names of the numbers and the order of the sequence correct right from the beginning, otherwise numbers which have been established wrongly or unclearly might interfere with later recall. This means limiting the numbers a child is asked to recite at any time carefully according to his memory capacity, as well as taking into account any articulatory or verbal discrimination problems (e.g. 'fee'-four-five can be a difficult sequence in that respect). Sometimes, to begin with, it might be necessary to limit the sequence to 1, 2, 3, followed by a new series 3, 4, 5; then 5, 6, 7; then 7, 8, 9, and so forth. An overlap like this seems advisable to ensure that later, when the triplets are put into a longer sequence, there are no or few problems with 'linkage' (i.e. a break in fluency at the points where the parts are put together when the full sequence is learned). For numbers over 10, the use of the system will allow more numbers to be practised together, as long as the sequence of numbers from 1 to 10 has been well established.

When to use written symbols

Finally, there is the question of when to combine written numerals with the oral counting sequence. In general, this seems unnecessary at an early stage (while learning the numbers from 1 to 10), where no system can be detected. On the other hand it is possible to use the writing of figures as a 'distracting activity', but only when the child is already thoroughly familiar with the mechanics of writing. Figure writing should be so familiar that it can be done in rhythm with the oral counting sequence when it is recited clearly, evenly and not too fast.

After such initial work, written numerals are then introduced as valuable aids to memory, since they mirror the system perfectly. Place value can be introduced as the most memory-saving principle of all. For such more advanced work see Chapter 1 and Units 3 & 4.

Learning Number Facts

What are the problems?

'Number fact' is a term used to describe elementary number combinations that are learned more or less 'by heart' (cf. Ginsburg, 1989: 121 ff.), for example children learn the 'fact' that $2 + 3 = 5$. A person's knowledge of 'number facts' is the full store of answers to number problems which can be given from memory without having to perform practical or mental arithmetical operations. Most people 'know' that $6 \times 6 = 36$. They have learned it at school and rehearsed it so often that it is well secured in long-term memory and easily retrieved when needed.

In general, the use of such instant memory retrieval for mental arithmetic increases over the years, and earlier strategies like 'counting-on' or 'decomposition' become relatively less important (cf. Dehaene, 1993: 8 ff.). The availability of such basic number facts allows more complex number problems to be solved more easily and quickly than would otherwise be possible. Generally, the more such basic number facts are remembered, the better; and a considerable amount of time in early mathematics is devoted to their acquisition.

Slow, uneven progress

For children with a memory weakness the problems are obvious: firstly, they will take longer to learn the facts; secondly, a lack of such readily available facts will become an obstacle when working out complex problems that make high demands on short-term memory; and finally, if the facts are there but cannot be consistently retrieved, performance will be uneven.

Which number facts – how many – how much time to spend on them?

The teaching of number facts to children with a weak memory poses awkward questions. What are the essential ones? How many is it realistic to aim at in each individual case? How much time can one afford to spend on them? Are they actually necessary? Would it not be better to concentrate on operational strategies? Perhaps there may even be an advantage in not being able to remember number facts: the weaker the memory, the more one has to rely on sound strategies or reinvention of the procedures, which can mean a gain in understanding. One can perhaps speculate that Einstein's achievements may have been due to his reported childhood problems with language and memory (Wheatley, 1977). However, there are few Einsteins growing up, and in ordinary daily life it must be highly inconvenient *not* to have some common number facts instantly available, thereby unduly burdening short-term working memory.

How can we help?

Teaching operational strategies

Number facts to be learned in elementary mathematics come mainly in two categories:

(a) addition and subtraction with low numbers, and
(b) basic multiplication in the form of 'times tables'.

In both cases it is possible to rely on concrete solutions for answers. For additions and subtractions one can add and take away objects; or one can tally quantities on paper and cross a number of them out; or one can count up and down the number line. For multiplication problems one can use counters and building blocks for 'multiple addition'; one can make patterns with tiles; and one can use squared paper for work with areas.

There is no doubt that these 'play' strategies will help to lay the foundations of basic arithmetic. The vocabulary will become familiar and the first memory associations will be established and constantly checked for correctness through the materials. It is important that the first associations should be strong and correct, since it has been shown (e.g. Campbell, 1987) that inadequately learned answers to number questions tend to interfere later as wrong responses to other problems. For instance, if one is unsure whether 5 + 9 is really 14, 14 has a high probability of being chosen wrongly in answer to other questions. Such interference is always undesirable; for children with memory difficulties it must be avoided at all costs.

These practical strategies with concrete means should be kept fresh and working by regular systematic revision, so that they can be used as a back-up system for memory failure at any time.

Number sketches

Later perhaps, the child can be taught to make quick and clear 'number sketches' (see Figure 3.3). For instance, if the child is familiar with structured rods, 16 can be drawn with a fairly long line representing 10, a line of half the length representing 5 and a small circle representing 1 (see Chapter 2). Teaching children systematically how to draw such sketches is probably one of the most valuable aids that can be offered in case of memory failure. Such teaching can often take more time than expected, especially with children who also have some organizational difficulties. Various methods can be developed, on plain paper or on one of the many kinds of lined and squared paper. One method which I have found successful for making fast and interesting number sketches is to use the hieroglyphic system of Ancient Egypt (see Chapter 1 and Unit 3).

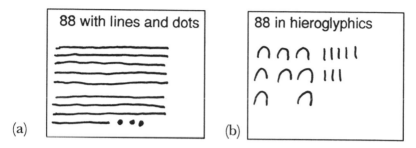

(a)   (b)

Figure 3.3 (a) and (b): Two kinds of number sketches

Whatever method one uses with individual children, in the end one ought to arrive at a kind of 'standard' method, so that the sketches can be made quickly and confidently. Any possibility of alternatives at this stage would slow children down and distract them from the tasks that the sketch is meant to facilitate.

Both practical number work and sketches play an essential part in promoting understanding and security. For some children they may be the best solution, and later they can perhaps be used together with a calculator. However, they are only supporting measures and have the disadvantage that they are generally slow or not practical in all situations. Are there better methods?

Using images to memorize addition and subtraction facts

As mentioned earlier, we cannot assume that weak verbal sequential memory is always compensated for by a relatively strong visual memory but it can be assumed that, in most cases, visual means of remembering can at least assist in one way or another. They can act as parts of the 'visuo-spatial sketchpad' of working memory, described at the beginning of this chapter. The question is how to make full use of visual means.

I am certain that there are different ways of providing the child with images to aid basic arithmetic. But whatever kind of method is chosen, it has to be used fairly consistently, despite any awkwardness or possible limitations. The perfect method has yet to be found, but as a teacher one has to act. One of the available 'second best' methods will have to do, as long as the teacher, and perhaps the child too, realize its limitations (cf. Globerson, 1989).

An appropriate visual back-up is the image of the structured 'field of 100' (see Chapter 1 and Chapter 2). I return to it repeatedly because I know from experience that, with all its rigidity, it can be used in many ways and can therefore provide consistent support in a number of different situations.

Specific work on learning addition and subtraction facts with the aid of the visual field of 100 is described in detail in Unit 4. The kind of effects that this work can produce is described in Marion Walter's (1986) *Mathematical Memoir*. Marion Walter grew up in Germany; she emigrated to England and later to the USA, where she became a well-known mathematics educator. She remembers learning early mathematics with the Slavonic abacus:

> Then there was school. We learned with an abacus (10 rows of 10 beads). I remember that, though I have almost totally blocked out my first years of school. I am pretty sure of the importance to me of learning with an abacus as I never had to 'learn' my number facts – I just knew them from my experience with the abacus. Numbers that added to 10 were very easy as were ones that added to less than 10. Then sums like 8 + 7 were easy; even today, as soon as someone says 8, I *feel* the missing 2 and the 7 obliges in 'breaking up' into 2 + 5. I often wonder why not more research has been done on *how* people cope with numbers and with what model they learned. I often ask my students to add two numbers, such as 27 + 15, in their head and then to tell how they did it. Some are 'breaker-uppers' but very many are column-adders. I am definitely a breaker-upper and I am sure it is because I learned with an abacus. I might add 27 + 15 by thinking 20 + 7 + 15 = 35 + 7 = 42 or 30 + 15 – 3. I couldn't possibly do it as the column-adders do it : 5 + 7 = 12, so write down a 2 and carry the 1, etc. My memory is far too poor to deal in my head with 'carrying' and recalling digits. (1986: 14)

It is interesting to notice that she not only 'sees' a 2 when she hears 8, but that she actually 'feels' it.

A drawback of using such intermediate non-verbal methods is that they tend to slow down the speed of performance in mental arithmetic slightly, since the answer is never a prompt automatic verbal response. If one has acquired some relevant imagery well, it seems almost impossible to suppress visual responses parallel to automatic ones, even when the visual back-up might not be necessary any more. On the whole, what is lost in speed is gained in certainty, since one response is checked by the other. And such certainty may lead to reduced anxiety.

For the present purpose, the aim of all work with such abacus methods (using the bead frame, the paper abacus, quantity pictures and selected Cuisenaire rods) is, in the long run, to establish a memorable mental representation from which one can 'read' the answers. This, one hopes, will facilitate retrieval from long-term memory and assist all subsequent demands in working memory.

The value of such mental representation has been shown by studies in Japan, where abacus work is common (although with a somewhat different abacus which uses five-unit counters). Hatano (1982: 219) actually defines an abacus as an 'external memory'. Japanese studies indicate that people who have learned to calculate on an abacus develop a mental representation of it through which they can calculate just as efficiently later without actually handling the beads (Hatano, Miyake and Binks, 1977; Hatano and Osawa, 1983; cf. also an observation by Whitburn on a visit to Japan, 1995: 357). Interestingly, Hatano (1982) reports on a study (Hishitani and Yamauchi, 1976) which showed that among skilled abacus operators memory for digits was not correlated with their high mental calculation ability (1983: 219); they presumably relied on their 'mental abacus' for that.

Such studies may give us confidence to make use of an abacus with language-impaired children, especially since we know that the majority of them show very low results in digit-span memory tests, with little hope of improvement over age (Haynes and Naidoo, 1991: 146 ff.).

There is another visual aspect of Japanese and Continental teaching methods that can certainly be valuable and is also found in work with the Slavonic abacus. It is the special emphasis on the number 5 as an intermediate higher unit and its use for 'privileged anchorage' (cf. Hatano, 1982; Yoshida and Kuriyama, 1991; Grauberg 1995; Bierhoff, 1996). The importance of the number 5 was naturally obscured in teaching that still had to do with imperial measurements. The English bead abacus of Victorian times had dozens or half dozens in one row with a colour break at 3, 6, 9, 12 (cf. White, 1971 and Figure 3.4).

White writes that 'in 1969 an abacus on a toy booth at Paddington Station had the groups of beads in tens and fives, perhaps looking forward to decimal currency' (1971: 140).

It may take another generation of English teachers to realize in full the advantages of giving the number 5 a privileged place in counting and early mental arithmetic.

Becoming verbally fluent (basic additions and subtractions)

Fluency cannot be achieved with compensatory measures only; it has to be tackled directly. We can assume that the children have acquired some experience and a certain degree of fluency in count-

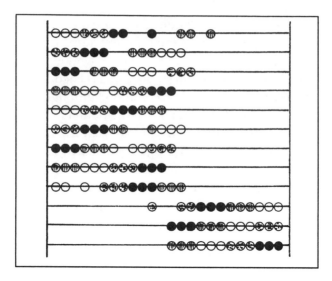

Figure 3.4: Victorian English abacus (after a picture in White, 1971)

ing by now, and that the vocabulary of number words is now fairly familiar to them. They have also used this knowledge in practical work or visually-based abacus practice, the latter having almost reached the stage of 'mental abacus work'. They know where to look for help if memory fails them, but now they have to become fluent through consistent verbal rehearsal of basic number facts.

Generally, all that has been said about practising counting is relevant here. Again one can employ 'distraction' to make practice varied and arrive at some degree of automatization. For example, ball- or bag-throwing can be used. The teacher might say: 'three add four', while throwing the bag to a child. The child catches it and answers 'seven', he then throws the bag back to the teacher while repeating the whole sentence ('three add (plus, and) four is (equals, makes) seven'.

It is difficult to say how many such number sentences should be practised at a time. In most cases I would try to start with three. These are practised daily in short periods for a week or so. Three different ones are practised the week after. In the third week the six sentences are worked on together, and so forth. If there is one sentence that a child finds harder to remember than the rest, a special session should be devoted to it, perhaps on the following lines:

– Don't worry, we all have our special 'tricky ones'; yours seems to be $x + y$. Let's see if we can find a reason why $x + y$ should be more difficult than the rest; yes, you often mix it up with $x + z$; perhaps you have learned the two too close together . . .

- See how $x + y$ looks on the abacus; now close your eyes and try to remember it; keep your eyes closed and say the sentence; can you see the abacus picture in your mind? Say it again.
- Here is a heap of counters; give me x, give me y, how many counters have I got now? Say the sentence. Let's do the same fast until the counters of the heap are all lined up on my side.
- What are your two best sums – the ones you can always remember? OK we will play ball with three sums, your two 'best ones' and the 'tricky one'.
- Good, you seem to know it well now. Tomorrow we will do the same to make sure it is still OK. If we meet each other on the corridor or on the playground you can ask me the tricky one; or I will ask you. I am sure it won't be tricky for much longer . . . [or something to that effect].

It is hard to state in general what the difficult number facts are likely to be. There seems to be quite a variation from person to person, although generally larger numbers seem to cause more problems than smaller ones. For a discussion of number facts shown to be harder to memorize than others, see below in the context of 'times tables'.

If children have learned how to use the written number symbols and are confident with them, they may find it helpful to write their 'tricky' sums down repeatedly and to have a reference card on hand to 'look – verbalize – and check'. This may also help them to look at the written number fact from all sides again with or without practical demonstration ($7 = 3 + 4$; $7 = 4 + 3$; $7 - 3 = 4$; $7 - 4 = 3$). On the whole, however, the emphasis should be placed heavily on oral work.

Testing

One day, when one has established a few sets of number facts this way, let's say 18, these can be 'tested' together, either orally or in writing. But it is essential to remember that, even if the child has scored 18 out of 18, this should not be taken as a sign that he 'knows' the facts. Specific short practice sessions as well as testing sessions have to be repeated again and again, perhaps over years. This should be made clear to the child; it can be put into context as 'fitness training' or 'maintenance' depending on the child's interests – the analogy with his football hero or with car maintenance should be used to strengthen motivation.

Learning multiplication facts ('times tables')

It is relatively easy to provide early practical experience of multiplication – it can be done with concrete materials like egg boxes, cubes and other building bricks, or with squared paper in art periods, or in introductory area work. Such activities will lay the foundations for understanding and give the child strategies to work out multiplication facts 'the long way' (cf. Freudenthal, 1986; Anghileri, 1991). These early strategies will mainly rely on the child's experience with addition. For a discussion of children's understanding of aspects of multiplication that are more complex than the additive one, see Nunes and Bryant (1996: 144–200); they look, for instance, at situations involving ratio, where a fixed one-to-many correspondence between pairs of sets has to be kept constant (e.g. 1 carton – six eggs; 3 cartons – 18 eggs . . .).

However, providing a mental visual back-up system for multiplication facts, a system which can bridge the gap between the concrete and purely verbal knowledge is more difficult than simply providing practical experience. One can certainly use some visual patterns but their usefulness for remembering individual times table facts rather than addition and subtraction facts is limited.

One way of using patterns for teaching multiplication facts is to build up times tables with Cuisenaire rods (the large Cuisenaire set is needed for this). The patterns follow the decimal system; for instance, for the three-times table the first row would be: 3;3;3;1; the second: 2;3;3;2; and so forth. This, incidentally, is perhaps the best method to introduce the rods to any adult who has not used them before. Such tables are visually quite impressive. A comparison between the first ten tables built up in this way shows interesting relations in which the colours play their part (odds versus evens; the numbers that 'fit' the system well; the special nature of nine; symmetry lines).

However, most of these patterns seem visually too complicated to be remembered in sufficient detail to help a child with the instant retrieval of individual multiplication facts. They are probably more suitable for general consolidation, to reinforce the understanding of the system and to practise number bonds. They can even serve as design patterns for slow finger weaving (with yarn or with paper) and thus, without conscious effort, they may strengthen traces of already memorized multiplication facts. Such patterns are certainly fun and should not be left out.

On the abacus the easier ten-times, five-times, two-times and perhaps the nine-times tables make quite memorable visual patterns. Other tables can be chanted in parallel with bead movements on the Slavonic abacus or changes with the clear plastic overlay on the paper abacus, but on the whole the number pictures are too varied and the visual impact will be low. For an illustration of the pattern of three- and four-times tables see Figure 3.5.

Such a limitation means that in the end the child will have to rely

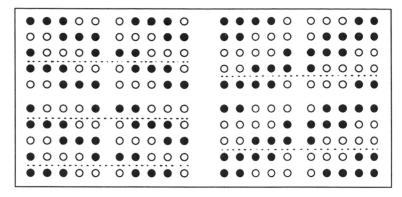

Figure 3.5: Three- and four-times tables on the abacus: examples of visually weak patterns.

heavily on non-visual memory and the teacher will have to provide ample practice.

Multiplication facts: how many, when and in which order?

It is difficult to say how many multiplication facts to be learned by rote should be part of *early* mathematics. This is a problem with children in mainstream education, but even more so with children who have a memory deficit. There may be a case for concentrating on just working out multiplication problems by practical methods, thereby laying sound foundations. Rote learning would thus be left for later years, perhaps even for secondary school.

If, however, a decision is made to tackle 'times tables' proper, Chinn and Ashcroft (1993: 84 ff.) show the task to be less daunting than it might seem. Their book is concerned with the mathematical problems of older dyslexic children, whose memory weakness is also often a matter of concern to their teachers. The authors point out that only 25 facts have to be remembered purely by rote. These exclude the tables which can be learned with the help of patterns (10, 5, 2 and 9 times tables); they also exclude all the reciprocal facts, assuming that if children know 3 × 4, they will also be familiar with 4 × 3. Therefore only one of the pairs is counted in the 25 facts to learn the hard way.

This still leaves the question of order: do we start with the easy ones, or do we try to get the hard ones settled in memory first? Which are the really 'hard ones'?

Difficult number facts: some research and its application

Most people will remember that some basic number facts are more difficult to learn than others, and most teachers will have experienced this with children. Campbell (1987) has addressed the question of 'which' and 'why' more systematically in a study where difficulties have been judged by the speed and correctness with which a basic number problem can be answered. He found, in summary, that:

(a) with some exceptions the greater the magnitude of the numbers involved, the more errors can be expected and the more time is needed to answer the questions; this has been found true for learning multiplication as well as addition facts;

(b) exceptions are facts that include the number five or that are 'tie (twin) problems' (like $2 + 2$ and 6×6); thus, in this respect, $4 + 3$ should be more difficult than $5 + 3$ and 6×4 more difficult than 6×6.

These exceptions as well as the factor of problem size seem to be widely confirmed by experience. Normally problems with lower numbers are met earlier and used more often; thus the order of acquisition as well as frequency of use may lead to better memorization; visualization may also still be possible with lower numbers. Twin problems have the advantage that problem and answer together only involve two different numbers instead of three ($2 \times 2 = 4$ versus $2 \times 3 = 6$) and therefore one can assume that the memory load is reduced. Children may also have had early practical experience with square numbers.

Perhaps these results make one wonder whether there *is* actually something like pure rote learning. In theory there should be no differences in memorizing number facts, as long as (a) the numbers of syllables involved in a number fact sentence are the same and (b) all facts are practised equally. However, we obviously do not see number facts just as nonsense syllables and there may always be some parallel rudimentary arithmetical thought in the mind; thus 3×12 normally takes more time to answer by 'mental arithmetic' than 3×4, although both sentences have three syllables. This finding may please some of us who feel at times slightly uncomfortable with teaching by rote; it also suggests that previous practical work still influences mental work when number facts are memorized.

Altogether, as Campbell points out, multiplication facts seem very difficult to memorize compared with non-mathematical facts. Even university students showed an error rate approaching 30% for certain basic multiplication facts (4×8, 6×9). Campbell suggests that such difficulties can be explained by 'associative interference' in the memory network: the more facts of a similar kind are learned and stored in close proximity, the greater is the likelihood of associative confusion. (For a summary of current cognitive models of simple arithmetic processing see Ashcraft, 1993; Campbell's network interference model is one of the three discussed there.)

If one thinks of the implications for teaching, one will come to the conclusion that, as far as pure memorization is concerned, one ought to teach the 'hard' facts early and in isolation, well spaced in time with adequate intervals. This is one of the suggestions made by Graham (1987) when he applied research findings in this field to teaching. His suggestions, seen from the associative retrieval point of view, can be summed up as follows:

- Accuracy should be emphasized from the beginning, together with reasonable speed.
- To promote accuracy one ought to minimize associative confusion by not practising one full times table after the other, but rather mix them (e.g. 2×7, 5×6 rather than 2×7, 3×7 etc.).
- The facts to be learned should be divided into small practice sets, each set containing problems from many times tables where the answers are widely divergent in magnitude.
- More difficult problems may be given a head start by placing them in the first set with a strict performance criterion before the next set is tackled.
- Special care should be taken with a few exceptional multiplication facts. These are the ones where the product is 12, 16, 18, 24, and 36 (i.e. a product that appears more than twice in the first ten times tables). To counteract the tendency to give such products as wrong answers to any problem not yet securely learned, it would be better to teach these facts once the rest of the basic 100 multiplications is well established.

Graham stresses that it is still very much an empirical question as to whether such alternative orders are better than the traditional way of learning whole times tables (i.e. one-times, two-times, three-times...). I have not tried such alternative orders systematically myself, but they make good sense to me and are in my opinion well worth a try, especially with children who have memory difficulties.

Becoming fluent

As was said before all facts once learned must be rehearsed repeatedly to ensure continued ease of retrieval. This is even more important when dealing with multiplication facts where visual back-up is limited. Again, one can try to bring variety into the daily practice sessions by employing 'distraction' activities (see above) – although these may have lost some of their attraction through frequent use.

Written work with figure notation could be used for reinforcement. Graham (1987) advocates individualized computer drills rather than paper-and-pencil work. Such general 'maintenance' programmes can be 'tailor made' and enriched with frequent occurrences of facts that have proved difficult in individual cases. It is, however, important to remember that the verbal aspect of proficiency is our main concern and must not be neglected. Independent work either with paper and pencil or with computer programs does not require verbalization. In this respect Lane and Chinn's method (described in full in Chinn and Ashcroft, 1993: 55 ff.), which makes use of a tape recorder, seems more suitable:

- The child records on tape the facts he wants to learn (e.g. $7 \times 8 = 56$, $6 \times 4 = 24$, and a few more).
- The child listens to his recording and is encouraged to repeat the number sentences.
- Finally, the child writes them down.

These measures certainly have their value as independent reinforcement but, in my opinion, they cannot be a substitute for direct child and tutor interaction where individual help is linked with instant and cheerfully supportive feedback, with elaboration as well as the real-life spontaneous unpredictability provided by human contact (intentionally or unintentionally).

Summing up the points to remember (addition, subtraction, multiplication)

All number facts that have to be learnt to automatization level should be treated *over years* with a combination of

- practical, visual and perhaps written back-up;
- consistent, ongoing verbal rehearsal in the form of 'maintenance drills' (even when the facts seem quite well known already);
- regular 'testing' (short non-standard 'home-made' tests catering for individual needs – mainly to document to the child that he is still proficient in what he has learned); and
- constant joint child/tutor elaboration aiming to make the child aware of (a) problems inherent in the subject matter; (b) his own specific problems; and (c) the general usefulness of knowing essential facts well.

Overcoming Retrieval Problems

I am concerned here with two aspects of retrieval difficulties: 'initial cluelessness' and 'tip of the tongue' problems. Neither is connected with any specific point in the syllabus, and for neither do I find it easy to give advice.

What are the problems?

All applications of memorized knowledge have to do with retrieval and only through retrieval can one check what knowledge a child has ready for use. All work described above had to do with improving retrieval through constant rehearsal, and in general there is a straight positive relation between frequency and recency of use on the one hand, and ease of retrieval on the other. However, in a small group of children, this relationship does not always seem to hold. Their retrieval capacity, at least as expressed verbally, is erratic.

Initial cluelessness

This is an elusive problem for which I have no better name. It seems to be a case of 'all forgotten/all remembered'. In a strong form it seems rare and in my experience it is often linked with some organizational difficulty; the child does not seem able to remember the learned procedures for organizing a problem so as to solve it. I have met it to a worrying degree in only a few children who

were normally careful and willing; –
had a reasonable memory for details, factual as well as situational; –
seemed to understand how number systems work and could act intelligently when these were explained and when they were asked to apply them; –
but did not seem to remember any previously gained structural insight without some clues; thus they were unable to carry their knowledge over into identical or very similar situations.

Any teacher will have witnessed some similar incidents of forgetting in children, but the striking feature of these particular children is that, when given a very small clue, they will say with infuriating speed: 'I know, I know' – and get it right. One feels that a minute external clue brings the memory back as a whole (time, place, procedure, content, application and all). Unfortunately, they are not able to find the initial clue that would trigger off the memory by themselves, and without help there is an absolute 'blank'.

'Tip of the tongue' problems

These problems seem to be more common than those due to 'initial cluelessness'. The child suffers from specific intermittent word-finding problems, resembling older people who have – and complain about – the experience that certain names, words or formulas are 'on the tip of their tongue', but cannot be expressed verbally at that particular moment.

Such problems are different from those of children who store and retrieve knowledge slowly and with difficulty. Children with 'tip of the tongue' problems often seem to learn facts relatively fast; in many circumstances they retrieve their knowledge without undue difficulty, but at times there are incidents when they are unable to do so. The child may have given the right answer to a number question yesterday. Tomorrow he will probably do so again. But today the answer to the same question is not forthcoming. The child knows he can do it. The teacher knows the child can do it. Just now, however, the question only leads to embarrassed silence and, often, the longer one waits the less likelihood there is of an answer. It is normally time to give up when the child says: 'I am thinking'. Thinking will only increase tension, and the right answer will not slip off the 'tip of the tongue'.

Sometimes erratic retrieval problems seem to take the form of 'erratic confusion' between verbal labels. The child may think of the right number (e.g. '4') and uses it in practical situations, but then he mixes up the label (calls it '5'). In situations without practical work it is thus possible for a teacher to reject an answer which for the child is factually correct. The child himself may not be aware of his labelling error and may rightly be puzzled by the rejection. 'That's funny,' he may think, 'what's wrong with it today, it seemed to be right yester-day.' In consequence, uncertainty and anxiety may develop.

How can we help?

I will start with some rather limited specific suggestions and finish with perhaps more helpful general advice.

Suggestions for 'initial cluelessness'

In most cases of initial cluelessness it is easy to give the initial clue, and then all will be fine. Where will the clue come from in out-of-school situations? How can one teach the child to look for and recognize clues?

One method that I tried (albeit with little conviction) was to reduce the clue to a minimum and let the children find the rest themselves (e.g. 'I spy' type of clues: 'think of something starting with' . . .).

One can try fuller elaboration of the structure or procedures; or give more practice. Either might be successful in some cases, but there could be the risk of irritating the child since he knows he has done it all before. Also, elaboration is generally not what is needed: the problem is a blockage rather than a lack of knowledge.

Perhaps one could devise some special language-therapy sessions with general 'clue-finding' activities. As mentioned before, such work would have to take place on a very long-term basis to result in any observable improvement, and one would wonder all along about the 'transfer' prospects.

Suggestions for 'tip of the tongue' problems

When a child with such problems seems momentarily unable to find a word that is needed as the answer to a number problem, he should be encouraged to say calmly and confidently that he 'knows it' but cannot say it at the moment. And parents and teachers should accept this just as calmly. The carer has to learn to hide any exasperation that may naturally occur in busy situations. If one is convinced that the child knows the answer, the best solution will be to give the answer oneself in a matter of fact way, perhaps with a side remark like 'I know you know it, it is just one of your special moments when you can't find the word.' If one has doubts about the child's knowledge, it is safer to show him or her the solution on an apparatus while simultaneously providing the verbal number sentence oneself. Alternatively one can ask the child to write down the answer (in figures) so long as this is not too disruptive in a situation of predominantly oral work. It is always best if one can bring the child to repeat the full sentence: although repetition is certainly not the cure, it may help. But again, I would not insist on repetition if that made the situation more tense.

When there is obvious or suspected confusion of labels, similar methods may help: one can correct calmly ('you said "five" but I think you meant "four"'); one can talk the child through the problem with the help of an apparatus (the teacher does the talking; the child repeats – if this is acceptable to him); or one lets him write down the answer. One ought to make him aware of his problem by talking about it and pointing out his 'danger numbers' – either as and when the confusion occurs, or in a subsequent session if that seems more suitable.

With regard to early numbers (mainly 1–10) the 'ruler game' (described in Unit 3) can be helpful for children with word-finding problems as well as for children with labelling problems. It gives opportunities to have fun while repeating the same first numbers over and over again.

General suggestions for overcoming retrieval problems

One has to realize that in both forms of retrieval problems help can only be very indirect: the child needs to learn strategies for self-help. This is more easily said than done and needs long-term teaching and therapy. In the end, the child must learn to provide his own help along the same lines as those provided by the teacher. Not all clue-giving and memory techniques can be expected to help all children, and most of the work therefore has to be done individually. Whatever approach is taken, the child must be *made conscious* of the techniques that the teacher/therapist has used with relative success.

The overall aim should be to turn a difficult free 'recall' situation into easier 'cued recall' or 'recognition'. This can generally be done by leaving the field of tension for a while and perhaps side-stepping into 'free word associations' or thinking of parallel situations.

In moments of acute failure the most helpful general advice to the carer is probably: 'know your child and keep calm!' Without knowledge of the child's normal performance one cannot be sure if an incident is due to a specific difficulty or if it is just a case of not knowing the facts. 'Keeping calm' is probably also the most generally useful strategy the child has to learn. One strict rule for the teacher is certainly not to show her own exasperation and most of all, *not to blame the child* by asking him to 'concentrate'. His problem is, in my opinion, not a matter of concentration, but one of temporary memory failure.

SUMMARY

A memory weakness may lie at the heart of most types of language impairment among children. Although research is by no means extensive or conclusive, the experience of practitioners as well as some research findings on short-term (working) memory tend to confirm this view. A memory weakness is a challenge in all aspects of learning and teaching, including early mathematics, and one cannot take it for granted that a language-impaired child is weak only in *verbal* memory.

The critical points in the early mathematical syllabus are obviously those where some rote learning seems the only way to achieve reasonable efficiency, like counting and learning 'number facts' by heart. The best help one can offer is probably *compensatory measures* which make the child rely on the decimal system as early as possible; or which appeal to his visual memory, if that is feasible. This still leaves some hard work to be done using direct rote learning. 'Rehearsal' activities have to be devised to a greater extent than would be normal and the challenge is to find ways of making 'the same old thing' look interesting and different.

Some forms of verbal memory problems are not limited to specific points in the syllabus; they seem to affect all school work. Certain retrieval problems show themselves, often unpredictably, in most aspects of mathematics, mainly as erratic word-finding problems. Although a few specific suggestions for reducing the problem can be made, these seem limited in their effectiveness. What is needed are general strategies that work in a variety of acute situations: the child has to learn to relax and divert his attention to fairly free but relevant associations which may help to overcome the blockage. Such strategies have first to be demonstrated to the child and then consciously taken over by him as a means of self-help. This is a long-term task which can sometimes be disappointingly slow and unreliable.

Chapter 4
Additional
Weaknesses

This chapter deals with two further problems faced by some language-impaired children:

1. Problems with relative concepts, and
2. A weakness in auditory discrimination.

These problems are more directly related to language than the previous ones. They can be seen as aspects of two different domains in language acquisition: the first belongs to the cognitive-conceptual domain; the second to auditory phonetics. Experience shows that they can lead to difficulties in some specific and identifiable areas in the elementary mathematics syllabus.

Problems with Relative Concepts

What are the problems?

All children seem to have some problems with the 'language of mathematics'. This is well documented and discussed in the mainstream literature; see, for instance, Dickson et al. (1984: 330 ff.); Shuard and Rothery (1984) (difficulties posed by mathematical textbooks); Mathematical Association ('Maths Talk') (1987); Wood (1988: 197 ff.); Durkin and Shire (1991); Rowland (1995).

Most teachers, therapists and parents of children with language difficulties are very aware of problems due to lack of concepts and vocabulary and realize that such a lack also hinders progress in mathematics. Concern about problems with mathematics is therefore often expressed in publications about children with general language difficulties and dyslexic children; see, for instance, Hutt (1986); Durkin and Shire (1991); Snowling and Thomson (1991); Miles and Miles (1992); Pollock and Waller (1994).

I want to concentrate here on one aspect of concept and vocabulary learning that seems to pose problems in many areas of early mathematics: the difficulty caused by concepts that have either variable points of reference, or unstable dimensions, or both (in short: relative concepts, a rather vague term which can be used for almost all language, but which seems to be used mainly in a restricted way for comparisons; cf. Donaldson and Wales, 1970; Bruner and Kennedy, 1966). Such concepts are expressed through words that are given their 'sense' through their specific relation to other words: 'before' does not make much sense on its own, but in a phrase like 'the day before Christmas' it means a lot. The difference between a non-relative and a relative concept becomes obvious if one compares 'circle' with 'right and left'. A circle is always a circle; it may be a big circle or a small circle, but the shape is constant and the concept evokes an image which makes sense on its own. In contrast, 'right' on its own is ambiguous; what is on your 'right' is not always 'right'; you only have to turn round and all that was right is now left; the world has not changed, but the relation between you and what you once called 'right' in the world has changed.

What makes relative concepts difficult for a child with language difficulties? It is probably the fact that the correspondence between the lexical item and the condition or object to which it refers is not fixed. Language-impaired children are often not at all at ease with things that are changeable, but such concepts are a vital part of the 'language of mathematics' and cover some aspects of 'time', 'space' 'comparison' and 'quantity'. Here are some examples.

Examples of relative concepts

- *Time:* On 24 December a child's mind may be filled with the thought that 'tomorrow' will be Christmas ('tomorrow' = 'Christmas Day'!). However, on 25 December at night-time he may think of tomorrow as a sad day ('tomorrow' = 'the day after Christmas': it is all over; it will take a whole year until it comes round again'). How different is the emotional content of the same word 'tomorrow' on the two occasions. Even worse, what was 'tomorrow' on the day before Christmas, is 'yesterday' today (for similar difficulties see Crystal, 1986: 163: 'Does after come before or does before come after?')
- *Space:* 'Right' as opposed to 'left' has already been mentioned. Another example is 'behind'. If two children sit opposite each other at a table with a built-up wall of wooden bricks in the

middle and are told to put their wooden toy animals behind the wall, they will have to put them in two different places. At an early stage this will be puzzling, and in the end the less confident child may quite possibly change the position of his animals and put them in front of the wall – in the same position as the one which means 'behind' for the other child.

- *Comparison*: If one compares a dog with a pony, the pony is the 'big one'; if one compares the same pony with an elephant, it is not. Or, if John compares his 18 conkers with Eric's 4, he feels he has a lot; but if he compares his same 18 conkers with Matthew's 46, they appear as just a few.
- *Quantity*: 'All' may equal 'three', as in 'you may have all the biscuits left in the tin' (and there are only three left); or it may equal 'hundreds' if one tries to blow 'all' the seeds off a dandelion.

The verbal label that is used in such relational situations may often be acquired quite early because its use is common, but this does not guarantee that the concept is understood. Even with normal children, such concepts grow bit by bit, acquiring new features until they have their full meaning. One would expect the child with language problems to be years behind in this process. Unfortunately there are quite a few such relative concepts in early mathematics. They can lead to confusion, and something has to be done about them.

How can we help?

The first thing is to realize that the concept of a common word expressing a relation like 'in front of' can be more difficult than the concept of a less common word such as 'oval'; and that some relational concepts will need long-term work over a period of years.

There are probably two main approaches for teaching, and in practice these will often go hand-in-hand. One can teach a concept when a good opportunity is offered through a naturally occurring situation; and one can also introduce a concept explicitly because the child seems to need it at that point in his development (see the example in Unit 1).

Keeping a 'danger list' in mind

For both approaches it would be useful to have a mental or written 'danger list' of such concepts available. Opportunities for teaching a certain concept can then be more easily spotted and will not be missed. One will also be more aware of the various concepts that may urgently need explicit attention, and of those that are already known but still need 'elaboration'.

Most words that may constitute the 'danger list' can normally be spotted naturally when teaching early mathematics. In the literature they are discussed under various headings, such as 'time and place relaters', 'dimensional relations', 'sense-relations', 'case', 'prepositions' (Lyons, 1968; Quirk and Greenbaum, 1973; Clark and Clark, 1977).

A word of caution may be necessary: when teaching such concepts it may seem easiest to explain them in terms of their opposites (e.g. 'before Christmas' versus 'after Christmas'). This should be avoided, at least at the beginning and with young children, and certainly with children who have language problems. The reason is that, if concepts are learned together, the two word labels may get mixed up: a child may say 'yesterday' when he means 'tomorrow'.

Elaboration

In the end, however, the concept is probably only really understood when seen in relation to the opposite, from 'the other side' as it were (so well expressed in one of Tom Waits' beautiful songs: 'I never saw the East Coast till I moved to the West'). The suggested teaching sequence is therefore:

- teach term A;
- leave an interval, let's say about 6 months;
- teach term B (the opposite term);
- leave another generous interval;
- teach both terms in relation to each other.

Summing up

The point I want to make is that one has to 'make a fuss' about these words and not to consider them as ordinary as they sound. In practical terms one should:

- have a mental (or written) list of such unstable concepts available;
- look out for occasions when they occur in natural settings and work on them there and then in an *ad hoc* way;
- elaborate in planned sessions at a later stage; or
- introduce a concept when it seems to be needed and work more explicitly;
- in both cases, provide some elaboration sessions fairly regularly, preferably in different contexts and in the end with a look at opposites;
- make the child aware why a particular word can be difficult;

- make the child aware of similar difficulties in other words (i.e. let him recognize such words as a special group;
- discuss the advantages of such words as well as their difficulties, so that the child can see a trade-off between difficulty and useful flexibility.

Problems with Auditory Discrimination

What are the problems?

Auditory phonetics, as a branch of general phonetics, includes both the field of *speech discrimination* and the *discrimination of prosodic features* like pitch, loudness, tempo, rhythm or stress (Crystal, 1980). In everyday perception of speech, both will combine, and if one says that a child has difficulties with auditory discrimination it can be with both 'pure' speech sounds and prosody.

But there is more to it: an additional factor, which makes the study of speech perception a complex one, is the part *knowledge* and *experience* (linguistic and otherwise) play in perception – a part that leads to highly individual *expectations* of incoming sounds. Sensible expectation of what a word or phrase could mean in a particular context is one way to compensate to some extent for an auditory deficit and should be fostered; the use of *visual clues* is another.

Auditory discrimination problems are widespread amongst language-impaired children (e.g. Haynes and Naidoo, 1991: 136). In some cases they can be severe (cf. Rapin and Allen, 1983, for 'verbal auditory agnosia'), but more often they seem to occur in a milder form as one feature among other others in children with language difficulties. Articulation can be affected, although the causal relation between auditory discrimination and articulation does not seem to be clear-cut (Haynes and Naidoo, 1991).

In learning to read, there is evidence that a weakness in auditory discrimination, especially in sequencing, is a contributing factor to 'phonological dyslexia' (Stackhouse, 1989). In elementary mathematics, even a milder form of such a deficiency can have a serious effect at one critical point in the syllabus: the discrimination between '-teen' and '-ty' (as in 'sixteen' and 'sixty').

'-ty' versus '-teen'

In English, the salient difference between '-ty' and '-teen' is one of stress. If the child's perception of stress is poor, discrimination is almost impossible. Thus a child may think of 'sixteen' when the teacher talks of 'sixty'. Such confusion in the initial stages may undermine the understanding of the decimal system and the child's attempt to make sense of it. The example in Figure 4.1. shows how a 10-year-old boy interpreted a tallied quantity of 17 as 52.

$$\text{IIIII IIIII} = 52$$
$$\text{IIIII II}$$

Figure 4.1: 17 = 52

This was done in writing. When I challenged the boy, he answered that 15 and 2 equalled 52. He thought of 'fifty' instead of 'fifteen' – against all possible experience and expectation, and against a given visual clue.

How can we help?

Two possible compensatory measures have been mentioned above: providing visual clues and fostering good expectations. A third measure would be to tackle the problem directly by trying to improve a child's auditory discrimination in general and with regard to '-ty' versus '-teen' in particular. I will try to discuss the three measures under different headings, but in practice as well as in the discussion they will fuse to some extent.

Using visual representation

The difference between '-teen' and '-ty' becomes visually clear when one writes numbers as words (e.g. *sixteen* versus *sixty*). It may thus help if the child learns to recite the counting sequence systematically with the words simultaneously presented in writing. This presumes that the child can read number words already; if not, both learning to count and learning to read number words can go hand-in-hand. Here is a suggestion for different exercises. The following sets of cards will be needed:

Set A: a pack of cards with number words (a selection, or a full set up to 100); the selection must include all words ending in '-teen' and at least the same amount of words ending in '-ty'.

Set B: a corresponding pack with quantity pictures (see Unit 4).

With such sets different kinds of work can take place where the child *sees* the difference between the numbers while using the verbal label.

Here is a first example:

(a) Take Set A (or a selection from it) and give it to the child in the correct order (the number of cards depends on the level of his reading and counting skills); the child looks at the first card, says the counting word and puts the card down; he looks at the next card... (e.g. eighteen, nineteen, twenty, twenty-one...); all cards should at the end be neatly lined up on the table.
(b) Now take Set B (or a selection corresponding to the selection from Set A) and give it to the child in the right order.
(c) The child puts the corresponding quantity pictures under the cards from the first set, again while saying the number word.

As the next step, this can be repeated with the cards given to the child in random order: the child has to say them, sort them into the counting sequence, and match the two sets. For more exercises, involving two additional sets with figures and 'system-words', see Unit 2. For an example of a matching exercise involving all four sets see Figure 4.2 (a) and (b).

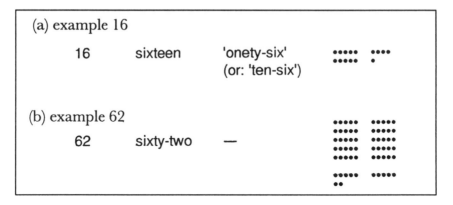

Figure 4.2 (a) and (b): Matching different representations of number

Such exercises give the child an opportunity to see the difference between '-ty' and '-teen'; they will not necessarily help him to hear the difference, but at least they will focus his attention on the difference.

Emphasizing correct expectations

Some of the exercises with the sets of cards emphasize the value of a number, either through order or through quantity pictures. It is to be hoped that this will help the child to understand what magnitude a certain number label stands for. This understanding will give the child certain expectations. Although one cannot guarantee that this will necessarily lead to an improvement in discrimination, the child will again have been made aware of the words that can cause problems. He will be on the alert when '-teens' or '-tys' are involved, and he may develop the desirable habit of always checking against expectation, which is determined by understanding and experience. He can then decide, on the basis of expectation, whether a larger number ('-ty') or a smaller number ('-teen') would make better sense. All the measures outlined earlier that were aimed at 'understanding what number words and figures stand for' are of value here.

Tackling the problem directly: improving auditory discrimination skills

One can assume that the language therapist of a child with a particular weakness in auditory discrimination will be doing some work to improve his or her skills. One can reinforce this in elementary mathematics sessions by work on the specific problem of '-teens' versus '-tys'. I suggest that one concentrates on the stress pattern and the length of the two.

Percussion instruments can be of use here. One will need two 'instruments' of different sizes (for example, an empty tissue box and an empty cigarette box). Real drums or other percussion instruments of two sizes will be more fun, and a variety of such instruments will make repetition more pleasurable. One also needs various sets of cards as described above. The aim is to make the child realize that in 'sixteen' there is a level stress, whereas in 'sixty' the stress is put on the first syllable. Moreover, '-teen' is longer than '-ty', both when spoken and when written. The difference in length may be an extra help for a child who may have difficulties in noticing subtle differences in stress.

One of the instruments is needed for '-teens'. It is probably best to use the smaller of the two for this. The instrument is sounded with two even beats ('level stress'), once for 'six' and once for '-teen'. In the case of '-tys', one uses both instruments, first the big one with strong beat for 'six-', followed by a light beat on the small instrument for '-ty'. A list of activities designed to bring variety into the work on discrimination concerning the difference between '-ty' and '-teen' given in Unit 7.

The effectiveness of such exercises in improving the child's auditory discrimination skills will vary, but they should at least result in an increased awareness of the problem.

SUMMARY

The two aspects of language impairment discussed in this chapter (difficulties with relative concepts; weakness in auditory discrimination) are less fundamental than the features considered earlier. However, in their sometimes undetected way they can cause considerable difficulties at specific points in elementary mathematics.

Firstly, a group of concepts to be learned causes difficulties because of their unstable *relative nature*. Some are very common and are often used early in mathematical contexts of time (e.g. 'before'), space (e.g. 'behind'), quantity (e.g. 'a few') and comparison (e.g. 'more'). It is important that the teacher is aware of the difficulties such words can pose and anticipates potential problems. The teacher can thus help in situations where a relative concept is used incidentally, or can create situations where it can be addressed explicitly. In the end the growing child himself should become more and more aware of the special nature of such concepts.

Secondly, specific problems can arise if a child has a *weakness in auditory discrimination* and is therefore unable to hear the difference between numbers like 'sixty' and 'sixteen'. Help can be given by using parallel visual support (quantity pictures, written numerals), by training discrimination skills with particular reference to the stress pattern in such numbers, and by strengthening correct expectations. Again, the child should become aware of this potential mathematical 'danger area' and of his specific difficulties with it.

Chapter 5
A Social Dimension

Problems with Social Interaction: Description of a Group Session

Anyone who has worked with language-impaired children will have witnessed the problems many of them experience in dealing with situations that call for social skills. One could almost add another feature to those listed so far: social inadequacy. If I have said very little about this up to now, the reason is certainly not lack of interest, but rather the fact that the feature is probably best treated in a much wider context than in early mathematics. However, mathematical group sessions are often places where social interaction is needed, and they can therefore be places where social skills are fostered. I will end the first part of this book with the description of a group lesson planned for four rather 'difficult' boys as a joint problem-solving session requiring the organization of mathematical materials.

The group consisted of four boys aged 11 and 12. They were attending a special school for children with language impairments and had been grouped together for a daily session of 20 minutes to improve their pragmatic language skills. Three of them, Philip, Victor and Stephan, had organizational difficulties in almost every aspect of learning; they had been at the school for 4 or 5 years. The fourth one, Harald, was able and neat in written routine work, but often lacked a sense of relevance, especially in new situations; he had been at the school for about 10 months. With the exception of Stephan, the boys had some additional behaviour problems and could be difficult at times.

The session (ordering quantities)

The session started with a fairly large heap of Cuisenaire rods in front of each child (for Cuisenaire rods see Chapter 1 and Unit 3). I explained that this was our pretend 'desert island' money for today, each stick was worth its length, the smallest piece (1 cm³) counting for 'one', and that we wanted to find out how much money we all had altogether.

First reaction

Three of the boys were familiar with the rods. Philip was enthusiastic and said spontaneously: 'Oh, I like these!'

Victor also said that he used to like them when he used them with Miss X, some years ago. Stephan, in his usual low-key way, answered my question about whether he knew them with 'yes', and if he liked them with 'they are OK'. The rods were new for Harald.

So there they were, each with a heap of rods in front of them and the task was to find out how much 'money' there was altogether. No one talked to each other. They all fiddled around with the rods in a rather disorganized way. After a while, Philip started to put them in a long row, as they came. Harald was obviously ill at ease. He looked around and did not seem to know what to do with the rods. He finally imitated Philip by rather hesitantly making a line. Victor, normally the quickest and probably the most intelligent of the four, sorted the rods horizontally flat on the table, one above the other but in no particular order. Stephan was the only one who made some attempt at ordering by sorting all the yellow rods on one side.

They seemed preoccupied with their heaps, at times muttering irrelevantly to themselves. None thought of suggesting a joint approach.

Philip then started adding up the units of his rods, again in no order; he just added them orally, taking them as they came in his line. I noticed some mistakes. He gave up soon. He asked if he could use my calculator, and I agreed. He started from the beginning, adding up on the calculator, not taking care to separate clearly the ones he had added from the ones still to be added.

Victor, in the meanwhile, had obviously 'left the field' and was absorbed in building something, commenting that this was going to be a little playground. Harald, after having looked around for a while, still uncertain of what to do, asked Philip if he could have the calculator. When Philip refused, Harald expressed his disinterest – or perhaps his uncomfortable feeling of uncertainty, by saying: 'I am not doing this.'

Stephan had continued to sort out his yellow rods, one above the other, and had proceeded to do the same with the orange ten-rods. He started to count and arrived at 65 for the yellows and 80 for the orange. He then looked around at what the others were doing. He muttered something that could not be understood, folded his arms ostentatiously and sighed, not doing anything. Taking his facial expression into account, one was tempted to interpret his mutterings as: 'You fools. This way we will never get anywhere. I might just as well give up.'

Harald was still mainly watching Philip, but he started to help to push Philip's rods and some of his own rods towards Philip and the calculator in a somewhat haphazard way. Philip declared loudly: 'We are already at 200.'

Victor was now looking up from his play. When he saw what was going on, he said: 'Can I have the calculator after you?'

First intervention

At this stage I thought it was time to intervene. I asked Stephan if he had given up, and he said 'Yes, *they* are not doing it'. I praised him for his ordering attempt.

I asked Philip and Harald, the two with the calculator, how they could be sure that they had not made a mistake. They agreed that they could not be sure. Philip cheerfully suggested starting again.

I reminded them of our objective: to find out how much we had altogether, and suggested looking at what Stephan had been doing and asked Stephan if he could suggest a way to get everybody working together.

Before Stephan had a chance to say anything, Victor suggested that they should all put their rods into one pile in the middle and each should do one colour. Stephan agreed, except that he was not going to put his yellow and orange rods back, the ones he had already sorted out. He announced that he was going to do all the yellow fives and orange tens. Victor protested. He said that this was not fair. They were the easy rods to count.

I intervened again by suggesting we could make the others 'easy' (i.e. easy to count). This gave rise to the question of why Stephan's were easy to count. It was agreed that if one boy took all the 2s and 8s, and if another took all the 3s and 7s, and so on, we could all count in tens.

Change of attitude

From now on there was a change of attitude. The boys knew what to do and they really started to work together. They agreed who should take which rods. Philip suggested that Stephan should stick to his 10s and 5s. I made the suggestion that Stephan, who was ahead of us, should be our 'gaffer', and make sure we were doing the right thing. The others agreed. Victor took all the 2- and 8-rods (because he liked the colours of the two rods). Harald took the 1- and 9-rods, Philip took the 3- and 7- rods and I took what was left: 4- and 6-rods.

Co-operation was good: rods were pushed across the table according to colour so that they landed in front of the person who sorted them. When all rods were sorted everybody started to build up tens, fast and enthusiastically. When Harald saw me putting my tens together in blocks of 100, he remarked – pleasantly generously for him – that this was a good idea. They now all put rods in ten rows of ten, ready for counting in 100s.

In the end Harald helped Philip who seemed to have the most rods to count. Steven suggested putting rows of 'left over' tens of different colours together to make more blocks of 100.

We just managed to count all the 100s and added up the relatively small remainder in time for the morning break. The total was 592. We were confident that we had got it right. A sigh of relief. Everybody was satisfied; and when I thanked Stephan for looking after us and suggested that I would do the clearing up for once while they went out to play, they left the room in high spirits, Philip's arms round Harald's shoulders, good friends all!

My reaction

I did not use the break for clearing up, but wrote down the notes to remember the session. It struck me as special among others because it seemed a good example of how the attitude to work and work-mates can change when one feels that the end of a task seems possible and the means seem under control.

Despite the 'happy ending', the beginning of the session had been worrying: all four boys had shown later in the session that they had the 'tools' to sort out the problem, but they did not see how this applied to the situation. They were able to make groups of ten, but they did not think of it. With the exception of Stephan, they used rather inefficient methods; the idea that working together could make things easier did not really occur to them, although the aim of the session had been worded so as to suggest a joint effort. Neither organization nor teamwork were spontaneously used as helpful means, they would have to be taught. What ought I to prepare for the next step?

Part Two

Practical Work: Additional Suggestions

Unit 1
Non-Count Work

'A Few, A Lot, The Lot': Description of a Lesson

The lesson was suggested in Chapter 1 for children who have problems with symbolic understanding and in Chapter 4 for those who find relative concepts difficult. It looks at the terms 'a few', 'a lot' and 'the lot' in relation to familiar numbers such as 'one', 'two', 'three' rather than at the grammatical distinction between count and non-count words, or between the defined and undefined article.

The problem

Some children seem to be uncertain about the meaning of these three terms. The difficulty is twofold. Firstly, they are *imprecise* compared with numbers. Secondly, they have a *relative* quality (see Chapter 1): 'a lot' of a large quantity is more than 'a lot' of a small quantity; similarly, 'the lot' can refer to everything in a small amount or to everything in a large amount. Sometimes 'the lot' can mean precious little, as, for instance, when a child expects a large number of cards on his birthday and only two or three come through the door. He may ask: 'Is that the lot?'

Setting

The setting is a maths lesson where a small group of children (in this case 6) and a teacher are sitting around a table. They must have some table space in front of them and each must be able to see the others' space. It is assumed that the children are familiar with at least the numbers from 1 to 3 and have perhaps some further knowledge of numbers up to 10.

Materials needed

The teacher has an open basket (box) full of playmatches (available from toy shops or craft suppliers, plain or in colour).

Description of lesson

The lesson starts with the children taking playmatches out of the basket.

- In the first round, they take *one* matchstick each out of the basket (the teacher goes first).
- The next round is the same.
- In the next round they take *two* each, one with each hand:

> We can now make a 'square' with our sticks (the teacher shows how, if necessary). Let's compare: we have all got the same.

- In the next round they each take two playmatches again, and two more again in the following round so that they can make another square.
- They repeat the process so that they have enough for a third square.
- They compare again: everybody has the same – three full squares.
- The next step would be for the teacher to say:

> Take enough for another square; two with each hand.

Some children may call this spontaneously 'four'; the teacher could take this up if it seems appropriate and from then on say something like: 'Take four, two with each hand, which will make another square.' In this way the image of four and the corresponding number words can be established. After four or five squares are completed and compared the teacher says

> Let's each take a few.

There might be hesitations and puzzled faces.

> How many?

> A few. Just take a few matchsticks out of the basket.

The teacher takes a few to demonstrate. The first child will probably take 'a lot' rather than 'a few'. Either the teacher or, with luck, the other children will protest:

> That's not a few, Peter! That's a lot.

The teacher helps Peter to a few.

Right Peter, that's better, that's a few.

Next one, can you take a few?

One child at a time is asked to take a few. There will still be some hesitation. Counting is not the answer. If a child counts, one can discourage this by saying

No need to count. Just take a few.

If the child still hesitates one can just give him a few and say:

Don't be shy, Tommy. Here are a few.

The teacher holds 'a few' visibly between her fingers for all to see and then drops them in front of the child.

When everybody has had a few, it is a good idea to give the children time to arrange the sticks into squares. The result will be that they will have different numbers of squares, including some half-finished squares (see Figure 2.1.1).

Figure 2.1.1: Different numbers of matchsticks arranged in squares

The children compare squares. It will become clear that the number of matchsticks and of full squares is not the same.

How did that happen? We all had a few.

It will be established that 'a few' is not a precise number, but one with uncertain numerosity. The discussion might go like this:

Can it be any number? – Yes/no/it depends. – It cannot be 'one'. – It cannot be 'two'. – Perhaps 'three'. – It cannot be 'a lot'. – What is 'a lot'?

The teacher may decide to stop the lesson there for the day, perhaps with a few more practice trials in taking 'a few'.

What is 'a lot'?

If the children are still attentive, it is advisable to continue letting them take 'a lot' (which they will love to do anyway). The term 'a lot' is probably more familiar than 'a few' (cf. Burroughs, 1970). By linking up the two terms, a mental 'hook' is provided on which to hang 'a few', and thus the less familiar concept is consolidated. To continue work on 'a lot' the teacher might say:

> Let's have *a lot* this time.

The children may quarrel a bit over the amount a child takes; this has to be welcomed as part of the learning process: it makes the non-specific character of the concept clear; on the other hand it takes some teaching skill to keep the situation amicable and to make each child feel that the distribution was roughly fair.

The next step would be for the teacher to say:

> Let's put our 'lots' into squares and compare.

This will take some time. One can let the children predict what will happen and, at the end, one will establish that 'a lot', like 'a few', is not a number with definite numerosity.

As a grand finale to this lesson, the teacher could introduce the third term, '*the* lot', in the following way.

> Let's collect all the matches back into the basket.

The children do so and the teacher asks:

> Is that *the lot*?
>
> Would you like to see the lot?
>
> Here is the lot!

With that I suggest that the teacher turns the basket over and lets 'the lot' scatter over the floor. (I've done it, and the result was utter delight on the children's part.)

What have we learned?

Once the chaos over collecting the matches in handfuls back into the basket has stopped, the teacher could round up the lesson by saying:

> Right. Let's see what we have learned today. I'll write it down, so we won't forget.

The teacher writes 'a few', 'a lot' 'the lot' (on the blackboard or equivalent) saying the words clearly whilst writing.

At the beginning of the next maths lesson one can then refer to the writing on the blackboard:

> Do you remember, 'a few'? You take a few, Tommy. You take a few, Peter. Have you got the same? What is 'a few'? What is 'a lot'? What is '*the lot*'? Say some numbers that might fit 'a few'. Say some numbers that might fit 'a lot'.

With some brighter children one could perhaps add and discuss the following questions:

Can you actually say a number out of your head that will fit 'the lot'?

Can you find one number that will fit all three ('a few', 'a lot', 'the lot')?

Understanding of the relative quality of certain concepts may now have been reinforced or at least it may have dawned on the child, but consolidation is probably needed.

This is the time to heed the advice of language therapists when they warn not to practise opposites together. Many children with labelling problems say 'tomorrow' when they mean 'yesterday', and may say 'a few' when they mean 'a lot'. Although it was suggested that the three concepts and their verbal labels should be introduced in one situation, this is now best followed up by sessions in which one term is practised at a time.

Consolidation and extension

For a week, a fortnight, or a term if necessary, one concentrates on 'a few' but one lets 'a lot' and 'the lot' come up now and then. In practice:

(a) A short daily period is arranged in which each child takes 'a few' sticks. If the children are familiar with tallying and know the numbers up to about 30 to 100, the sticks can be tallied instead of 'squared'. This is faster and the numbers can be compared more easily (for tallying see Chapter 1).
(b) A variety of counters is used (wooden bricks, corks, straws, conkers, dots, lines) to take, show and draw 'a few'.
(c) One can leave the field of mathematics and put 'a few raisins in our cake', gather 'a few pretty leaves', and have 'a few visitors for our puppet show', thereby *broadening the context.*
(d) Periods of work on 'a lot' and 'the lot' can follow after a while.

Proceeding from there, in similar settings, the teacher can fill in the gaps that are apparent when one looks at the whole field of non-specific quantity words (see the next section).

Revision

A need for revision may become obvious later. Even if this is not the case, one day – perhaps after the holidays, or when a year has passed – the teacher should ask:

Can you remember when we had the whole lot of matchsticks on the floor?

(Thus one appeals to the children's 'episodic memory'; see Chapter 3.)

Can you still show me 'a few', 'a lot', 'the lot'?

As many revision sessions are organized as seem necessary, using different counters and naming them with the terms. The whole process is repeated at a later time if that seems necessary.

Sequence of Work with Non-Specific Quantities

This is a list of suggestions for early mathematical work that does not presume any knowledge of specific numbers but concerns itself mainly with global indeterminate terms like 'a few', 'many', 'big', 'more'. It is adapted from a syllabus (1986) developed for the teaching of early mathematics at Dawn House School, UK (I CAN), a special school for children with speech and language disorders.

In Chapter 4 it was suggested that this work might be helpful for children who need practice with basic concepts and vocabulary. It was also recommended for children who do not yet have a secure knowledge of number names, of written symbols, or of the counting sequence (Chapter 1).

The order of suggestions is not to be taken as rigid. The carer chooses activities which seem to be useful at a certain time with a certain child. However, a rough check to establish that the child can manage earlier activities is generally advisable. Some suggestions may require the knowledge of a few low numbers (mainly 1, 2, 3) which could be developed alongside the respective activities.

Inside a section the more 'hands-on' activities are always listed first, although sometimes they are slightly more complex than the paper-and-pencil suggestions which are listed later. It is possible, and sometimes advisable, especially with very young or immature children, to take from each section the activities with concrete materials first, and then have a second or third 'round' with increasingly formal materials, in order to deepen the understanding of the concepts.

There is quite a difference in the complexity of the concepts covered. The work is thus meant to be spaced out over several years, almost from the first day ('sorting' and 'pattern-making') to the stage where the children are ready to leave primary education ('less' and 'least').

The list of activities may give an impression of repetitiveness. Repetition is indeed one of the aims, but the list has been compiled with the experience that for a young child the same activity with a new material is a 'new' activity.

Materials needed

The activities involve a variety of materials, some of which are standard equipment in most schools, whereas others (mainly packs of cards) will have to be specially made. Most activities will involve the classroom becoming cluttered with materials. Useful toys and teaching aids in early mathematics seem to have a large number of parts – the more parts the better. Thus teachers, therapists or parents taking up some of these suggestions should be prepared to have their organizational skills tested to the limit and to show tolerance for situations which may border on the chaotic.

List of activities

The following are suggestions that are given as instructions directly addressed to the carer.

(1) Sorting

Let the child sort materials (with at least three different categories) by:

(a) function, e.g.:

> sort a set of wooden toys into trees/animals/vehicles;
> sort bottle tops into those for jam jars/beer bottles/plastic bottles;

(b) shape, e.g.:

> sort wooden toy bricks into blocks/rounds/roofs;
> sort commercially available or 'home-made' two-dimensional shapes into triangles/squares/circles (perhaps better first in one colour, later in different colours);

(c) colour, e.g.:

> sort objects into three colours, using sets of toys like plastic cups and saucers;
> sort the different coloured shapes used under (b);
> sort bits of yarn; bits of paper;

(d) size, e.g.:

> sort sets toys of three different sizes into big/medium/small (for instance: three Russian dolls, three bears, three billy-goats, three marbles);
> sort Poleidoblocs (see Unit 6) or similar bricks that come in different sizes;
> sort Cuisenaire rods (see Unit 3), limited to three or four obviously different sizes;
> sort two-dimensional plastic shapes that come in different sizes;
> sort shells (or other objects with less clearly defined sizes);

(e) revise by asking the child to do the exercises under (a) – (d) but with pictures on cards rather than with concrete materials.

(2) Grid-sorting

Let the child sort:

(a) 2 × 2 grids, see Figure 2.1.2;

	shape	shape
colour	red square	red circle
colour	green square	green circle

Figure 2.1.2: Example of grid-sorting (2 × 2)

(b) more advanced grids, e.g.:

> 3 × 2; 3 × 3; 3 × 4; 4 × 4, depending on the materials available (tip: to make good grids for bigger items, use open boxes of the same kind, glued together with tape).

(3) Patterns

Let the child make (copy, continue):

(a) ribbon patterns (beads, pegs, rods, cut-up drinking straws)

> with one change (e.g. one red/one green – one red/one green, etc.; or two red/two green – two red/two green, etc.);
> with more than one change (e.g. red/green/blue – red/green/blue, etc.);

(b) simple cube patterns, see Figure 2.1.3;
(c) two-dimensional peg patterns, see Figure 2.1.4;
(d) paper-and-pencil patterns, see Figure 2.1.5.

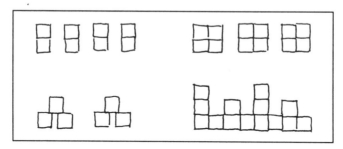

Figure 2.1.3: Examples of simple cube patterns

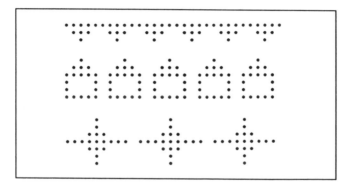

Figure 2.1.4: Examples of two-dimensional peg patterns

Figure 2.1.5: Examples of paper-and-pencil patterns

(4) Unordered masses

Ask the child to 'give me':

'1, 2, 3'; 'a few'; 'lots and lots of'; 'all'; 'none' (or, in different terms: 'some'; 'a lot of'; 'the lot'; 'nothing'; 'no'); use different small counters, such as beans, melon pips, corks cut up into discs, beads and commercial materials.

(5) More (mainly: much more)

Let the child:

(a) indicate a set with 'more' out of two sets where the difference is very obvious ('much more', e.g. 20 versus 40);

(b) change two roughly equal sets so that one set definitely has more ('much more'); there should be no counting; use a mass of counters to avoid this;

(c) indicate a set with 'more' out of two smaller sets where the difference between the sets is less obvious (e.g. 7 versus 10);

(d) indicate (intuitively, no counting required) a set with 'more' out of two small sets where the difference is 'one' (e.g. 2 versus 3; 3 versus 4; 4 versus 5);

(e) sort out pairs of cards (or, later, dominoes) into two columns, one containing all those with 'more' (there must be two cards showing the same object, animal or mark but in different quantities) – see Figure 2.1.6;

(f) draw two sets of something, one of which definitely has 'more'.

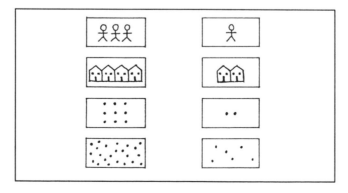

Figure 2.1.6: Sorting cards ('more' versus 'not-more')

(6) Same ('same' in the sense of 'equal number')

Let the child:

(a) produce two sets that are roughly the same out of a mass of counters (50 or more; no counting);
(b) change two obviously uneven sets from a mass of counters into two sets that are roughly the same;
(c) share a small even number of counters (2, 4, 6, 8) into two equal sets (no counting required);
(d) share a small uneven number of counters (3, 5, 7, 9) into two equal sets and keep 'the rest' apart;
(e) change two small equal sets (2, 4, 6, 8) into two unequal sets (one with 'more') by taking one or two counters away from one set and 'giving it to the other' ('not the same now');
(f) match two cards which show the same number of dots (these have to be prepared in advance: two equal sets of cards each with, for instance, 100, 40, 20, 10, 5 and 3 dots; the two sets are mixed and the child has to find the pair that matches as being 'the same'); at this pre-numeral stage the difference between the numbers chosen should be large and obvious (e.g. 100, 40, etc. rather than 12, 13, etc.).

(7) Big

Although it seems natural to teach 'small' at the same time as 'big', this is not done here in order to avoid the labelling confusion between the two opposites which is often seen in language-impaired children. There is, however, no harm in using the term 'small' incidentally.

Let the child:

(a) take all the 'big ones' out of a box of objects with two sizes (initially the objects should be the same kind, e.g. big and small jam jar lids; later a box with mixed objects can be used – with two of each kind, e.g. two differently sized toy trees, toy cars, cereal boxes, or lids);
(b) cut papers into one big piece and one small piece; collect the big ones;
(c) cut paper into two pieces 'roughly the same' (consolidation of 'same');
(d) take all the 'big ones' out of a box with objects of the same kind but with more than two different sizes (e.g. shells, lids);

(e) sort picture cards showing big and small objects of the same kind (e.g. a picture with a big tree and a picture with a small tree) into two heaps, and then hand over the heap with the 'big ones' to the carer;

(f) name any 'big things'.

(8) Long

Avoid teaching 'short' here so as to prevent the terms from being confused. Let the child:

(a) take out all 'long ones' from a box with straws (rods) of two different lengths (at first the differences should be obvious; later they can be not so obvious);

(b) cut straws (strips, strings) into two so that one piece is definitely 'long' (ignore short ones and collect long ones);

(c) cut straws (strips, strings) so that the two pieces are roughly the same (consolidation of 'same');

(d) find all the 'long ones' from a box with straws of more than two different sizes;

(e) find all the cards with long lines (from a pack of prepared cards with, for instance, lines of 5, 6, 7 cm versus 1, 2, 3, cm) and hand them over to the carer;

(f) name 'long things' (e.g. long hair, long string, long nose, long ladder); discuss the difference between 'big' and 'long'.

(9) Heavy

Avoid teaching the opposite, 'light', here. Let the child:

(a) find the 'heavy ones' out of a collection of objects. This should consist of two or more objects of roughly the same size, but with one definitely 'heavy' and not just 'heavier' (e.g. a brick and a cardboard box of same size; empty washing powder boxes and one full one; a large empty plastic bottle and the same kind of plastic bottle filled with sand);

(b) name 'heavy things'; discuss the relationship between 'big' and 'heavy'.

(10) Bigger

The next three sets of activities deal with the comparative. It is open to question whether it is easier to deal first with the comparative (-er) or with the superlative (-est). For a young child, the superlative (biggest) seems to have the greater appeal and requires a less complex grammatical structure (it avoids 'than' as in 'bigger than'). However, the comparative is taken first here because the child has only to choose between two items and not three; thus the activity will make fewer demands on his concentration span. If one wants to reverse the order with a particular child one can go to the activities listed under the heading 'biggest' (13) below.

Let the child:

(a) 'make it bigger' (e.g. prepare a ball of Plasticine to be made bigger; start a house with wooden bricks); avoid tasks which could lead to confusion between 'longer' and 'bigger' (e.g. a paper-chain);
(b) find 'bigger ones than the one I've got' (first use boxes, bottles, shells etc., later use more structured materials like wooden bricks, Poleidoblocs etc.);
(c) take the 'bigger one' of two similar objects (both fairly big so that the contrast is 'big versus bigger' rather than 'big versus small');
(d) take the 'bigger one' when represented on pictures (two objects of the same kind);
(e) make natural verbal comparisons (e.g. 'elephant' versus 'horse'). if the grammatical structure 'bigger than' seems too difficult, use 'which-of-the-two' questions.

(11) Longer

Let the child:

(a) 'make it longer' (e.g. start a row of toy houses or a string with beads);
(b) make one of two equal linear sets 'longer' (e.g. two rows of toy houses, two rows of pegs on a peg-board, two strings of beads, two daisy-chains); in all cases both sets should be fairly long so that the contrast is 'long versus longer' rather than 'long versus short';
(c) give the carer a rod that is longer than the one the carer has in her hand (out of a box with a variety of lengths);
(d) give the carer the 'longer one' of two rods which are almost of the same length (both fairly long);
(e) indicate the 'longer one' when presented with two objects or pictures of objects that are identical except for length; the objects should be long rather than short and lend themselves to such comparison (e.g. ruler, rope, pencil, thread, daisy-chain, worm);
(f) make natural verbal comparisons like 'my hair is longer than

yours' (other objects that can be compared are: trousers, legs, candy sticks etc.).

(12) Heavier

Let the child:

(a) indicate the 'heavier one' out of two fairly heavy objects (e.g. two buckets of water or bottles containing sand, one fuller than the other; two box files, one with files, the other filled with less heavy materials; two pieces of wood of roughly the same size but of different specific weight);
(b) show an understanding of the concept by weighing (in play) any objects in his enviroment (by hand or with two-pan balance scales; do not use standard weights at this stage).

(13) Biggest

Let the child:

(a) find 'the biggest' out of a collection of objects of the same kind where one is definitely the biggest amongst others (e.g. a sack full of cardboard boxes where one box is very big);
(b) find 'the biggest' named object out of a collection of different objects where there are more than two of the same kind (three shells, four lids, three paper-clips etc.); the reason for having more than two is to avoid the concept of the opposite ('big one' versus 'small one') at this stage; there should be definite differences in size between the items of one group; use 'natural materials' as well as Poleidoblocs and other structured materials but only those where 'big' is more appropriate than 'long';
(c) find 'the biggest' out of any collection of different items of different sizes; once the 'biggest' is taken out, go on to 'which one do you think is the biggest now?' until all items are gone (perhaps this will lead to a discussion about relative size, i.e. the biggest is not always very big).

(14) Longest

Let the child:

(a) find 'the longest' out of a box with many rods of different lengths but with one (only one) definitely longer than all the others;
(b) find 'the longest' named item out of groups of different items (e.g. three rods, four sticks, five screws; see 13(b) for the reason for having more than two items in a group);

(c) find 'the longest' out of any collection of long items (see 13(c); see also under 11 for examples).

(15) Heaviest

Let the child:

(a) indicate 'the heaviest' out of three or more fairly heavy objects with clear differences in weight;
(b) find 'the heaviest' of a collection of objects, first through estimation and then by weighing (by hand or with two-pan balance scales).

(16) Most

Let the child:

(a) find the set with 'most' out of three sets with obvious differences (have one open box containing perhaps seven toy cars, another box with three, and another with two);
(b) find the set with 'most' out of more than three sets with obvious differences (e.g. sets of 3/3/2/4/8);
(c) find the set with 'most' out of three or more sets with less obvious differences (e.g. sets of 6/6/5/4/8);
(d) determine 'who's got most' of a group of children (or carer and child) when a fairly small number of playmatches or other counters are randomly dropped in front of each person.

Revision and extension through opposites

So far the exercises have focused on the positive dimensions of mathematical aspects – big rather than small, long rather than short and so forth. The reason for doing so is the greater attraction that positive dimensions normally have for a child, as well as their more frequent use and earlier developmental appearance. From now on the focus will be on their opposites – small rather than big and short rather than long, for instance. It seems natural to *contrast* the opposites now. However, as mentioned earlier, the teacher may in some cases like to avoid opposites even at this stage (i.e. with one concept fairly well established) in order to avoid errors in children with labelling problems. This may mean leaving out the suggestions under 18, 20 and 22 ('small versus big, 'short versus long' and 'light versus heavy'). For such children it is also advisable to leave a substantial time gap between teaching the positive concepts and teaching the negative ones.

On the whole the following can be seen as an extension and revision of the aspects covered so far. Some activities will be more or less the same as those described earlier, except for the focus on the opposite aspect. Likewise, suggestions for materials would often be the same.

(17) Small

The exercises are essentially the same as for 'big' (see 7 above) but with the focus on the concept of 'small'.

(18) Small versus big

Let the child:

(a) sort out sets of 'real' objects (e.g. spoons, cups), objects on picture cards, or sets of counters of two sizes and two other qualities into a 2 × 2 grid (e.g. red/green × big/small; paper/plastic × big/small). Avoid objects which are 'short' rather than 'small'; reinforce verbal and written labels;
(b) as for (a) but with more than two other qualities;
(c) make bead patterns with beads of two sizes by following written instruction cards (see Figure 2.1.7).

---

big-big-small, big-big-small, big-big-small,..........

big-big-big-small, big-big-small, big-big-big-small,.........

Figure 2.1.7: Examples of instruction cards (bead patterns)

(19) Short

The exercises are essentially the same as for 'long' (see 8 above) but with the focus on the concept of 'short'.

(20) Short versus long

Let the child:

(a) sort out rods and/or a pack of cards with lines into short and long ones (perhaps write 'long' or 'short' on the cards as preparation for instructions under (g) below);

(b) sort materials into a 2 × 2 grid when lines are in two colours;

(c) sort materials into a long/short grid with more than two colours;

(d) produce patterns with Cuisenaire or similar rods of two different sizes as suggested by the teacher (for example, the teacher might say 'short-short-long, short-long, short-short-long', etc. and the child would produce this pattern using different-sized rods);

(e) produce patterns like the one above under (d) but with rods where the colour does not help – for example, with natural wooden strips (straws) cut into two different lengths;

(f) produce and continue patterns with rods when the pattern is given as lines on instruction cards;

(g) read the words 'long' and 'short' and produce continued patterns according to written instruction cards, similar to the ones shown above under 18 ('small versus big').

(21) Light

The exercises are essentially the same as for 'heavy' (see 9 above) but with the focus on the opposite concept of 'light'.

(22) Light versus heavy

Let the child:

(a) estimate and check by hand a collection of objects with definite differences in weight ('which ones are heavy/light?');

(b) name two items within one category where one item is heavy and the other one light (e.g. plastic chair versus wooden chair; sheet of glass versus sheet of paper); avoid 'big versus small' (for instance in the category 'animal' avoid a comparison of 'mouse versus elephant') and discuss differences between 'big versus small' and 'light versus heavy'.

It is probably better to use scales for weighing when one compares lighter with heavier.

(23) Smaller
See activities under 'bigger' (10).

(24) Shorter
See activities under 'longer' (11).

(25) Lighter
See activities under 'heavier' (12).

(26) Less

'Less' is dealt with at the end of this section on negative comparatives because it seems to have little attraction for children. They naturally prefer sentences such as 'He's got more!' to sentences like 'I've got less!'

Let the child:

(a) indicate two sets of counters that have 'less' than four other sets. (e.g from four sets of ten and two sets of four the child has to pick the two sets of four; later the difference could be less obvious, e.g. sets like 3, 3, 3, 3, 2, 2). Starting with at least six sets of which only two qualify for 'less' makes the sets with 'less' more special and they are thus more likely to attract the attention of a child; furthermore, by having two sets with 'less' (rather than just one set) one may avoid possible interference from the term 'least';

(b) indicate the set with 'less' out of two unequal sets with an obvious difference;

(c) indicate the set that has 'one less' after one counter has been taken away from two initially equal sets that were *obviously* equal, like two even rows of counters;

(d) change two equal sets so that one set has 'less';

(e) find the ones that have 'less' out of a pack of cards with pairs of objects in different quantities (for examples of such cards see Figure 2.1.6 under 'more' above).

(27) Smallest

See activities under 'biggest' (13).

(28) Shortest

See activities under 'longest' (14).

(29) Lightest

See activities under 'heaviest' (15).

(30) Comparison (absolute / comparative / superlative)

Let children show their understanding when comparing materials that have previously been used (e.g. big/bigger/biggest).

(31) Least / most

'Least' is a term that is relatively unused by children. It should be taught after the other superlatives in conjunction with the oppositional term 'most', which should be well-established at this stage.

Let the child:

(a) find the sets with 'most' and 'least' out of three different sets with obvious differences (e.g. sets of 9, 5, 2,);

(b) find the sets with 'most' and 'least' out of more than three sets with obvious differences (e.g sets of 10, 7, 7, 6, 3);

(c) find the sets with 'most' and 'least' out of three or more sets with *less* obvious differences (e.g. sets of 7, 6, 6, 5, 4).

Unit 2
Early Number Work

Starting with Counters

Early work with counters was suggested in Chapter 2 for children with organizational problems. It may also be useful for general teaching at a pre-counting level.

Materials needed

One will need up to about 100 counters for each child; there should be some counters suitable for tallying.

Setting

The child (or a group of children) must sit at a flat table with space to accommodate a heap of counters safely. There must also be enough space left to organize large quantities next to the original heap. An adult must be in charge who also has a heap of counters to join in and model the activities.

Procedures

The first two steps are described in Chapter 2; they are in short:

(a) Working with a single line (straight, curved, in a ring, close together, spaced out).
(b) Working with double and multiple lines (e.g. lines of 'twos' bent over into lines of 'fours'; a single line combined with a double line to make a line of 'threes').

The following suggestions aim at continuation of this work.

Dividing

Let the child divide and subdivide the counters

(a) roughly in two parts;

(b) exactly in two parts (check by making a double line);
(c) roughly in four parts;
(d) exactly in four parts (check); and so forth.

Making groups

A low number ('2', '3'or '4' at the beginning) is suggested for 'rounding up'; for example, the teacher may say: 'Let's round up twos'. This means that two counters at a time are taken (pushed away) and separated from the heap 'in one go' until the whole heap is sorted out in twos. The pairs (or later the small sets) should be neatly spaced out over the available table space. When separating the two counters ('rounding them up'; or 'catching them', i.e. sliding them away from the heap) the child can either use two fingers of one hand, or one finger of two hands, as preferred. The teacher joins in and adds the verbal label by continuously saying in a kind of rhythm 'two' – 'two' – 'two', slowly enough for the child to be able to follow the rhythm with his movements. Keeping up the rhythm makes it necessary for the child to take the counters *simultaneously* – 'in one go'.

This can be followed by working with:

(a) groups of threes (three fingers of one hand, or two and one of two hands);
(b) groups of fours (four fingers of one hand, or two fingers of two hands); and so forth.

The question of 'left-overs' will arise. One could emphasize the 'be good to your partner' principle: 'If something is left, give the rest to a partner who might be able to use it to make up another group; tomorrow he might do the same for you.' If that principle does not work, surplus counters can be put back into a box. For an example of how the counters might look 'before and after' see Figure 2.2.1.

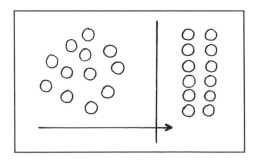

Figure 2.2.1: Turning an unordered quantity into orderly groups (example: 'two')

(c) Paper-and-pencil work: The same exercises can also be practised as paper-and-pencil tasks. This has the advantage that the child can keep and show the work to others. Work sheets with unordered quantities are prepared and the child 'rounds up' various amounts with a pencil (see Figure 2.2.2). 'Left-overs' are dealt with by simply crossing them out.

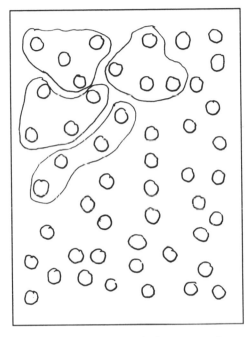

Figure 2.2.2: Sorting an unordered quantity into groups (paper-and-pencil work)

Gradually the child should learn to work fairly systematically on the sheet, so that he is not left with single marks at the top, bottom and middle which could make up a new set.

Tallying

Tallying has been described in Chapter 1. One will need a large number of playmatches or other small sticks as counters (about 100 per child); they are ordered into fives and double-fives in tally fashion. For a more advanced child with some counting skills, this task is a good way of building up a first image of the 'field of 100', which will be used later as the basis for work in the decimal system. He can learn to count and work in fives and tens. If this is not yet advisable, the work can represent just another way of creating some order out of an unordered heap.

Examples of Number Sequences

Number sequences seem generally useful when numbers are first introduced to young children. Work with such sequences was specifically suggested in Chapter 1 for children with problems in symbolic understanding and in Chapter 3 for children with a memory weakness.

Materials needed

A variety of counters is needed; some should be cubes.

List of sequences

Some sequences suitable for early number work were described in Chapters 1 and 3. The following is a full list with more examples.

The 'doubling sequence'

The doubling sequence is mentioned in Chapter 1 and Unit 1. It is the sequence of 2, 4, 8 (and perhaps further), which can be introduced by letting the child sort out an unordered mass of counters into lots of 'twos'. The 'twos' are then pushed together into half the amount of 'fours'; and the fours are then pushed together into 'eights'. This means that eight for instance is not understood as 'one more than seven' or 'the number before nine', but is visually and perhaps through active movement kinaesthetically remembered as the number one gets when one pushes two 'fours' together.

The 'pyramid sequence'

This is the sequence of triangular numbers. It is one of the finest for a young child to 'build' and is discussed and illustrated in Chapter 3.

The 'sequence of squares'

This is the sequence of square numbers. It can easily be built up with cubes put down flat on the table. No child will need much encouragement to get down on his knees and peep at the squares from all sides to establish that they really look alike from each side.

The plus-one sequence

Although this is the most basic and widely used counting sequence, it was suggested in Chapter 3 that it might not be the most interesting way to introduce a child to numbers because of its rather dull nature (increasing by one at a time). It certainly has its place later, and an example of how to introduce it with Cuisenaire rods as the 'staircase of cardinality' was given in Chapter 3. The same sequence can be built up with other materials (such as cube towers, soap boxes, plates or saucers, or beads on vertical rods). The advantage of such work is in all cases that the ordinal aspect of numbers can be seen and practised verbally while it is still linked to cardinal images.

The sequence of even numbers

This sequence has to some extent already been covered by the 'doubling sequence'. It can also be developed by work with simple symmetrical patterns (with counters or with pencil on squared paper); see Figure 2.2.3.

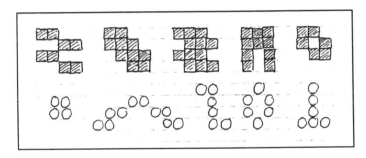

Figure 2.2.3: Patterns with even numbers

The sequence of odd numbers

Patterns of odd numbers can be developed with counters or pencil and paper similar to the patterns of even numbers shown above. But this sequence perhaps deserves some extra time. Here the discussion aims at 'an event' through which one tries to establish a concept. This section can thus partly be seen as an example of how to make use of 'episodic memory' (see Chapter 3).

The suggestion is to link concept and sequence with nature study, either on a special outing or, if one is lucky enough to have some plants on or near the school grounds, as an ongoing study. Odd numbers seem to be 'nature's favourites' and a sequence of odd leaves (leaflets) can easily be built up which should include, perhaps as the 'finale', the 'oddest' number of all – the common and therefore pale and unmemorable number 'one' (see Figure 2.2.4).

As elaboration on 'oddness' one can look at flowers like the common chickweed, which shows the most beautiful little star made out of five petals and five sepals; or at the buttercup, dog-rose, crane's bill and pansy. A contrasting session can take place where one looks

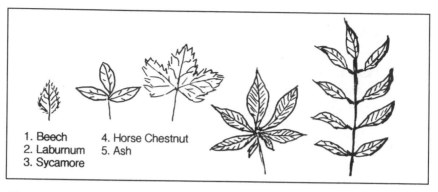

1. Beech   4. Horse Chestnut
2. Laburnum   5. Ash
3. Sycamore

Figure 2.2.4: Nature's patterns with odd numbers

for even numbers in nature; one can (in moderation) turn odd numbered leaflets into 'evens' by pulling off the odd leaf which often takes the prominent position at the top. In springtime one can let the child look at the petals of a daffodil as revision and for further consolidation. He may realise that the flower is made up of 2 × 3 petals. This may be the point to start the 'doubling sequence' again, but now with odd numbers, which will help to make clear that 'two odds always make an even' ('and what about two evens?'). If further revision is needed, this can take place once a year in festive mood when the first fine spring or summer day arrives.

All in all it is hoped that, with the help of episodic memory, whenever the question of odd numbers is raised in subsequent school years, an image like the leaf of a rowan tree will come back into the child's mind, representing the essence of 'oddness', even when the verbal sequence of odd numbers to be learned by rote might still cause difficulties (see Figure 2.2.5).

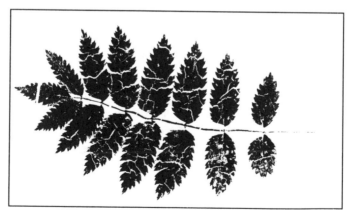

Figure 2.2.5: A rowan leaf as representation of 'oddness'

List of 'System Words'

'System words' were mentioned in Chapters 1, 3 and 4. I use the name 'system words' for number words that one might want to use in elementary mathematics instead of those conventional ones that do not strictly follow the decimal system, and therefore make the system less accessible to young children.

Such traditional 'irregular' numbers are few, but since they are the numbers that children need to learn early on they may need special attention. They are mainly the numbers from 11 to 20. Table 2.2.1 shows the list of such words. There are two categories, the irregulars and the mildly irregulars; from 60 onwards all English number words follow the system (cf. Fuson and Kwon, 1991).

Table 2.2.1: List of 'system words' (with corresponding Hindu-Arabic figures, conventional number words and the Chinese way of saying them)

Figure	Conventional English	'System words'	Chinese
1. Irregular			
10	ten	onety	ten
11	eleven	onety-one	ten one
12	twelve	onety-two	ten two
13	thirteen	onety-three	ten three
14	fourteen	onety-four	ten four
15	fifteen	onety-five	ten five
16	sixteen	onety-six	ten six
		etc.	
2. Mildly irregular			
20	twenty	twoty	two ten
21	twenty-one	twoty-one	two ten one
22	twenty-two	twoty-two	two ten two
		etc.	
30	thirty	threety	three ten
40	fo(u)rty	fourty	four ten
50	fifty	fivety	five ten
60:			
3. Regular from here onwards			

If one hesitates to use system words in teaching because they have an unfamiliar sound I can only repeat that once children are first made familiar with 'sixty-four', they will have no problems with 'threety-four' (Grauberg, 1985).

Sometimes older children seem to need the help of system words. In this case one may prefer to introduce such words first as a 'joke' (show me ninety-two, sixty-two, 'twoty-two'). One can then continue with questions like: 'This sounds funny, but is it only a joke? Does it make sense?' This should be followed up by pointing out the fact that in some other languages a combination like 'twoty-two' is taken for granted as the regular one and is used exclusively in everyday life. Finally one can give children some figures (such as 65, 35, 85, 15, 45, 25) and ask them to write them out as full number words according to the system.

If matching exercises are used where sets of cards include system words (spelled out in letters; see Chapter 4, Figure 4.2), a symbol could perhaps be added (e.g. a 'smiley face') to indicate that this is a system word and that a different card can also be found with the 'proper' name.

Unit 3
Understanding
Sums and Symbols

Introducing Sums in 28 Steps

All children who are introduced to 'sums' may benefit from the activities that follow, but they are especially aimed at children who have failed to understand what they are doing when they are given 'written sums'. The length of this section can be taken as an indication of my concern. I have seen too many young children doing sums without understanding them (cf. Bierhoff, 1996).

Materials

One will need a variety of counters, Cuisenaire rods, coloured paper strips and two-pan balance scales.

Problem and aim

Understanding written 'sums' means understanding written symbols: numerical ones and relational/operational ones. The expression '1 + 1 = 2' is utterly meaningless unless you know what the figures, the cross and the two small parallel lines stand for. Most children 'get the idea' somehow; others may feel baffled for years although they use the symbols obediently. General suggestions were made in Chapter 1 concerning how to foster conscious understanding of arithmetical symbols right from the start, namely:

- delay written work at the beginning;
- provide an obvious need for symbols;
- use children's own inventions;
- use intermediate iconic systems;

- aim at the widest understanding of the three symbols traditionally used at the beginning, i.e. '+', '−', and '=', so that they are understood as relational symbols as well as operational ones.

The following is a more detailed list of the steps one might take, and is an attempt to suggest a sequence in which teaching might take place. It makes the unrealistic assumption that the child has never seen, never heard of, and never used such symbols. Thus it has to be adjusted to the individual child or group of children, according to their previous contact with the symbols.

I would like to start with a general word of caution. The idea of using certain sequential steps for teaching is often fraught with difficulties when it comes to applying the sequence to an individual case. Essential previous learning may be lacking, or it may have occurred randomly and thus will interfere (negatively or positively). Generally, the teacher ought to feel free to override any given sequence, even with commercially produced 'highly structured' schemes and materials, if that seems to make sense and promises to lead to more efficient learning.

There could be many reasons for such deviation: for instance, one sees the need for side steps to consolidate a certain aspect; one wants to broaden a step to accommodate knowledge which is already there; one realizes that it is possible to skip a step or two; or that it is better to delay a step because it seems impractical; or one might reach the conclusion that it is better to break up the sequence altogether for the time being because it does not seem to lead anywhere. In writing the steps, I thought of the most difficult problems I have encountered. Thus one might feel the list is full of 'ritardandos' – steps which are almost there to 'hold back' the child rather than make him progress. Such steps are meant as safeguards, in case the development of a child is slow. In short: the sequence should be taken as one possible way of proceeding – a model to be modified and selected from to fit the carer's circumstances. At the end of this section a table of the steps in the sequence is provided to facilitate easy entry and exit (Table 2.3.2).

As was pointed out in Part One, before children are asked to 'operate' in a formal way, they ought to be familiar with the 'tools of the trade': the quantities and their order from 1 to 100. They should know their way around the 'field of 100' and be fairly familiar with the names and the appearances of quantities as ordered according to our 'base-ten' system and as represented, for instance, through Dienes materials or the Slavonic abacus. Perhaps they should have learned to write conventional figures for recording quantities up to ten, although the first steps can happily be completed without such knowledge. If necessary, 'figure writing' can be learned 'as one goes along'.

Step 1: 'sharing' rather than 'adding'

In order to work towards an understanding of the most general meaning of equations, I suggest that one starts analytically: not with 'adding', but rather with 'sharing'. Here this means 'even sharing by two'. This way one starts with a known quantity visibly in front of the child, which includes the sub-quantities that are asked for. All is there for the child to work with.

Counters of any kind could be shared, and the procedures might be like this:

8 shared evenly means 4 for you and 4 for me ('me' is the child who does the sharing);

7 shared as evenly as we can means 4 for you and 3 for me (remember: 'be kind to your partner and give him one more!'); or

7 shared could mean 3 for you, 3 for me and 1 for an absent friend;

100 means five tens to you and five tens to me;

and so forth.

Checking is carried out:

(a) by lining the counters up against each other; and
(b) by using two-pan balance scales – 8 shared means 4 in one pan, 4 in the other, and then watch if it balances.

When working in this way, numbers are analysed and quantities are experienced as wholes and sub-wholes. A notion of the state of equality, which will be expressed at a later stage by the use of a sign ('='), might dawn on the child. Oral labelling is constantly consolidated and the child works in the emotionally comforting frame of 'fair sharing' – something not to be underestimated.

Step 2: 'making things easier for us'

This step introduces structured material (Cuisenaire or similar rods, see Unit 3 below). It will enable the child to work directly with wholes and sub-wholes rather than with groups of units (counters) and will thus lead him gently away from the counting mode of dealing with numbers. Remember, the aim is to help the child to understand equations as expressed with figures and signs. The one rod standing for three units, for instance, is a better way of representing the figure '3' than three separate units.

Motivationally this should be an easy step, since the children will normally be quite ready to see the advantage of dealing with a few larger counters instead of lots of fiddly units. Conceptually, however, this step should not be underestimated since it involves substituting the whole for an equivalent made up of parts. Sharing a 7-rod, for instance, means 'swapping' it first for two 3-rods and a unit, or for a 3-rod and a 4-rod. (I use the term 'swapping' here rather than 'exchange', since this definitely seems children's preferred option.)

One will need an adequate supply of coloured rods, including unit cubes. The procedures will to some extent depend on how familiar the children are with the rods. The steps could be:

— Take out the dark green (6) rod.
— Take a handful of white cubes (1) and measure how many you need to make a row of the same length.

Establish that a 6-rod is as long as (good as) 6 small units.

The teacher might then take the lead:

> If you and I want to share a 6-rod what would we have to do? Saw it in half? Any better idea? Yes, swap it for the 6 unit cubes and give each of us 3.

> Could we make a quicker swap for the 6-rod? Yes, we can swap it for two light green ones (3) and we have a 3-rod each.

A challenge could be added:

> Could we swap it for a (red) 2-rod and a (pink) 4-rod? Not a good idea if we want a fair share for each of us. We want to break up the large rod as evenly as possible.

The teacher might sum up:

> We had a (dark green) 6-rod; we swapped it for two (light green) 3-rods which make up the same length as the 6-rod; now you and I can each have a 3-rod.

Similar work can be done by starting with rods of even numbers (8, 4, 2, 10) and perhaps a 100-flat.

In a new session the teacher might start with a challenge:

> What will happen if we start with a 7-rod?

We have to use units (1-cubes), 4 for you and 3 for me.

No, we can use larger rods: a (light green) 3-rod for me and a slightly larger (pink) 4-rod for you; that is as fair as we can get, unless we have a 3-rod each and leave one unit for a third friend.

Similar work is then done with other uneven numbers and with both even and uneven numbers mixed as they come (perhaps taken randomly out of a bag). Make sure the child understands that in fair sharing we want the two sub-wholes to be as similar as possible (no more than a variation of one).

Step 3: 'recording' sharing with rods

So far we have dealt with proper even sharing – the quantity which was the starting point was actually shared out, or the original rod was exchanged for parts and then the parts were shared out. Now we want a record of what has been happening. This can be done with the help of the rods. I am using the term 'recording' here since the arrangement of rods can be seen as a pictorial representation of what will later be recorded in writing as an equation with figures and signs. As an example, six shared by two would look like the arrangement of rods shown in Figure 2.3.1.

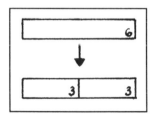

Figure 2.3.1: 'Six shared by two' recorded with Cuisenaire rods

This exercise should be introduced with care, perhaps as follows:

We have been 'sharing' for some time now. Today I want to show you how we can make a kind of picture of what we have been doing with our rods. Anybody looking at the 'rod-picture' can then see how we worked. How can we make a picture of our work? Any ideas?

Let's start with an easy one. Take a 6-rod. We want to tell others that a 6-rod is to be shared between two people. We know by now that each will get a 3-rod. So take two 3-rods but leave the 6-rod there as well. Put the 3-rods under the 6-rod. That is our picture of what we have been doing: 6 shared by 2 (you and me) means that there is a 3-rod for each of us (one for you and one for me). One can 'read' the picture and tell what we have been doing.

I'll make another picture and you see if you can read it (e.g. 8/4/4; 7/3/4).

> You make a picture with your rods and ask your neighbour to read the 'sharing story' from it.

Depending on the child, a few more examples or a longer period of work should follow.

A word of caution: we are so familiar with the process of 'recording' in all kinds of ways that it is hard to see where the difficulty lies for a child. If we take the example pictures in Figure 2.3.1, there will at the end be a potentially confusing amount of 12 units to be seen on the table, 6 to represent the starting point, and 6 to represent the outcome. The critical moment comes when we ask the child 'to leave the 6-rod' as a record. The 6-rod at the top must not be taken as the one we actually share. It is not part of the solution but must be left alone as a pictorial record of the past, of 'what it looked like before we started to share'.

Our difficult task is to ensure that the child develops some understanding of how one can represent an action with stable materials. The 'freezing' process of all recording should dawn on the child. Also, through these exercises the child should begin to gain some first insights into the usefulness of recording, realizing that it can tell what was done to someone who did not take part in the action; or that it helps us to remember what was done.

Step 4: 'breaking up' quantities into unequal parts

From even sharing it seems a natural step to analyse a number like 7 in different ways; see Figure 2.3.2.

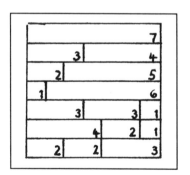

Figure 2.3.2: The analysis of 7 with Cuisenaire rods

If a 7-rod is left on the top, there is a 'record' which can be 'read off'. For example, 'a seven can be broken up into a six and a one'. This will prepare the child for more formal addition exercises later. Predictions can be made about how many possibilities there are for each number.

Sidestep 4a: using 'weight' of rods instead of 'length'

The same analysis can be done by working with the two-pan balance scales where one pan is kept constant (containing, for example, a 7-rod); again, what is seen on the scales can be read off as a 'record'.

Step 5: 'building up' quantities (reverse of step 4)

So far we have started with a given quantity. Now the process is reversed: 'building up' means that at the onset of the process the final quantity has to be 'imagined'. One could start by saying:

> Let's see if you can 'build-up' a seven with two or three different rods without looking at the 7-rod.

When this is done:

> See if you are right: take the 7-rod and 'measure' as a check. Let's see if we can remember all the different ways we found earlier (Step 4).

Thus one introduces the reverse of analysis: synthesis – a form of addition that can be done using 'weight' as well as 'length'.

Step 6: 'taking it home' or 'recording work more permanently on paper'

The idea is to represent the rods with colour on paper. This is quite a step into the abstract. The 'frozen' quality of an action is emphasized by the stability of a record on paper as compared with a record on the table (see Step 3). However, the task is made easier by a motivational asset: children like to make pictures and take them home; now they could take home their 'number work picture' and show it to parents, big sister and anyone else interested. If a child is taught at home, the work could be shown to someone other than the instructing carer.

Another factor that could have motivational value and should be pointed out is the fact that 'recording on paper' will help us to remember 'what we have been doing'. What we have done today can be seen and recalled tomorrow, in a week's time, even over a year and longer: 'if you don't lose the piece of paper, you could show it to your grandchildren'. Figure 2.3.3 gives an example of such 'recording'.

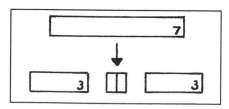

Figure 2.3.3: '7 shared by 2' represented through a drawing of rods

Some children may have considerable difficulty in drawing the rods with reasonable accuracy. In such a case I suggest providing the children with sheets of coloured strips prepared beforehand; each child then chooses those he needs, cuts them out and glues them on paper. Although I originally followed this procedure because of some children's difficulty in drawing, it could actually help in another way – in the smoothness with which the child progresses from the very concrete to the less concrete (two-dimensional paper strips instead of three-dimensional rods). In this case the materials can still be 'handled' before they are turned into the more static representation on paper resembling the drawing of Figure 2.3.3.

What will children experience when they take these sheets of number work home? At home people may not be familiar with the rods. The child may have to explain what the coloured strips or lines stand for – which could be an asset. The parents may interpret the picture as 4 + 3 = 7 (i.e. starting to 'read' from the bottom). The child then will have to explain again what happened in school (sharing) but the '4 + 3' suggestion' may also appeal to him. In any event, the next session should definitely start with the children reporting what happened at home.

Step 7: adding as the reverse of sharing

After experiences from home have been exchanged (see above), one could raise the question of what would happen if one put the largest of the four rods at the bottom; see Figure 2.3.4.

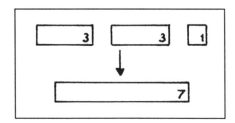

Figure 2.3.4: Reverse of Figure 2.3.3 suggesting 'adding'

The teacher takes the lead again:

> What if we had a 3-rod and a 4-rod at the top? It would then mean that a 3-rod and a 4-rod are as long as a 7-rod; or: a three and a four together come to the same as (gives us; is as much as) a seven;

Let's just check this: we can *see* that a three and a four are 'as long' as a seven. But does three and four always give us seven? What about 'as heavy as'? What about 'as much as'?

Checking can then be done with the two-pan balance scales; and, if appropriate, counting can be done with and without an abacus. In the end it should be established: yes, it comes to the 'same'.

Step 8: 'the same' versus 'equals'

This is a difficult topic and needs treatment that will make it memorable. The following is one way of introducing the word 'equals' as a 'treat'. Bring two gingerbread men into the situation, one broken into two bits (head or leg off) and one intact. A teacher-led conversation might follow:

Which one would you rather have? Are they the same?
     No and yes. The broken one is not so nice. They were the same before the head broke off. You still have the same to eat.
     Now then – what about these rods in my two hands (3- and a 4-rod in one hand; a 7-rod in the other), have I got the same in my two hands?
     Yes and no. We know they come to the same length, to the same weight and to the same counting units. But strictly speaking they are not the same. One lot is in two small pieces, the other one is just one big piece. Wouldn't it be nice to have a special word for things that are 'the same and not the same'?
     There actually is a word which adults use and we might just as well learn it today and use it for ever after: the word is 'equal'.

Write the word on the blackboard and explain carefully:

* *If things are equal it means that things are the same when you measure them somehow* – the same in counting, in length, or weight, or number (in quantity).

     Let's look at the gingerbread men. How can we measure them?

Establish that they are equal in weight (perhaps in length and width?). Finally, fun:

     Let's eat the gingerbread men. We'll all have a piece – I'll try to be fair – and after that we'd better start practising the new word.

Step 9: practising the term 'equal to'/'equal(s)' orally

It is open to question which of the two terms ('is/are equal to' or equal/equals) is better at the beginning; 'is equal to' seems to have the slight advantage that it corresponds in form to some extent to 'is the same as'; use what comes naturally (to you or the children).

Start by demonstrating the build-up of a 'picture' with three rods, two of which make up the third in length (e.g. 3/4/7, as in Figure 2.3.2 above, first two lines). Let the child 'read' the picture, using 'equal':

$$3 \text{ and } 4 \text{ is equal to } 7$$

Change the order back by putting the larger rod at the top:

$$7 \text{ is equal to } 3 \text{ and } 4.$$

The children build up 'pictures' of the same kind with three rods ('a + b = c'; or 'c = a + b'). They 'read' their own picture and those of their partners aloud. The aim is to familiarize them with concept and word 'equal' on well-known tasks.

Revision question (after some practices as above): what is the difference between our old 'sharing by two' and the work we are doing now?

> The two smaller parts don't have to be 'equal' or 'as equal as possible'. We can have 7 is equal to 2 and 5, or 1 and 6 (i.e. not only 3 and 4); or 6 equals 2 and 4 (instead of 3 and 3).

Sidestep 9a: working with more than two numbers added

This is an extension of Step 4 and might serve to consolidate Step 4 as well as the fairly new term 'equal' (which is still only used orally). Examples might be:

$$2 \text{ and } 2 \text{ and } 2 \text{ and } 1 \text{ is equal to } 7;$$
$$7 \text{ is equal to } 3 \text{ and } 3 \text{ and } 1.$$

Step 10: the familiar two-pan balance scales seen as a symbol of 'equal'

This step will again be to some extent a revision session (revising even sharing, analysing, adding, recording) using the term 'equal'. But the main aim is to let the children see the balance scales as a representation of their newly learned word 'equal'. For some children this could be an aid to memory and understanding, because they can link an abstract term with a concrete object (the pointer of the scales) and a picture of balance in their minds. It is assumed that the children have used the scales before and are familiar with them.

Present the balance scales as a good tool to tell us that things are 'equal in weight'. I suggest starting with 'the obvious': '7 is equal to 7'. This is one of the cases where 'the obvious' is taken so much for granted that children could find it far from obvious and they might find it strange to express it in words. Nevertheless it seems a basic factor in understanding the general nature of equations.

The first step is therefore:

> Put a 7-rod on each pan of the scales and let the children see that 7 is equal to (equals) 7; and let them say it.

The next step could be:

> Put an 8-rod in one pan and a 7-rod in the other and let the children see that 8 is *not* equal to 7; and let them say it.

Next:

> Put a 4-rod and a 3-rod in one pan, and a 7-rod in the other. Let the children see that 3 and 4 are equal to 7 – and that 7 is equal to 3 and 4; again, let them say this.

Point out that: 'equal' always lets us think of something that is 'balanced', like the two pans of our scales. Talk about 'balancing' in general, preferably on the playground and in a PE lesson as well as in the classroom.

Step 11: 'cover-up work' (subtraction)

This step is meant to be an introduction to subtraction. As a starting point I suggest that the children work with coloured rods. This way it is easy to link the exercises to previous work.

The teacher takes the lead by saying something like this: today we want to make 'cover-up stories' with our rods:

> Take a 7-rod. Cover it up in part with a 3-rod: put the 3-rod on top of the 7-rod so that on one side the two rods are flush. What can you say about the uncovered part of the rod?
> It fits a 4-rod (check it by putting a 4-rod next to the 3-rod so that the 7-rod is fully covered).
> How can we say what we see? 'A 7-rod covered with a 3-rod leaves the length of a 4-rod uncovered'; or (shorter): '7 with 3 covered leaves 4'.
> Does it matter which side we put the 'cover-up rod'? No, so please yourself.

Do more exercises with different rods after the following model:

> Take a 9-rod and cover it up with a 5-rod.
> What is left uncovered? Check (by putting the complementary 4-rod on the 9-rod).
> What can you say about it? (Nine with 5 covered leaves 4; or a longer version; see above.)

Let the children work as partners. One makes a 'cover-up story' (e.g. a 7-rod with a 5-rod on top); the other one finds the right complementary rod (2-rod) and 'reads' the story.

Step 12: recording 'cover-up stories' with coloured pencils and paper

Cover-up stories can be recorded using paper and coloured pencils. It will help if the children use lined paper or if they draw around the rods they want. The procedure is as follows:

– let the child draw the outlines only using a pencil of the same colour as the rod (e.g. 7-rod in black);
– let him 'cover-up' the part representing the longer rod (7) with a smaller rod (2-rod) by shading in over the required length with the correct coloured pencil (red for a 2-rod);
– let him find the correct complementary rod (5-rod) and let him shade the rest in the respective colour (yellow for a 5-rod);
– let him 'read' the story (7 with 2 covered leaves 5).

Challenge: There is another story here. Can you find it?

7 with 5 covered up leaves 2

or as an analysing/adding story:

7 is equal to 5 and 2.

Sidestep 12a: recording 'cover-up stories' in black and white

The same exercises can be done in black and white. This is faster and loses the scaffold effect of the colour system (see Figure 2.3.5).

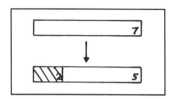

Figure 2.3.5: Recording 'cover-up stories' in black and white (example: 7 with 2 covered up means 5 left)

Step 13: 'take-away stories' on the two-pan balance scales

One will need the two-pan balance scales and coloured rods, including a substantial number of unit cubes. The exercise is basically the same as in Step 12, but using weight instead of length. It also differs because it involves counting units; and one needs a different kind of phrasing.

Introduce the session by saying something like this: today we do not want to make 'cover-up stories' but something similar, which you could call 'take-away stories'. After all the work you have done with 'cover-up stories' I am sure you will find them quite easy.

> Take a 7-rod and put it into one pan.
>   Take some unit cubes and make the scales balance by putting some into the other pan. You can count them if you like. How many will you need? Yes, 7 cubes. Remember? 7 is equal to 7.
>   Now, we will spoil the balance by taking 2 unit-cubes out of the second pan. How many are left? Yes, 5.
>   Can you say a 'take-away story'? It helps if you
>   first look at the pan with the rod (7); this is your 'checking pan' which tells you how we started;
>   then look at the cubes in your hand (2);
>   and then look at the cubes left in the other pan (5).

The phrasing of this example could be: '7 with 2 taken away leaves us (balances with) 5'.

In case a child has difficulty with the phrasing and only responds to questions with a one-word (or better: one-number) sentence, I suggest modelling it for him for some time until he – spontaneously or with some encouragement – feels like trying it himself. I would not ask him to repeat the sentence after me (it generally does not 'make sense' – cf. McTear and Conti-Ramsden, 1991: 205).

Later one could repeat the exercises and use more precise formulations, gradually working toward the final version, '7 minus 2 equals 5' (see below: Step 14 (equals) and Step 25 (plus and minus)).

Sidestep 13a: 'take-away-stories' with the two-pan balance scales using unit cubes or other unit counters (no rods)

As consolidation of Step 13 the child can be asked to follow the sequence of:

– putting an equal number of counters of his choice into both pans (numbers from, say, 4 to 10);
– taking some away from one pan;
– telling you what he has done and what the result is, using the same phrasing as in Step 13; this is best done as a 'running commentary' while he is acting.

Step 14: applying 'equal' to 'take-away' stories

The child should now be familiar enough with the technicalities of 'take-away' stories to learn to apply the newly learned term 'equal' to this situation (see Step 8). Ideally it should come spontaneously from the child (see the end of Step 13). In most cases it will have to be introduced. In all cases it ought to be consolidated by practising it for at least a couple of sessions. One can use rods only; or rods and unit-cubes; or unit-counters only. The work can be done either on the table or with the balance scales. I prefer the slightly more cumbersome use of the balance scales because it will consolidate the link between 'equal' and 'balance'.

The teacher starts by asking the child:

Does 5 balance with 7? (answer: no). Prove it (on the scales)!

What will we have to do to make the pans balance? (Add 2 to the pan with 5.)

Or? (Take 2 away from 7.)

We've been working with 'take-away' stories, so let's take away 2 (either by taking unit counters out or by exchanging rods).

Say the story (7 from which 2 is taken away balances with 5.)

Can you think of another shorter way of saying 'balances with'? You learned a word for it some time ago. Yes, 'equals'. (Or, if the answer is not forthcoming: remember 'equals'?)

Let's try using it.

There should now be some practice, following the suggested procedure but using the term 'equals'. It is beneficial to slip a question like 'does 7 equal 7?' into the series of examples. ('Yes – prove it – what have we got to do? Nothing.') At a later stage, this work can be done as partner-work, provided the children have the language skills to give and follow each other's instructions.

Step 15: work with three specifically related numbers ('number triplets')

This relates to what was said about number triplets in Chapter 2. It is meant as a 'ritardando', a step to slow down the pace of new learning; or as a summary of the work that has been done in the previous steps. It can also be taken as a preparatory step for the work described below under Step 17 (number triangles).

One will need as many rods as possible and some squared paper (preferably with 1 cm² squares). The lesson starts with the teacher taking the lead:

Did you notice that most of the time lately we have been working with *three* numbers?

Let's take three rods and put them on the table: an 8-rod, a 3-rod and a 5-rod.

What can you say about them?

Table 2.3.1 gives a list of the responses that might be expected (or a list from which the teacher can choose for demonstration).

Table 2.3.1: Possible responses to the number triplet 8/3/5

---

8 as the 'whole' can be broken up into the two parts 3 and 5
$(8=3+5)$;
8 can be built up out of 3 and 5
$(3+5=8)$;
you have 3 but you want to have 8, so you have to add 5
$(3+[5]=8)$;
you have 5 but you want to have 8, so you have to add 3
$(5+[3]=8)$;
you have 8 from which you take 3 away which leaves you with 5
$(8-3=5)$;
you have 8 from which you take 5 away which leaves you with 3
$(8-5=3)$.

8 is more (bigger, longer, heavier) than 5
$(8>5)$;
5 is more (bigger, longer, heavier) than 3
$(5>3)$;
therefore: 8 is also more (bigger, longer, heavier) than 3
$(8>3)$

3 is less (smaller, shorter, lighter) than 5
$(3<5)$;
5 is less (smaller, shorter, lighter) than 8
$(5<8)$;
therefore: 3 is also less (smaller, shorter, lighter) than 8
$(3<8)$.

Work is still only done verbally and for some time a variety of correct formulations should be accepted. In the end it is probably best if one agrees on a 'standard set' of formulations. For this I suggest the following four main statements:

(a) 8 can be split into 3 and 5 (later: 8 equals 3 and 5)
(b) 3 and 5 equals 8
(c) 8 with 3 taken away equals 5
(d) 8 with 5 taken away equals 3

Again, the teacher can challenge the children:

Will any three numbers do for such four sentences?

Let's try 2/5/8; put the rods on the table.

What is wrong here?

> 8 can be split into 2 and 5 and 1; we need four numbers (an extra rod);
> 2 and 5 do not equal 8; there is something (one) missing;
> 8 with 2 taken away is not 5 but 6;
> 8 with 5 taken away is not 2 but 3.

So, let's think, what is special about the three numbers we have worked with? Let's take a different lot: put 7/3/4-rods on the table and look at them. Now put 8/2/5-rods on the table and look at them.

See Figure 2.3.6.

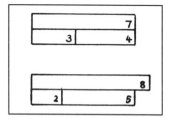

Figure 2.3.6: Comparison of two sets of three numbers

What is different? Yes, with 'our' numbers the two smaller rods make up the length of the larger rod; with the 'wrong' numbers the two smaller rods don't make up the length of the larger rod.

Let's call 'our numbers' 'triplets' (explain the name; find a better name if you can (see Chapter 2)); they are not just any three numbers, they have a special relation to each other.

Let's put three more rods on the table that make a triplet.

Let's put down as many different 'triplets' as we can find; remember: all sets must have three rods and they must make a triplet; if you run out of rods here is some squared paper – you can cut strips off and make more groups.

The session should end with one child at a time choosing one of his triplets and orally formulating some or all of the four statements that are listed above. While talking, he could point to, or handle, the rods or strips (splitting the smaller rods; or putting the smaller rods on top of the larger ones; or covering part of the larger rod with a smaller one – according to what he says). Ask the children to keep the squared strips for the coming sessions.

Step 16: finding easy ways of recording 'triplets'

The sequence of procedures in this step is difficult to write down.

Ideally it should be left open so that it can be determined by the child. It is a step where, if things go well, each child or each group of children can contribute in different ways. I am writing a somewhat hypothetical sequence, the one I would like to happen spontaneously and the one I frequently *made* happen because the child was not able to contribute at all or only contributed in a limited way.

This step is an introduction to one way of representing the relations between numbers in a triplet on paper – a 'number triangle' (see Chapter 1). Here it is mainly a vehicle to make children consciously familiar with different possibilities for recording. They will explore – or be carefully led along – a route from the concrete to the more abstract. It is a crucial step because it will end with a representation of numbers where the symbols bear no relation to the size of the quantity they represent: they are just colour, number words and number figures. This is a kind of representation that has been avoided so far.

The session could start with the following procedure:

–   The child is asked to make a picture of a number triplet by gluing three appropriate strips that now represent number rods on paper. If in the previous session there was no need to work with such paper strips, the strips are cut now.
–   Let the child formulate the relationships orally in four statements, more or less to the model in step 15.
–   Work on a series of examples; there can be partner work: children make 'pictures' for their partners to 'read'; partners together make sure that all four statements are made.

Establish in the end: we now have a 'record' of work that can be taken home and can be kept for future reference. Following on in a new session one could start with the suggestion:

> This takes rather a long time, all this cutting and gluing. Can you think of a quicker way of putting down on paper what we have been doing?

Let the children make suggestions. These will probably be almost as time-consuming as cutting and gluing squared paper strips, which can be somewhat frustrating to the teacher but it pays to 'hold back' at this moment. Let children go through with their own clumsy suggestions. These suit their level of understanding, and good (if slow) consolidation takes place. In the end the child will appreciate all the more the efficiency of the conventional system for representing quantities and relations through number figures and relational signs.

Possible suggestions (listed in the 'ideal' sequence, from the more concrete to the abstract) are:

(a) drawing the rods;
(b) drawing only coloured lines instead of full rods;
(c) making only coloured marks (the first step into the truly abstract);
(d) writing the number words, with or without colour;
(e) writing number figures, with or without colour.

Figure 2.3.7 gives an example of each of the possibilities. It can be seen that a kind of 'number triangle' emerges. When colour is used as a 'symbol', it is best to keep to the same colours as those used previously (e.g. for the Cuisenaire set: yellow for '5').

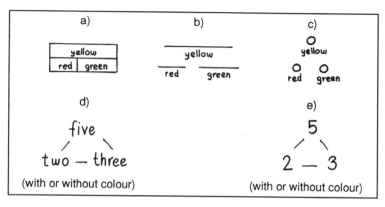

Figure 2.3.7: Different representations of a number triplet on paper

It is up to the teacher to decide how much time and practice one gives to the different possibilities. Ideally each step should be tried out for some time, though this may seem too elaborate. But if one wants to consolidate the verbal formulations that go with the 'triplets', the time thus spent will be helpful. More importantly, I like to repeat: the more cumbersome this process seems to the child, the more obvious the advantages of the conventional ways of recording will become and the more the use of abstract symbols will make sense.

Step 17: working with 'number triangles'

This step assumes that the children are basically familiar with the look, the formation and the value of number figures. The work will lead to more opportunities to practise the term 'equal' by application. It will also provide a general consolidation period if one feels that this is needed before the symbol for 'equal' and the next terms 'plus' and 'minus' are introduced. In my experience, the more familiar a child is with the actual number tasks involved, the easier it is for him to acquaint himself with the terms and symbols to be learned.

If one has more or less followed the steps above, only the form of the number triangles will seem new to the child: triplets are now put down on paper with figures in form of a triangle (see Chapter 1). Basically this is 'doing sums' written down in another form. The advantage is that the components of a 'sum' are seen in relation to each other. Figure 2.3.8 gives some examples of number triangles.

Figure 2.3.8: Examples of number triangles

The procedures are:
- The child is asked to make up number triangles. In the beginning it is advisable to work with rods and figures in parallel (i.e. the child makes a triangle with rods and then writes it down in figures).
- After some time one can start with figures, and use rods only for checking, or as 'inspiration' in case the child cannot think of another triangle.
- Each session should end with the children choosing at least one triangle and 'telling us all about it'. This means verbally formulating plus and minus relations, perhaps using the four statements outlined in Step 15. For instance:
  (a)   7 can be split into 3 and 4 (7 equals 3 and 4)
  (b)   3 and 4 equals 7
  (c)   7 with 3 taken away equals 4
  (d)   7 with 4 taken away equals 3.

The two-pan balance scales and rods should always be on hand and the child should be allowed to work with them while formulating the four sentences, if he so wishes. It may also be helpful if the child jots down the three figures of the triangle in each sentence while he says them. Thus he has a check that all three are there. If working with a group, the children who are not speaking can write the numbers down and approve each sentence. This will mean fuller involvement and an aid to concentration.

Step 18: more work with number triangles

There should now follow a period where the triangles are used and the relationships recorded orally. The formulation should gradually be 'standardized' to the form used in the example above, although it may sometimes be beneficial if there is a period when various formulations are used in parallel, according to the child's preference.

The four main statements illustrated in Step 17 cover the example 7/3/4. Staying with the number 7 as the top number one could suggest to the child:

Starting with 7, can you make up another triangle and tell me all about it?

The answer should be something like:

(a) 7 can be split up into 2 and 5 (7 equals 2 and 5);
(b) 2 and 5 can be put together to give us 7 (2 and 5 equal 7);
(c) if we take 2 away from 7 we are left with 5 (7 from which 2 is taken away equals 5);
(d) if we take 5 away from 7 we are left with 2 (7 from which 5 is taken away equals 2).

If the child is reluctant to use 'equals', the two-pan balance scales should be used to make 'equals' visually clear again. Gradually the child should become well accustomed to the 'rules' when working with number triplets:

- there should be at least four sentences;
- each sentence must have three numbers;
- the two smaller numbers must make up the larger number.

Step 19: challenges

This seems a good time to pause and let the child think about certain points concerning number triplets and triangles. Some of these will have already come up during previous work but it seems profitable to go through certain aspects more systematically. Posing the following questions may help to do that. Counters, rods and scales should be used for demonstration if necessary.

Question 1:

What will happen to the four sentences when we have three numbers, two of which are the same, like 6/3/3?
– Establish: in such cases there are only three sentences.

Question 2:

What will happen if we put four numbers into our triangle, like 7/5/1/1? (See Figure 2.3.9.)

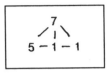

Figure 2.3.9: A 'four-number triangle'

The first answers in the following dialogue might be:

> You can't call it a triplet anymore. They won't make a triangle. Oh yes they can! What about our four sentences?

— Establish: we can put two of the numbers together so that we have three numbers which are a triplet and make a proper triangle.

Question 3:

What do you think of these three numbers: 7/5/4? The following dialogue might take place (revising Step 15):

> They don't make a triplet. Why not? The two smaller numbers are too large. How can we turn them into a proper triplet? We change the number which is the odd one out. Which one is it? It could be any of the three. So, how many ways have we got here to turn the numbers into a proper number triangle?
>
>> We could change the 7 – into a 9 (show with rods).
>> We could change the 5 – into a 3 (show with rods).
>> We could change the 4 – into a 2 (show with rods).

— Establish: only certain numbers make a 'number triplet' (we must get the right ones, otherwise our rules don't work; if we are not sure, we can always build the triangle up with rods; one can then see straight away if something is wrong).

Question 4:

Can we have an 'empty corner', or better, can we have a '0' at one corner?
The teacher writes down a triangle where '0' is one of the three numbers (e.g. 7/7/0). This is discussed, perhaps with the children saying something like this:

> 7 can be split into 7 and 'nothing' (0) – that is not really splitting!

- Establish: one can 'think about' such triangles; they are not wrong, but the only sentence that 'makes sense' is the last one of our four (7 with 7 taken away equals 0).

Question 5:

We have always put the largest number at the top. Do we have to do that? Could we write 7 / 3 / 4 in another way? A discussion like this might follow:

> We have always put the largest *rod* on the top. We have always started our sentences with the largest number. But what about this? (See Figure 2.3.10.)

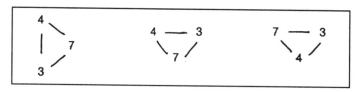

Figure 2.3.10: The number triangle with the largest number in different positions

The discussion continues:

> No, the largest number need not be at the top, as long as we read the triangle the right way (starting with the largest number). Can we do the same with the rods? Try it!'

Yes, we can (see Figure 2.3.11).

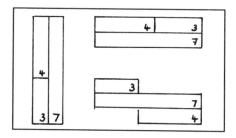

Figure 2.3.11: Three rods representing the number triangle with the largest number in different positions

- Establish: the largest number can be at any corner (but for the time being: let's agree that we will always write it at the top, because that is what we are used to and that way we don't get confused; that is our way of making things easy for ourselves.'

One might mention that grown-ups call this a 'convention' – something that they agree always to do in a certain way, although it could just as well be done differently. The British convention of driving on the left-hand side of the road might be a useful example.

I always like to take the opportunity to elaborate on the term 'convention' as a mutual agreement with alternatives. It is a concept that seems to cause problems for many children with language difficulties. They tend to see only one way of doing things and they view arbitrary conventions as restricting laws (see Chapter 1). Here it is a good preparation for the 'convention' of arithmetical symbols which are going to be introduced.

Question 6:
Can any number be a 'top number'?

A dialogue may develop:

> Yes. What about 1? Thinking of rods, we would have to saw a 1-cube into half. 1 is possible but difficult. What about 2? Possible, but boring. The larger the top number, the more interesting our work. Why? We can make different triangles with the same top number.

— Establish: any number can be a top number but some numbers are for various reasons better than others.

A special activity may be suggested here (chains of triangles; see Chapter 2, Figure 2.6 for an illustration):

> We can actually make 'chains' of triangles. I'll show you. Let's start with a nice big top number: 12.

Each child takes paper and pencil and draws along with the carer. Examples are:

(a) a long chain: $12/9/3 - 9/4/5 - 4/2/2 - 2/1/1$;
(b) a short chain: $3/2/1 - 2/1/1$;
(c) a 'side branch' of (a) starting with $9/4/5$, followed by: $4/3/1 - 3/2/1 - 2/1/1$.

Step 20: 'target work' – another way of doing the same thing

Target work has been briefly described in Chapter 1. This is a more detailed account. The session could start with an introduction like this:

> Today we want to work with 'targets'. Do you know what a target is?

A discussion of the word 'target' should follow (with the use of a safe dart board; or a ring of targets chalked on the classroom/playground floor into which counters have to be thrown from a certain distance; paper balls or used bottle corks with chamfered sides are suitable as safe counters).

For the following activity each child will need coloured rods and a beer mat (or a piece of thin card/paper the same size). The procedure is roughly outlined below and illustrated in Figure 2.3.12:

> Take a 6-rod and put it on the beer mat. 6 is our 'target'.

> Take the rods I am going to tell you and put one under the other in a neat column below the beer mat; listen:
>
>> take a 5-rod; a 4-rod; a 7-rod; a 1-cube; a 6-rod; and a 2-rod.
>
> Look at the first rod (5-rod) and look at the target rod (6-rod). What will we have to do to reach our target? – Add 1.
>
> So, put a 1-cube next to the 5-rod. 1 and 5 equals 6. Measure it with your target rod if you are not sure.
>
> Look at the second rod (4-rod). What will we have to do...? (as above).
>
> Look at the third rod (7-rod). What will we have to do here? Cut 1 cm off?
>
> Cover one unit up with a 1-cube: 7 from which 1 is taken away (with 1 covered up) equals 6.
>
> What do we put down next? (1 add 5).
>
> The next one is interesting (6-rod). What do we have to do here?

and so forth, as illustrated in Figure 2.3.12.

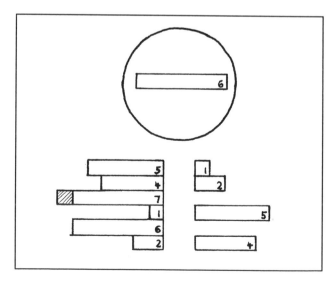

Figure 2.3.12: Target work with rods

Additional activities could start with the following question:

> If you look at the rods and think of the numbers they stand for, can you think of something familiar?

- Establish: each set of rods makes a number triplet. We could write them down if we wanted to (e.g. 6/2/4; 9/3/6; 6/0/0).

This should result in two exercises:

(a) The children take any 10 rods and make up a column. The teacher determines the target.
(b) The children choose any target they like. The teacher determines the rods which make up the first column.

Step 21: a step into history: the application of number triplets by the merchants of medieval Germany (see Chapter 1)

One could start the lesson by elaborating in language appropriate to the children the following historic points:

> Today we will do some history in our number work lesson. About 500 years ago the merchants and shopkeepers in medieval Germany used something like our target work with number triplets to check whether they had the right amounts of goods in the sacks, barrels and boxes which they were buying or sending out. For instance, if they were buying boxes which were supposed to have 25 silver mugs inside each, they would make sure that each box actually had 25 mugs inside. Or if they bought a load of sacks due to have 20 pounds of precious salt inside each, they weighed the sacks and made a note in their books that told them if the goods were 'overweight' or 'underweight' or 'just right'.

If possible the teacher should give colourful historical impressions of the times, the towns and the goods that were transported and sold. Such topic work could anchor the mathematical facts to be learned in 'episodic memory' (see Chapter 3). This can include acting out the merchants' work (counting the goods and recording the 'overs' and 'unders') which will – one hopes – lead in the end to an understanding of plus and minus and the corresponding symbols.

One will need:

(a) a variety of 'goods' – anything that is available in sufficient quantities: real things like nuts, paper clips, pebbles; and finally school 'counters';
(b) containers in which to pack the 'goods': boxes, egg boxes, plastic bags, brown paper bags, tins – any container of which one can find a fair number of the same kind;
(c) a kind of 'record sheet' on which one records any discrepancy

between the target amount and the actual content in the containers. See Figure 2.3.13 for a possible version of such a sheet.

In general, the more interesting the 'package' and the 'goods', the more memorable the event will be. However, the following is an example of how to work with somewhat dull but easily available materials.
     Prepare, for instance,

 — 5 or more egg cartons by putting different amounts (between 4 and 8) of single 'goods' (nuts, counters) into each; close the carton. Start by telling the children that the 'target' – the amount of nuts that should be in each carton – is 6.

Work will then proceed roughly like this:

 — a child opens a carton and reports that there are only 4; which means 2 are missing (triplet 6/4/2);
 — this is recorded on a record sheet;
 — the next box is opened: 6 nuts;
 — just right, none missing. This is recorded; and so forth. The record sheet for the 5 boxes may look like the one in Figure 2.3.13.

	Target: 6	
Counted goods	missing / too much	action
4	short 2	add 2
6	just right	—
8	over 2	take away 2
5	short 1	add 1
7	over 1	take away 1

Figure 2.3.13: Example of a 'warehouse record sheet' (nuts in egg cartons)

One may feel that the terms 'short' and 'over' used on the record sheet will be confusing for some language-impaired children because the terms are normally used with different meanings. In such cases one could use '2 missing' and '2 too much' instead.
     As a final activity one may want to 'spot' some triplets on the record sheet and write them down, either as 6/4/2; 6/6/0; 8/6/2 and so forth; or as triangles.

More interesting packages will be those where the amount of goods is not so easy to establish as it is in an egg box. One could, for instance, obtain large sacks (garden centres sell old potato sacks cheaply) and fill them with various quantities of empty soap powder boxes (saved over the last 30 weeks). If one happens to have a plum tree in the garden and the season is right, plums in brown paper bags are of interest, especially when they are shared and eaten afterwards. They will certainly be remembered – maggots and all.

Step 22: step 21 with different measurements

These suggestions involve more demanding tasks and such work can be delayed. It presupposes that the children are fairly familiar with various measuring units. Also, two kinds of systems have to be handled simultaneously – counting units and measuring units. On the whole, however, these exercises are good fun, and this may counteract the initial difficulties.

(a) *Weight.* The task is to establish the weight of certain goods contained in identical kinds of bags (boxes, sacks, tins) and to compare the weight with the target weight. In this case the three measurements (target weight, actual weight, discrepancy) are recorded in ounces, grams or pounds rather than in single items. It is best to use 'non-countable' matter such as sand, rice, water (preferably in closed containers!) rather than easily countable items, which would turn the task into the one described in the previous step. The target weight can be established by real or improvised weights.

(b) *Length.* The task is to establish the total length of a line made up from stick-like materials, and compare it with the target length (suitable materials: pruned branches from the garden, chopsticks, dowelling bits, Cuisenaire and similar rods). The teacher divides the chosen material beforehand and puts it into bags fairly randomly. The child lays out the content of a bag into a line, measures the total length and compares it with the target length (this would have been set differently according to the materials, e.g. 50 cm for rods, 3 m for branches). The discrepancy is recorded.

(c) *Time.* Moving a step away from the merchandise, personal time targets in physical exercises can be established and discrepancies recorded. (Beware that unrealistically high levels of aspiration may lead to an experience of failure; on the positive side, setting of realistic levels can be taught here.)

Step 23: finding short cuts in writing out warehouse records

After a period of lively work pretending to be merchants, the children will have experienced that there is quite an amount of writing to do; thus they will readily agree that it would be good if one could reduce the amount of writing. How?

The following dialogue may take place:

Can you think of a way of avoiding some writing?

If the children have no answer one could say:

Let me ask you a funny question: Do you know what M1 means?

This could be discussed:

Why don't we use 'Motorway 1'? How would that look on the signs?

It should be established that 'M', the first letter, stands for the whole word. More abbreviations, such as PE, AA, TV, 'e.g.' can be discussed. Perhaps it is also worth mentioning that sometimes, mostly in phrases, a full stop shows that words are abbreviated.

This should now be applied to the warehouse task with an introductory question like:

Could we use it for our warehouse sheets?

A prepared warehouse sheet is shown; or a sheet is written with the help of the child, using abbreviations; see Figure 2.3.14.

	Target: 6	
Counted goods	missing / too much	action
4	sh. 2	a. 2
6	j. r.	—
8	o. 2	t. aw. 2
5	sh. 1	a. 1
7	o. 1	t. aw. 1

Figure 2.3.14: The record sheet of Figure 2.3.13 with abbreviations

Further discussion might follow:

That looks complicated. Would your mother/father/friend understand? No, because they don't know what the first letters stand for. We must make it easier for them:

(a) we only shorten the longer words because it is hardly worth shortening the short ones;
(b) and we make a list which shows them what whole word the letters stands for.

An additional question could be asked:

> Why don't we need a list for abbreviations like M1, PE, TV?

The abbreviations of the warehouse sheet are now altered:

> for 'a.' we write 'add';
> for 'n.' we write 'no';
> for 't. aw.' we could write 'out'.

Thus the list for parents would now be quite short and look like this:

> sh. stands for 'short'
> j.r. stands for 'just right'
> o. stands for 'over'

The new-look sheet is shown in Figure 2.3.15. Some work is now done using the new form of recording.

Target: 6		
Counted goods	missing / too much	action
4	sh. 2	add 2
6	j. r.	—
8	o. 2	out 2
5	sh. 1	add 1
7	o. 1	out 1

Figure 2.3.15: The record sheet of Figure 2.3.14 with altered abbreviations

Step 24: introducing the first relational symbols, plus and minus ('+', '−')

After some work with the new record sheets one could start a lesson by saying something like this:

> Our way of working with the shortened words seems to be quite good. Have you perhaps seen or can you think of any other ways we could save some writing? Have a look at this (write out or show Figure 2.3.16, perhaps together with Figure 2.3.15 above):

Target: 6		
Counted goods	missing / too much	action
4	− 2	+ 2
6	—	—
8	+ 2	− 2
5	− 1	+ 1
7	+ 1	− 1

Figure 2.3.16: The data of the previous record sheets (Figures 2.3.14 and 2.3.15) with the use of '+' and '−' signs

This is followed by a discussion and some explanation:

> Can you make sense of the record sheet? Have you seen those signs?
> This is roughly the way we think the merchants of Germany wrote their
> warehouse sheets about 400 years ago. They had names for those signs: '−'
> was called 'minus'; and '+' was called 'plus'. The words are from an old
> language (Latin) which in those days was the language used in books and
> when talking to foreigners who could not understand the language of the
> land. Not everybody understood Latin, but all people who went to school in
> those days (only some, mostly the rich) learned Latin at school, no matter
> what their own language was. That was one way people of different coun-
> tries could talk and write to each other.
>
> We still use these signs and names today. Everybody learns them at
> school all over the world, because they have been found very useful. Let's
> look at them:
>
> (a) *Plus* – 'Plus' means 'more' in Latin, and everybody agrees that we use it
> when something is 'added', or when something is 'too much'. (Mention
> 'plural', 'plus points' 'surplus' etc. if appropriate.)
>
> (b) *Minus* – 'Minus' means 'less' in Latin (or 'not enough' for the
> merchants), and everybody agrees to use it when something is 'taken away',
> or something is 'missing'. (Mention 'minor', 'mini', 'minnow', 'minute',
> 'minus points' etc. if appropriate.)
>
> What do you think of the signs? Nice and easy to write!

– Establish: from now on we are going to use the names and the
signs to help us with our number work, like your big brothers and
sisters do. I'm sure you will find out soon how useful they are.

A period of practical 'warehouse' work should follow, with record
sheets in which the plus and minus signs are used. Here is a possible
example:

– Collect ten yoghurt pots and number them.
– Fill them randomly with a handful of counters (playmatches,
coloured rods, beans etc.; larger counters are better for smaller
children).
– Take a pot that is filled with a fairly average number of counters;
find out how many counters there are in the pot.
– Set this number as the target.
– Prepare record sheets with the target number written in.
– Let the child establish the over/under amount and the required
'action' (how much has to be taken out or put in) using the terms
'plus' and 'minus' (orally and in symbols); Figure 2.3.17 shows
such a record sheet filled in.

Target: 20

Number of container	Goods (counted/tallied/weighed)	Plus/Minus	Action
1	23	+3	−3
2	18	−2	+2
3	20	—	—

[etc.]

Figure 2.3.17: Example of warehouse sheet, using plus and minus signs (containers: 10 yoghurt pots; goods: playmatches; target: 20 per pot)

The 'action' can be carried out either:

(a) while filling in the sheet; or
(b) after the sheet is completed; or
(c) the filled-in sheet can be given to a partner to perform the action; or
(d) two children can work as partners, one acting, one filling in the sheet.

At some stage the children are told:

> As far as we know, the busy merchants did not actually bother to write down what action to take. They knew what to do by looking at what number was shown with plus and minus. How?

— Establish: if we have too much (plus), we must take something away to get our target; if we have not enough (minus), we must add something.

From now on two kinds of record sheets are prepared (perhaps marked with different colours), one still showing 'Action', one without 'Action'. The children are given a choice of the two, hoping that they will all prefer the shorter version in the end and thus show that they have understood the relation between action and plus/minus and that they feel confident enough to use it.

Step 25: target work with 'plus' and 'minus' signs

The aim of this step is to reinforce the newly learned signs on a task which is familiar. Practice sessions could start by saying something like this:

> The merchants had to do such number work day in, day out. Some still do. We can now use their plus and minus signs and make things easier for our work. Let me show you:

The following is now demonstrated, developed and established using paper, blackboard or overhead projector:

Target work involves the familiar three-number relation (number triplet), now seen as

(a) 'target number';
(b) given number (goods);
(c) number to 'figure out' (action: plus/minus x).

This can be shown and checked with Cuisenaire rods; it can be summarized as shown in Figure 2.3.18.

```
Target:  7

Given    plus/minus
  4        +3
  9        -2
  7        — (or : ± 0)
[etc.]
```

Figure 2.3.18: Target work with plus/minus signs

While developing such a target sheet, and when first practising the task, ample opportunity should be provided to use the terms 'plus' and 'minus' verbally in parallel with the written form, so that the written sign and the word become securely linked.

The time spent on this step will vary. If one feels that a lot of reinforcement is needed (of the signs as well as of simple number skills), the step can be prolonged. If, however, one is keen to reach the stage of more formal work (like $3 + 4 = 7$), the step can be treated in one session as a demonstration step to facilitate what comes next.

Step 26: using plus/minus signs in a combination of 'target work' and 'number triplets'

The aim of this step is again general consolidation. It is also another way to ensure that the children remain flexible when they look at numbers and do not think relational signs can only appear in the customary linear way of $3 + 4 = 7$. In the end, however, that will be the form we want to establish as the most common one.

Perhaps one could start in the following way:

Do you remember our triplets and number triangles? Here is one (write a triplet in form of a triangle; e.g. 7/3/4). Does it remind you of something? Think of our target work. It looks a bit like target work all done for us.

It should be established that here:

The target is 7;
the given number (counted goods) is 3;
4 is the number we need to add (+4) in order to reach the target.
We can now put the plus sign where it belongs (in front of the 4) and 'round up' the two parts in the triangle that 'balance': the 7 against 3 + 4. (See the first number triangle of Figure 2.3.19.)

The next question could be:

Does the target always have to be the largest number? What happens if we think of 3 as our target?

If the child is hesitant, let him jot down the three numbers in 'target sheet fashion' and establish:

The target is 3;
the given number (counted goods) is 7:
−4 is the number we need to reach the target.

Further examples with the 7/3/4 triangle would be: 4/7/−3; 7/4/+3.

One may want to record the examples on paper; see Figure 2.3.19.

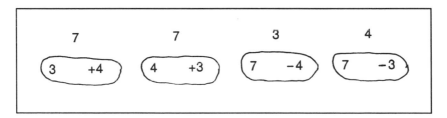

Figure 2.3.19: Relational signs in the number triangle

Perhaps a last question can be asked which leads to new triangles:

What will happen if we make 4 the target and 3 the number of counted goods?

− Establish: then +1 is the number we need to reach our target. We lose the '7'. It's fine, but we end up with new triplet (4/3/1).

There should now follow some practice sessions where the children are given the 'target number' and the 'number of goods' and have to find the missing 'action number'. At the beginning it is best to let them sketch the triangle, or let them use a 'record sheet'; rods or counters should also be on hand in case there are difficulties with procedures or the number facts.

In the end children should be able to give the 'action number' when 'target number' and 'goods number' are given in the following form:

6 as target, with a circle drawn around: ⑥
9 as goods
Action? −3.

The short representation for the completed triangle would be: ⑥/9/−3; or, another example, if the given part is ⑧/4, the completed written form would be: ⑧/4/+4.

It is perhaps advisable to draw a circle around the target number for some time until it becomes established that the first number is always to be taken as the target. Now and then one may want to do a short proper 'warehouse' session again, to keep the task mentally 'concrete'.

Step 27: combining 'plus/minus' and 'equals' with the use of balance scales (verbally)

The aim is to combine the two terms 'plus/minus' and 'equal', and approach the traditional form of equations. One will need two-pan balance scales. The starting point is the work done in the previous step: triplets to be completed, like 7/3/+4; 8/10/−2; 7/7/ ±0. After some examples have been worked out, one could suggest:

Let's check your work with the scales. How do we go about it?

 — We had 7 as the target (put seven into one pan, either as counters or better as a 7-rod); 7 is what we are aiming at.
 — We had 3 as the 'counted goods' (put a 3-rod in the other pan).
 — That was not enough, so we had to add something: plus 4 (add 4); this can be done either with a rod or with single counters (perhaps single counters are preferable here, because the children can see the scales gradually reaching full balance, i.e. reaching the target point).
 — We check whether the two pans are fully balanced.

One could continue with questions and explanations like this:

Can you remember our word for things that balance? (Answer: equals). Good, we have a fine balance here and can say: 7 equals 3 plus 4. I'll write it down (it is important that the children can see what is written).

Could we swap the two pans and have the 3 and the 4 on the left and the 7 on the right? Try! Yes. It comes to the same (just as we can swap seats on a see-saw). Can you say the sentence the other way? 3 plus 4 equals 7.

I'll write it down again (this is done – for all to see – in full writing unless a child says spontaneously: why don't you use '+' instead of 'plus'?).

The next step should probably be an example with a 'minus triplet':

– We have 8 as the target (put 8 into one pan).
– We have 10 as the 'counted goods' (put 10 in the other pan).
– This is too heavy! (Not balanced! Not equal!) We will have to take something out. What is our third number? 2. Take out 2. (This may call for an exchange if one has worked with rods – perhaps a 10-rod for a 5-, a 3- and a 2-rod).
– We check: does it balance? Fine.
– So, we can say: 8 equals 10 minus 2. Or, if we start with the other pan: 10 minus 2 equals 8. I'll write it down.

After some more examples one can suggest:

This takes me a long time to write. Can you think of something that would make it faster?

Either the teacher or, with luck, a child suggests using '+' and '-' signs to 'speed things up'. More examples are worked through, so that the child becomes accustomed to the verbal use of the three terms in combination (the writing is still best demonstrated by the teacher, using '+' and '–' signs but writing 'equals' in full).

Step 28: writing equations

This is the final step towards conventional 'sums'. I suggest starting the session by saying something like this:

Yesterday I did all the writing; today you will have to do it. We also want to try to do without the scales unless we are not sure and need to check something. But we could draw something like the scales. I have prepared a drawing for each of you with target numbers and goods filled in; you just have to find the 'action' and write the sentences. We will do the first ones together.

Figure 2.3.20 shows such work, see also Chapter 1, Figure 1.13.

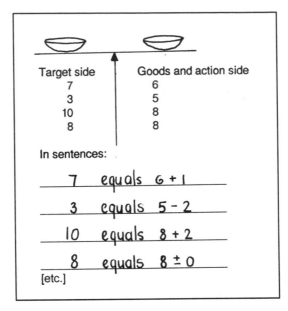

Target side	Goods and action side
7	6
3	5
10	8
8	8

In sentences:

7   equals   6 + 1

3   equals   5 - 2

10   equals   8 + 2

8   equals   8 ± 0

[etc.]

Figure 2.3.20: Example of worksheet showing 'equal' as balancing point on the scales

After the worksheets are completed, the question is raised:

Would it not be nice if we also had a short sign for 'equals'? Any ideas?

The children may or may not have ideas. The most likely idea will probably be the pointer of the scales; or some may know the proper sign '=' already and see the connection. One can either work with their possible suggestions for some time or go straight to the historical introduction of the conventional equals sign outlined below:

We are not the only ones to have looked for a short way of writing much used words. Several hundred years ago people did the same. They looked for a quick way of writing 'equal'. First they too wrote the whole word. Later they only used the first letters. And then – about 400 years ago – there was an Englishman called Robert Recorde who grew tired of writing 'equal' all the time and decided to use a sign instead (see Chapter 1 for a fuller version). He used two lines like this: '=' (draw the equals sign).

And this is the sign people still use today: two equal lines. Everybody seems to agree that it makes sense and is quick to write. All over the world pupils learn it in school. You may have seen your older brothers and sisters using it. Of course, among ourselves, we could use any old scribble for 'equals', but then we could not be sure that other people would understand our work. The two equal lines have become a 'convention'. So from now on we too will use them. That should make things easier for us.

Let's get the balance scales out and try it. I'll work the scales. You watch and write down in the shortest way what I do; listen:

the target is 7 (put a 7-rod into one pan);
the goods number is 5 (put a 5-rod into the other);
I'll make it balance (put 2 single or one 2-rod into the second pan).
What have you written? '7 = 5 + 2'. That's fine.

From there on one can gradually drop the target, goods and action idea and work with equations as 'balancing stories'. It should be explained that such balancing stories are called 'equations' and the name should be discussed. The children are asked to write as many equations as they can think of:

You can use scales, rods or counters if you wish. All targets are up to you. I can assure you that there are millions and millions of possible equations to find.

The worksheets are now filled with equations. Some children may need some help to get started. Perhaps one can insist that the children always write the equal signs in the same column; this can be made easier by writing on squared paper. One might also suggest that the children leave some empty space before and after the sign so that, if a child puts the numbers in the wrong positions, it will still be possible to line up the equal signs.

The kind of equations children will make depends on their number knowledge and their willingness not to take the easiest way out. It is possible that a clever Dick (or his more modest female counterpart Molly Whipple in one of the finest English fairy-tales) will only write equations of the type given in the last example of Figure 2.3.20: 8=8 (i.e. they could write 1=1; 2=2 etc. up to infinity). Do not worry: today, everything goes, tomorrow the teacher can prevent such work by setting targets again. This is not a session where number skills are practised, This session is to be remembered as something special; it is meant to bring home the written form and the meaning of '='. What better way than writing '1=1'.

The children are thus equipped with the tools for writing equations and doing simple 'sums' in the efficient conventional way. It is hoped that they will have also acquired a good understanding of what the signs stand for. This can now be applied to all number work, old or new, at increasing levels of difficulty.

It is advisable to have a fun revision session occasionally, where the pupil is taken back to some of the previous steps (e.g. number triangles, 'warehouse target work', use of balance scales, writing everything in 'long hand'), just to make sure that even in the more mechanical practice sessions and in application of the 'tools', the meaning is still alive.

Table 2.3.2 summarizes all 28 steps.

Table 2.3.2: Reference List: Introducing sums in 28 steps

1. 'Sharing' rather than adding
2. Making things easier (introducing structured materials)
3. 'Recording sharing' with rods
4. Breaking up quantities into other than equal parts
    4a. Using 'weight' (of rods) instead of 'length'
5. Building up quantities (reverse of 4)
6. 'Taking it home' (recording more permanently on paper)
7. Adding as the reverse of sharing
8. 'The same' versus 'equals'
9. Practising the term 'equal to'/'equal(s)' (orally)
    9a. Working with more than two numbers added (consolidation of 4)
10. The familiar two-pan balance scales seen as a symbol of 'equal'
11. 'Cover-up work' (Subtraction)
12. Recording 'cover-up stories' with coloured pencils and paper.
    12a. Recording 'cover-up stories' in black and white
13. 'Take-away stories' on the two-pan balance scales
    13a. Using single unit counters (i.e. no rods)
14. Applying 'equal' to 'take-away stories'
15. Working with three specifically related number (number triplets)
16. Finding easy ways of recording 'triplets'
17. Working with 'number triangles' (i.e. triplets with number figures)
18. More work with number triangles (standardized oral recording)
19. Challenges (revision 15–18)
20. 'Target work' (work with triplets/triangles in another form)
21. Historical application of number triplets
22. Extension of 21 with different measurements
23. Finding shortcuts for written recording of triplets ('warehouse sheets')
24. Introducing the first relational symbols ('+', '–')
25. Target work with plus/minus signs
26. Triplets, targets and plus/minus signs
27. Combining 'plus/minus' and 'equals' (orally)
28. Writing equations

Working with Hieroglyphic Number Symbols

The idea of using hieroglyphic number symbols came to me through Graham Flegg's book *Numbers: their History and Meaning* (1983); see also Ginsburg (1977, 1989); Grauberg (1985); Hughes (1986). Although the last three publications relate hieroglyphic numbers to the understanding of symbols in early mathematics, there have been no attempts, as far as I know, to suggest in detail and on the basis of some experience how such symbols can be used in practical teaching for that purpose. The following is such an attempt.

To some, such a detour into older systems might appear an additional complication or a waste of time but it is my experience that at certain stages children seem to be really happy with hieroglyphic numbers, probably because these symbols fit well into their stage of development as they move from the more concrete to the abstract. Although the ancient system is certainly more cumbersome in use than our conventional methods, it is easier to 'handle' and definitely prettier to look at. It will make number work fun for any child who gets pleasure out of pattern-making.

Generally, all children could benefit from using hieroglyphics, whether they have specific problems with understanding symbols or not. More specifically, hieroglyphic number symbols seem to be particularly beneficial:

(a) as a 'mediating method' when the step from concrete materials to recording numbers with our more abstract number system seems too great (Chapter 1);
(b) when the use of relational signs like '+', '−', '=' and the use of place value seems to be too advanced for a child (see Chapter 1);
(c) when a new start is wanted with older children who have failed with conventional methods (see Chapter 1), especially if they have developed some kind of 'maths anxiety' (Morris, 1981);
(d) as a reinforcement of conventional methods, especially if children seem in danger of losing the meaning behind conventional symbols and seem to work too mechanically (see Chapter 1);
(e) as one way of making 'number sketches' (see Chapter 3).

My suggestions here are mainly concerned with showing the hieroglyphic system as a tool that can be used in parallel with our written system, so that the latter can be better understood.

The symbols

A description with an illustration is given in Chapter 1 (Figure 1.5; see also Figures 1.6, 1.11 and 1.15). Some of the didactic advantages are also outlined there with reference to addition and subtraction. To show the possibilities, Figure 2.3.21 is a kind of summary where the examples are on a more difficult level than those in Part One. One can expect that most of the time work with children will be done on a much lower level.

The following is a list of materials and suggestions for activities. All materials will have to be home-made and instructions of how to make them are given.

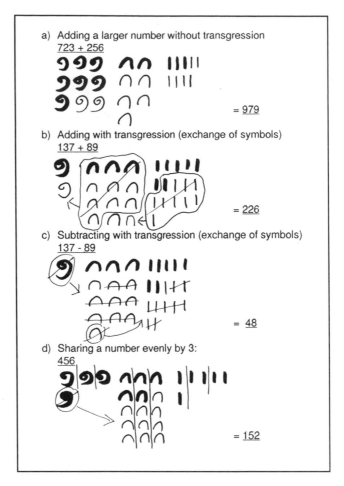

Figure 2.3.21: Working with hieroglyphic numbers (showing fairly difficult examples)
Note: work is meant to be done in two colours

Set(s) of cut-out symbols

How to make the symbol sets

The symbols are best made out of thin plywood – especially for small children or children who are clumsy and cannot easily pick up bits of paper or cardboard things with their fingers.

> An electric fretsaw is a good tool for making wooden symbols. It is possible to stack-saw a number of the same symbol in one go (stack plywood together with double-sided tape). If this is not possible, however, they can easily be made out of fairly strong card (e.g. old birthday or Christmas cards of the stronger type; coloured bits need not be avoided).
>
> The symbols for the numbers 1, 10 and 100 ought to be roughly of the same height (perhaps 5 cm), whereas the 1000 ought to be somewhat taller (perhaps 7 cm).

One will need one set of master templates of the symbols from which all the others can be made, even by children themselves (pencilling around the templates and cutting out the shape). When the cardboard symbols become old or are lost they can be quickly replaced. It is advisable to have a stock of spares on hand.

Each child will need an individual set with

(a) ten symbols of the numbers 1, 10 and 100 (sticks, hobbles, coils);
(b) one or several symbols of the number 1000 (lotus flower), depending on the range of numbers used at any stage.

Actually only nine of each symbol will be needed, but it is sometimes good to have the extra symbol to show a child the full equivalent of the next higher symbol (for example, one hobble stands for 10 sticks). The set for each child is best kept in a flat box with a lid (e.g. an old chocolate box), large enough to make it easy to choose the symbols one wants.

How to use the symbol sets

The following are some suggestions (given as instructions directly addressed to the carer).

- As an introduction: tell the child to take certain symbols, for example, 4 of the 'curly ones' (100s), 6 of the 'arches' (10s) and 5 'sticks' (1s); let him make a pattern with these; tell him that this is actually the number 465 in the way an ancient people used to count and write; talk about ancient Egypt.
- Let the child make more patterns; you read back the number they represent.
- With luck some children might find out how the system works, otherwise you take the lead; talk about the origins of the symbols: what is a 'hobble', what is a 'coil', what is a 'lotus-flower', and why these symbols? Could one use others? What would people today choose from their environment?

This is followed by more focused work. The carer says or writes down a number, the child builds it up (the number will depend on the child's knowledge of conventional number words and number figures). It is important to ensure that a clear representation of 10, 100 and 1000 is somewhere in view as reference, so that the child can constantly see how large a quantity a specific symbol represents. This could, for instance, be an abacus for 100 and ten quantity pictures for 1000 (see Unit 4); or one could use Dienes rods, flats and cubes or any other suitable structural materials.

The work in detail could be like this:

- let the child build up a certain number and share the number evenly between two;
- build up a certain number and then 'take-away' another number;
- build up a certain number and then add another number;
- share a number evenly by three (e.g. child, partner and a 'charity of their choice').

I suggest the following sequence:

(a) start with even numbers and numbers which do *not* involve transgression of the symbol boundaries, for example:
426 shared evenly by two (rather than 325 shared by two),
426 minus 223 (rather than 325 minus 17),
426 plus 262 (rather than 325 + 92).

(b) move on to exercises *with* transgression. This will mean that the idea of 'exchange' (i.e. the substitution of a single symbol of high value for an equivalent of several symbols of the next lower value) will have to be introduced. With luck, a child may think of it himself, especially if he has some experience with money.

For sharing and transgression exercises a child may need more than one set of symbols, so it is important to have a box with spare ones on hand. Alternatively, the child may be able to decide how many more he needs and then cut himself the appropriate amount out of rough paper.

Sharing an uneven number means of course that someone 'gets more'; let the child deal with this in his own 'fair' way if he can.

Pack(s) of cards with hieroglyphs

Such cards are useful for consolidation of number knowledge and for first arithmetical operations. They will take some time to make but this should not be too difficult.

How to make the cards

I suggest proceeding like this:

- cut about 20 fairly large cards (perhaps 5 × 2 inches) and number them unobtrusively in one corner of the card;
- write a hieroglyphic number symbol on each (same side);
- make a second set with identical numbers but in different colours;

– make a corresponding pack in conventional figures.

If more than one pack is desirable, the packs can be colour-graded according to difficulty (perhaps: one pack with numbers under 20, one pack with numbers over 500, one pack mixed; one pack which is easily 'shared evenly by two', etc.).

How to use the cards

All activities presume that the child has some knowledge of conventional numbers; if some of the examples seem too difficult, adjustment to easier numbers should not be a particular problem. Start with matching exercises:

– let the child name (i.e. 'translate' into conventional numbers) orally the hieroglyphic numbers, card by card;
– let the child match the numbers on the cards of both sets;
– give the child the conventional set and let him write down the corresponding hieroglyphics, card by card;
– vice versa: give the child the hieroglyphic set and ask him to write down the conventional numbers;
– if the child is used to working with quantity pictures (see Unit 4) these can be used for matching: give the child a set of cards with quantity pictures; give him also a card with a hieroglyphic number and ask him to build up the same number with his quantity picture cards. For example, for a hieroglyphic 333 the child will have to put down three separate cards with full hundreds and add one quantity picture with 33 (if these are not available, he may be able to draw them on squared paper and cut them out).

Sometimes such work can be made fun:

– give the child one card at a time from the hieroglyphic set and let him represent the same number in different arrangements and in colours that please him (i.e. let him make pretty patterns with them; let him cut out his 'pictures', let him mix them, match them or 'read' them to you or to a friend);
– play the game 'Memory' (also called 'Pelmanism') with both sets.

To play the game the cards of the two sets must look the same on all reverse sides; the cards are shuffled and laid out in neat rows on the table, each card separately and face down. The aim is to find a pair that matches.

The procedure is as follows: the first player chooses two cards and turns them over, with the other players able to see the two cards. If the two cards match, the first player removes them and collects them as his winning pair;

if they do not match, everybody tries to remember what they are and where they are. They are turned back over in exactly the position they were originally. The next player has his turn. The game ends when all cards are matched; the winner is the player who has collected the most pairs.

For younger children, or children with memory problems, the memory load can be made easier by creating two sets, each with one member of a pair; the two sets are laid out separately, with a clear space between the sets.

More formal work can follow. Start by giving the child the hieroglyphic set (at the beginning it might be advisable not to use the full set but only a suitable selection):

— *Simple sharing*: give the child the hieroglyphic set and let him share the number on the card (one after the other) evenly by two (either visually/orally, or by making new 'pictures'); start with 'easy-to-share cards' (e.g. 684 rather than 573).
— *Simple adding*: give the child the hieroglyphic set and let him add a given number in hieroglyphics (the same number for all cards); he will have to copy the number from the card and then add the new number symbols in a different colour. It is advisable to start with numbers that need no transgression over the 10- or 100-boundaries (e.g. 256 + 723 rather than 256 + 70); let the child read the 'number story' back to you;
— *Simple subtracting*: give the child the hieroglyphic set and let him 'take away' a given number by crossing out; he will have to copy the number from the card and then cross out the relevant number symbols. Again, start with numbers that need no transgression (e.g. 256 − 144 rather than 256 − 70); let the child read the 'number story' back to you.
— *More advanced sharing*: give the child the hieroglyphic set and let him share the number by three (by finger movement, or visually/orally, or by drawing 'pictures'). Start with numbers that are easily shared by three (e.g. 936 rather than 825); or
— give the child the hieroglyphic set and let him share numbers that involve exchanging symbols (e.g. 571 shared by two or three).
— *More advanced adding*: give the child the hieroglyphic set and let him add numbers that involve exchanging symbols (e.g. 137 + 89);
— *More advanced subtraction*: give the child the hieroglyphic set and let him 'take away' numbers that involve exchanging symbols (e.g. 137 − 89).

See Figure 2.3.21 for ways to exchange symbols and to transgress over symbol boundaries (e.g. over the 10- or 100-boundary). This is, of course, done much more easily when the symbols are actually handled than is suggested by the rather complicated looking pencil-and-paper figure.

A set of booklets (variation of the pack of cards)

Booklets can easily be made in various grades of difficulty. For example, each page shows about four to six hieroglyphic numbers (clearly separated by a horizontal line); each hieroglyphic is numbered right through the booklet for easy checking. The booklets can be used for most exercises suggested above with cards and are best used for consolidation. They provide plenty of material for independent exercises with hardly any new instruction required. It pays to make sure that the child uses the booklet as a 'textbook' rather than as an exercise book, so that it can be used again until it becomes too tatty.

Further suggestions

Using a tape recorder

If there is no time for supervising the child directly in oral work, a tape recorder can be used for recording the answers to be checked later (make sure that the child starts by saying the running number of the card or in the booklet).

Using transparent overlays

Sometimes a transparent overlay (the same size as the booklet) can be helpful. The child can then make his marks (added symbols, crossed-out symbols, division lines for sharing) onto the overlay with a non-permanent marker; he can then 'read-off' a page of finished work to his teacher or parent from his booklet with the overlay, or he can write the sum onto the overlay in conventional numbers; thus the overlay saves copying the hieroglyphics if such copying does not seem a valuable exercise in itself any more.

Translating numbers from one system into the other

Some 'translation work' has already been described in the exercises listed above in connection with operational tasks. However, I would like to emphasize the value of 'pure' translation work for children who feel particularly insecure with the way numbers are written in our abstract conventional system. Such children will benefit from translating numbers from one system into the other without having to do any arithmetical work with them. The 'semi-abstract' nature of the hieroglyphic system will help them to attach meaning to the conventional numbers.

Parallel work with Dienes blocks (or similar materials)

Sometimes, or with some children, there is a need for additional intensive work before the children are ready for formal number work. In this case a period of work using Dienes blocks (or similar materials) and hieroglyphic symbols in parallel can be beneficial. Such blocks mirror the hieroglyphics symbols exactly (see Chapter 1, Figure 1.19 for an illustration; see also this unit, below). Indeed, all exercises mentioned for work with hieroglyphics could in theory also be performed with Dienes materials. In practice, however, one would probably not have enough of the rather large and expensive Dienes pieces. Also, the attraction of working with a real historic system rather than with 'teaching' materials would be missing, a point which is especially valuable for older children.

Some exercises are given below to reinforce systematically the meaning of what a symbol stands for (e.g. one hieroglyphic coil for one 100-flat). They should be seen as a preparation for understanding our conventional recording system, where the 'symbol' for 'hundred' is 'nought-nought' (e.g. 'one hundred = 'one-nought-nought' = 100). In practice the suggested exercises will be limited by the stock of Dienes materials available:

— the teacher (or a child) builds up a number with Dienes blocks; the child (either the same child or a partner) puts down the same number with his hieroglyphic cut-outs;
— the teacher (or a child) builds up a number with Dienes blocks; the child (either the same child or a partner) writes down the number in hieroglyphic symbols;
— both exercises above can be carried out with partners exchanging roles;
— simple operations (adding, subtracting and sharing evenly) can be carried out in both systems, one as a check on the other.

The Chopstick Game

In Part One it was suggested that the game be used:

(a) with children who find it generally difficult to understand the nature of symbols and tokens (Chapter 1);
(b) with children who find it difficult to see the logic behind our money system, especially its arbitrary nature (Chapter 1);
(c) with children who have organizational problems (Chapter 2);
(d) with children who need practice in basic arithmetical skills, such as children with memory problems (Chapter 3).

Advantages

The game makes the child see that money is an arbitrary token system which can be changed as long as everyone agrees. It also puts the child 'in charge' by letting him set the value.

A variety of specifically targeted number skills can be practised during the game at a semi-concrete level (i.e. at the important intermediate stage between fully concrete work and fully symbolic work). And, last but not least, children seem to have continuous fun with the game.

Setting

The game is best played on a table with two or three players, one of whom must be a person competent in arithmetic (for a teacher it can be a diagnostic session; but it is also a good game to play with grandparents).

Materials needed to make the game

Any set of 'Pick-a-Stick' or 'Mikado' sticks can be used. The instructions here show how a larger set can be made with chopsticks. Figure 2.3.22 illustrates the materials needed to make the game:

(a) 42 chopstick-like sticks (chopsticks, or cut-to-size dowelling rods; or – for older children – toothpicks with sharp ends cut off);
(b) a container (a tall rectangular or cylindrical box or tin is best, preferably with a lid; if this is not available a bag with a drawstring will do).

One will also need some safe paints in four colours.

The sticks are coloured at one end. The distribution of colours suggested is as follows:

red – 20
yellow – 12
green – 6
brown – 3
multicoloured – 1

The sticks should fit comfortably into the container without leaving too much free space. They ought to protrude about 20 to 40 mm from the container so that they can be picked out easily. If there is a lid, this must be deep enough to let the sticks protrude when the lid is removed (see Figure 2.3.22). The bottom of the container should be fairly heavy so

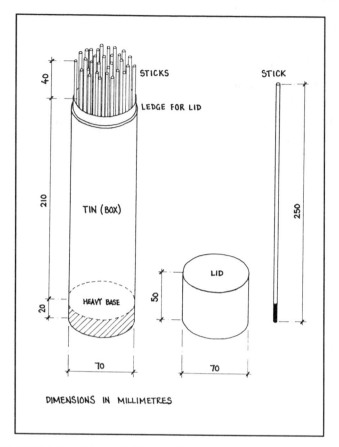

Figure 2.3.22: Materials needed for the Chopstick Game

Table 2.3.3: Examples of values for the Chopstick Game

'Standard' value		Mixed value: pence and pounds	
red	5 pence	red	2 pence
yellow	10 pence	yellow	5 pence
green	20 pence	green	20 pence
brown	50 pence	brown	£1.00
multicoloured	100 pence (£1)	multicoloured	£5.00
Pupil's naive (difficult) value		**Pupil's 'funny' value**	
red	$ 100	red	£100
yellow	$ 500	yellow	£50
green	$ 700	green	£10
brown	$ 900	brown	£5
multicoloured	$20000	multicoloured	£1

that the box can stand upright without tumbling over when the sticks are inside (a piece of hardwood or metal in the bottom might help).

Playing the game

The sticks can be introduced as some kind of 'desert island' money. At the beginning of each session one player (or the pair/group together) assigns a number-value to each colour. These 'values of the day' are written down for reference. For instance:

red   £1   (20 sticks)
yellow   £2   (12 sticks)
green   £5   (6 sticks)
brown   £10   (3 sticks)
multicoloured   £50   (1 stick)

The values can take any form: points, pence, pounds or dollars. For more examples of values see Table 2.3.3.

The sticks are now put into the container, with the coloured end down. In the first round, each player in turn takes two sticks from the container and adds up their value. The player with the highest value at the end of the round gets a plus point (or token); if it is a draw (all players end up with the same value) everyone gets a plus point.

Subsequent rounds are played in the same way as the first. The game ends when all sticks are taken out. The winner of the game is the player with the highest score.

Variations

Some variations are possible:
(a) The game can be made more difficult by taking 3 or more sticks at a time.
(b) The game will differ with each set of values; see Table 2.3.3.

Tips and thoughts for assigning values

Perhaps the following points will be helpful:

– Always write down the values for the day, so that one can refer to the agreed values during the game.
– Keep the written-down values; sometimes it will be nice to choose from the stock: 'Let's have Peter's value today'.
– It is a good idea to take turns in setting the values; when it is the teacher's turn, values can be set that reflect the current money system or that emphasize another teaching point.

- A pupil might sometimes set a 'funny' value, mostly one where the highest values are given to the most frequent colours (see Table 2.3.3). This can be seen as a mature idea if it is done as a 'joke' but often is set naively with a lack of understanding that the rarer colour should represent the more precious token. Children soon realize that it makes a dull game when most of the values are high. All this will provide a chance for a good discussion: why dandelions are never sold in flower shops and why roses are expensive; why diamonds and pieces of gold have such high values, and so forth.
- Children will normally soon learn that some values are 'hard' to add up (e.g. values with 7 and 9) and are therefore avoided in money systems.

Using a record sheet

If a child needs practice in matching the oral number word with written figures (or practice in just writing figures), one can use a prepared record sheet which the child has to fill in, as is shown in Figure 2.3.23 ('+' indicates the winner of a round; the score is the sum of the rounds that a player has won, so in the example the overall winner of the game is David).

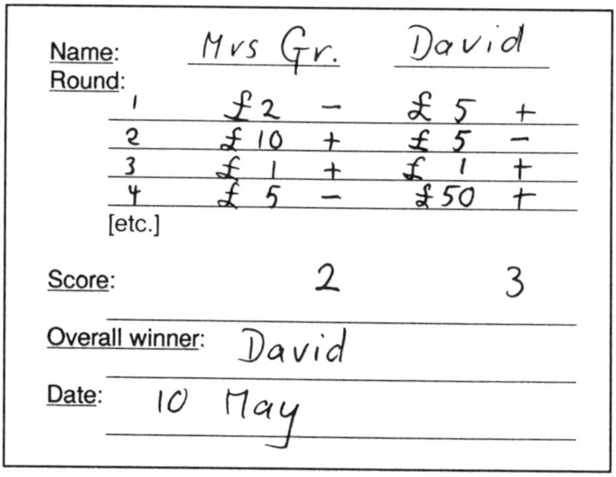

Name:	Mrs Gr.		David	
Round:				
1	£2	–	£5	+
2	£10	+	£5	–
3	£1	+	£1	+
4	£5	–	£50	+
[etc.]				
Score:		2		3
Overall winner:	David			
Date:	10 May			

Figure 2.3.23: Record sheet for the Chopstick Game

Other activities using sticks

1. *Adding up values of fairly large numbers of sticks.* This can be done individually as an exercise or as a partner game (who has the highest total of values?).

- Each player takes 10 sticks and adds up their values.

- Each player (two players only) takes half the total number of sticks (21) and adds up their values.

Both activities give the child the essential experience that one can have the same number of tokens but different end-values (i.e. neither a stick nor – in real life – a coin necessarily represents the unit of value).

2. *Sharing values evenly*. Such activities will contribute to arithmetical competence and again reinforce the insight that one token (stick) can be of a higher value than two, three, or more. The values of a handful of sticks are shared evenly by two, three, four. It should be emphasized that here it is the *value* one shares, not the number of sticks. This needs organizational skills like:

- sorting the sticks according to colours;
- starting with the highest value (good preparation for long division);
- exchanging a stick with a high value for two or more sticks with a low one (good preparation for 'borrowing' in written subtraction);

It is possible to add a social dimension to these activities:

- sharing between 'you, me and a charity of your choice'; the children will soon realize that sharing between three is a much more complex task than sharing between two;
- if one stick is left over, the child is encouraged to 'be kind to your partner', which means: 'if it is your turn to be in charge, your partner will get the extra one.'

3. *Use of sticks as tokens*. The sticks can be used for any game which needs tokens (or tokens of different values).

The Ruler Game

In Chapters 1 and 3 it was suggested that this game be used:

(a) when numbers are introduced (linking quantity with written symbols);
(b) with children who need to learn grouping strategies with low numbers (subitizing and minimal counting);
(c) with children who have general memory difficulties or specific labelling and word-finding problems;
(d) with children who need help with reading and spelling number words.

Setting

The game can be played with two to four players (the ideal situation is two players). One of the players must be competent in the skills required and must be able to act as a supervisor. The players sit at a table, facing each other.

Basic materials

There are three kinds of materials needed:

> a 'racing track' (ruler),
> counters in the form of cubes or rods, and
> a pack of cards with number symbols.

The materials can vary in some respects, depending on the version of the game played and its aims:

(a) The track may take the form of a 30 cm ruler; or a 1 m ruler; or some home-made rods (wooden strips of any desired length); or the length or width of the table;

(b) The cubes may consist of a heap of 1 cm³ cubes, perhaps from Dienes or Cuisenaire materials (or slightly bigger cubes for young or clumsy children, although these cubes must still be small enough for the child to take three cubes simultaneously with one hand); if preferred, selected Cuisenaire rods (including the unit cube) can be used, either right from the beginning or at a later stage. For older children a boxed set of materials combining a ruled track with all the cubes and rods needed is especially useful and attractive ('Computrack', for example);

(c) A large pack of cards is required (about forty cards or more). According to the children's needs the representation of quantities can vary; it may be pictorial (2 houses, 4 trees etc.); or it could be just dots; or the figure symbol; or written number word (see Figure 2.3.24). Later one can mix the sets and have a pack with all kinds of symbolic representations. A selection or a full set of a standard pack of playing cards is also suitable, especially with older children. The numbers represented on the cards of all sets can be selected and limited according to the needs of the child.

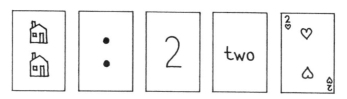

Figure 2.3.24: Cards for the Ruler Game (example 'two' from different sets)

First version of the game (beginners' version)

Aim

The aim of this version is to enable the child to recognize quantities from 0 to 3; to name those quantities; and to take those quantities simultaneously without counting.

Materials

Some preparation will be required:

– Take a 30 cm ruler and mark a clear line in the middle.
– Place the ruler across the table, one end close to each player.
– Sort out a pack of cards where there are only 'no', 'one', 'two' or 'three' objects (or marks). There ought to be several cards of each number, perhaps 10, but for motivational reasons only a few cards with '0'.
– Add one single card showing six objects (marks). This card ('lucky number') is only there to make the game more exciting, but incidental learning can take place (six as a 'double-three').
– Mix the cards and put them face down on the table.
– Empty a number of 1 cm³ cubes onto the table (not less than 15 cubes per player).

For a summary of the materials see Figure 2.3.25.

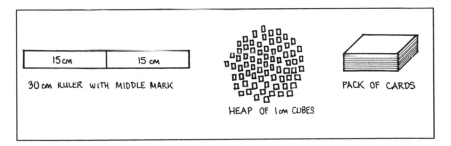

Figure 2.3.25: Materials for the beginners' version of the Ruler Game

Procedure

With the help of the supervising player the game proceeds roughly like this:

– The youngest player takes a card from the top of the pile, turns it over and names the number (number of objects/dots). He takes

the amount of cubes indicated by the card (simultaneously in *one go* with one hand, except for 'six', when two hands can be used) and places them neatly in a row along the right-hand side of the ruler, starting at his end of the ruler. He then discards his card face up on a new pile.
–   The second player does the same, starting at the opposite end of the ruler (i.e. his own end, see Figure 2.3.26).

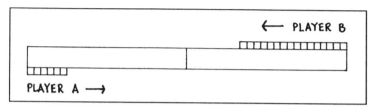

Figure 2.3.26: Positioning of cubes (Ruler Game, beginners' version)

–   The game ends when the cubes of one player reach the middle mark of the ruler; the player who reaches this line first is the winner.
–   If there are more than two players, two rulers are used.
–   The player with the least number of cubes along the track should be given the advantage of starting the next game.
–   If all cards from the original pile are used up, the pile with the discarded cards is turned over, shuffled and used as the next pile.
–   It is the task of the 'supervisor' to ensure that the number indicated by the symbol on the card is called out correctly and clearly, and that the right amount is taken.

Variations on the beginners' game

Lengthening the game

Depending on the children's ages and their ability to concentrate, the game could be lengthened by using the full length of the ruler (without a middle line), by using a longer ruler, or by 'racing across the table' (each player starts on his side of the table and aims to reach the other side). However, for motivational reasons a succession of short games is normally preferable to one long game because the chances of becoming a 'winner' are more evenly distributed. With older children one can divide the activity into 'sets' and 'games' by making a record of the 'sets' played. This means keeping a tally on a record sheet next to the player's name each time he is the winner, thus establishing an overall winner for the game of the day.

Different tracks

Instead of using rulers, a number of special tracks could be made by painting square rods of a suitable length in pretty colours or with patterns. Each player can then have his personal track; this will have an added attraction, especially for younger children.

Different cards

Instead of using cards with pictorial quantities one can use cards with other number symbols (figures, number words) according to the teaching aims; see Figure 2.3.24 above.

Alternative versions

Introducing a special rod as a 'unit of five'

If one plays with higher numbers (five and upwards) it is advisable to use a mixture of 1 cm^3 cubes and yellow Cuisenaire rods representing '5'. This helps the child learn to see 'six' as 'five plus one', 'seven' as 'five plus two' and so forth. The length of the track should increase as the value of the numbers on the cards increases. Again, it is fun to include one very high number (perhaps 20) as a special lucky card.

Using the full set of Cuisenaire rods

An excellent way of making children familiar with the values of the Cuisenaire rods for later work is to use the full set of rods. If one 'runs out' of one colour, children spontaneously seem to take the equivalent in rods of different colours. Some children like to 'go for' a specific colour or value (for example, they might like to have the whole track made in 'yellow'). This should not be discouraged since it makes for good 'swapping' exercises.

Learning to write the symbols

It is possible to use the game to reinforce the link between the written symbol and the quantity it represents by making a written record of each quantity that is put down. In this case it is best to prepare 'record sheets' beforehand onto which the child writes the figures (or number word) for both players.

Dealing with individual difficulties

It is possible to fit the game to children's individual needs by selecting particular cards (more of the ones that seem to cause difficulties). For

example the visual discrimination of 'four' and 'five' may need practising; or 'three' ought to be articulated more clearly.

Introducing 'minus'

It is possible to mix positive numbers with a few negative ones that
have to be taken off the track, thus introducing or reinforcing the
meaning of the symbols '+' and '−' (for motivational reasons there
should not be too many in each set, one is often enough).

Starting reading

Sometimes there is an older child who has totally failed to learn to
read. One wonders where to start. In such a case one can use the
game as a starting point for acquiring some first sight-vocabulary:
the written number words 1 to 10 or higher. The words will be
constantly linked to their 'meanings' since the pupil has to read and
immediately act upon what he has read by taking the right quantity
from the pile of rods. The ability to read these number words is
bound to be useful, and there is nothing 'babyish' about the reading
matter. Repetition is a natural requirement of the game. The game
can be made more attractive for older children by letting each player
choose the name of their race horse, which then appears on the
record sheet instead of their name. This idea came from a pupil who
happened to be a great fan of 'Silver Streak'; I have since used his
idea successfully with other pupils.

Teaching writing/spelling

If one has a child with specific spelling problems one can make him the
record keeper and insist that he writes out the entries of both players in
full. A record sheet might then look like the one shown in Figure 2.3.27.

```
┌──────────────────────────────────────────────────────────┐
│                                                          │
│  Name of player:___Anne___ Name of player:__Gary___     │
│                                                          │
│  Name of horse: Silver Streak Name of horse:_Red Rum_   │
│  ____four____            two_____                      │
│  ____six_____            twenty____                     │
│  ____one_____            one_____                      │
│                                                          │
│  [etc.]                                                  │
└──────────────────────────────────────────────────────────┘
```

Figure 2.3.27: Example of record sheet when the Ruler Game is played by an
older child with spelling problems

Andrew's idea

Andrew, an older boy with severe spelling problems came up with a further idea. After having used the game to learn to spell all the number words correctly, he was keen to go on playing the game. He convinced me that this would still make sense if he 'weighted' the words on his current spelling list of function words: for example, 'is' counted for 2 (easy); 'they' counted for 6 (difficult). Not only was this a rather sophisticated use of numbers, but it also demonstrates the popularity of the game.

In this case there must be a pack of cards with 'spellings' to be learned – perhaps 10 words coming up several times; and possibly a reference list with the assigned value of each word.

Cuisenaire Rods, Dienes Blocks and Similar Structured Materials

Cuisenaire and other rod systems have been part of elementary mathematics teaching in mainstream and special education for more than four decades up to this day. They were frequently recommended in Part One for children with problems in symbolic understanding, with organizational problems, and with memory problems.

Cuisenaire rods

Description

The rods consist of sets of white 1 cm^3 cubes and nine different unsegmented but colour-coded rods of various lengths (length × 1 cm × 1 cm), where the length and colour represent the number (e.g. 3 cm light-green stands for 3). Table 2.3.4 gives the details.

Table 2.3.4: Cuisenaire rods (dimension and colour)

1 cm cubes: white	6 cm rods: dark-green
2 cm cubes: red	7 cm rods: black
3 cm cubes: green	8 cm rods: brown (tan)
4 cm cubes: pink (crimson)	9 cm rods: blue
5 cm cubes: yellow	10 cm rods: orange

The rods were devised in the early 1930s by Georges Cuisenaire (schoolmaster and later Director of Education) in Thuin, Belgium. His idea stems from the notation of musical scales where certain tones have specific relations to each other. He substituted colour for sound to express relations between numbers. Thus there is, for instance, a 'chord' of 2/4/8 indicated by colours based on a red pigment (a chord of 3/6/9 based on blue; 5/10 on yellow). The materials were 'discovered', explored and have been made public in many countries since the 1950s by the untiring efforts of Caleb Gattegno (then a lecturer at the London Institute of Education).

The original sets were made from hardwood. Now they are only available in plastic (for suppliers see Appendix). There are similar rods on the market, sometimes with slightly different colour codes and mostly linked to somewhat different didactic ideas (e.g. 'Colour Factor rods', and 'Computrack' set).

General use

Although these rods were originally meant as educational materials, I think they are still a 'best buy' as a Christmas present for home use. In my opinion, free play, pattern-making and construction work with the rods is beneficial at all levels, up to adulthood. I believe that any child who is able to handle the smallest parts (1 cm^3 cubes) would benefit from free or guided play with them at an early age and would thereby absorb a feeling for quantities and their relations.

Note, however, that according to the CE and USA Toy Safety Regulations, children under three years should not play unsupervised with the smaller pieces as there is a choking hazard. Therefore, unless supervision is guaranteed, one would to have to take the 1 cm^3 cube and the 2, 3 and 4 cm rods away until the child is old enough.

More structured use

For more formal teaching the rods can be used in the systematic ways suggested by Cuisenaire and described in various publications by Gattegno (e.g. 1963a and b). The importance given to colour varies with the different systems. Nowadays the systematic use of colour as an aid to early mathematics is in debate (e.g. see Resnick and Ford, 1984: 120). However, a child using the coloured rods in free play may unconsciously absorb the system and be able to use it as an aid (e.g. for memory or understanding relations). My own point of view can be summed up thus: in general it seems better not to make systematic use of colour at the beginning, but if one sees a child responding to it, it may be worth picking up the response and making the child more conscious of the relations indicated by the specific colour choices.

Organization

I suspect that the reason why the materials and their didactic advantages have been neglected to a certain extent might have to do with the organizational difficulty of keeping all the parts under control in large classrooms. A full box makes a terrible clatter when it is upset and a child's attempt to pick up all parts again is likely to result in the neighbour's set being knocked down. This is a serious drawback but it can be overcome by organizing the full sets into selected smaller sets if they are wanted for specific teaching purposes.

For use with individual children or with a small group of children, however, the full box with its tray of special compartments is in itself a teaching tool. Tipping the rods out and replacing them into the various compartments in the course of different games promotes familiarity with quantities linked to their word labels. It also fosters manual dexterity. There is always a feeling of satisfaction and achievement when all the pieces are back in the box, in their right place and with nothing missing.

Examples of use

Here are two examples where a special selection of rods is used for specific purposes (work with numbers from 1 to 100):

1. *Number building box*. Each child has a box with the following rods only (15 pieces):

> one 50-piece (made-up flat)
> four 10-rods
> one 5-rod
> five unit-cubes.

The 50-piece can be made up of 5 ten-rods, held together with an elastic band of appropriate size, kept flat; or it could be made by sawing a Dienes 100-flat into two equal parts (see the section on Dienes materials below).

With this selection any given number between 1 and 100 can be built up (on the desk in rows of 10 on an imaginary 100-square, i.e. in the fashion of the 100-bead abacus). For an illustration see Chapter 1, Figure 1.2.

2. *Halving box* Each child has a box with the following rods only (20 pieces):

> nine 10-rods
> two 5-rods
> nine unit-cubes.

With this selection any number up to 100 can be built up and then halved; Figure 2.3.28 shows the halving of 84 and 57; the difference in the halving of even and uneven numbers will have to be discussed.

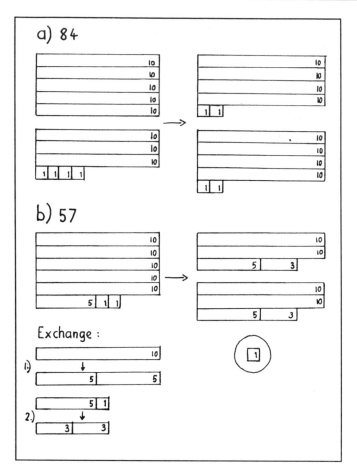

Figure 2.3.28: Halving even and uneven numbers with a selection of rods (example: a) 84; b) 57)

At the beginning the halving is performed by the actual separation of the two parts; the two equal quantities are then named. Later it can be done visually: the child looks at the built-up number and runs his finger round half the quantity while naming it. Halving uneven numbers manually may involve 'swapping' some pieces. For instance, in order to halve 57 one would have to exchange one 10-rod for two 5-rods, and if one has built up 7 as 5 + 2 one would have to exchange the 5-rod for units. One will end up with one unit as 'rest'; perhaps the concept and label of ½ can be introduced here.

When children are more familiar with the process of halving, one can ask them to say or write the full 'story' in appropriate forms (e.g. 84 halved gives us two 42s; or 84 shared evenly by two means . . .; or 84 divided by two . . .; or 84 = 42 + 42; or 42 + 42 = 84).

'Doubling' of a number can be done with the same set, but only for numbers under 50.

Dienes materials

Dienes materials have been used in elementary mathematics for decades. Their use was suggested in Chapter 1 for children who have problems in symbolic understanding. A basic set of Dienes materials was shown in Chapter 1, Figure 1.19.

> The materials are the products of Zoltan B. Dienes, who was influenced by Piagetian theory and worked with Jerome Bruner at Harvard. His concern was the relevance of concrete materials for young children's mathematical learning and he has written extensively about his ideas and the use of his materials (e.g. Dienes 1959, 1964; for an overview see Resnick and Ford, 1984: 116 ff.).

The original Multibase Arithmetic Blocks (MAB) materials in plain hardwood are still on the market, but there is also an extended plastic version available. This can be bought in a multi-colour version, or in wood-coloured plastic to go with existing wooden stocks. The name in the UK seems to have changed to 'Multibase' (see, for instance, the NES Arnold UK catalogue).

The basic base-10 set consists of

1 cm^3 cubes (representing 1)
10 cm × 1 cm × 1 cm 'longs' (representing 10)
10 cm × 10 cm × 1 cm 'flats' (representing 100)
10 cm^3 cubes (representing 1000)

There are also base-2 to base-5 sets available in wood (base-2 to base-6 sets in plastic only). This means that – if one includes the base sets – rods are available from 1 cm to 6 cm, plus a 10 cm rod. A special feature of the materials is that all pieces have scored grooves on one side which give 1 cm segmentations and add to versatility in use.

In general, as with Cuisenaire rods, the value of the materials lies in their adaptability for all kinds of teaching purposes, from using the different coloured base blocks as first building blocks for pre-school toddlers to intensive work on different base systems. The most unconventional use I have made of this was probably as a clumsy embodiment of our current money tokens to show a child with lack of symbolic understanding how practical our paper money is (see Chapter 1, Figure 1.19).

Stern materials

Stern blocks also come in unit cubes and number rods. The dimension of the unit is larger here (¾ inch). The blocks are coloured and scored and are part of a set of apparatus called 'Structural Arithmetic'. The full materials and their possible highly structured uses are described in Stern (1971). The materials come with very neat, specially designed boxes and trays which show the careful thought given to organization.

Alternatives

If one hesitates to invest in such sets it may be possible to make them up out of single linking cubes that may already be part of the school's stock (e.g. 'Multilink Cubes' which come in 10 different colours similar to the Cuisenaire colours). In this case I suggest that one decides on a fixed colour code system and adheres to it. One should not be tempted to produce individual multi-coloured rods because they will give unnecessarily diffuse images of the quantities they stand for.

One can also make rods by cutting up (and perhaps scoring) wooden lengths of 1 cm squares as sold in most hardware shops.

In any case, before one thinks of ordering an expensive set for school use or before starting to making one's own, I suggest that one looks into the darkest corners of the school's storeroom. There might be a slightly incomplete dusty set of Cuisenaire rods left on the shelves, probably made of fine wood and in subtle faded colours, ready for use.

Unit 4

Understanding the Decimal System

The Slavonic Abacus

The abacus can be used at many levels, from the very first pre-school activities with any toddler up to preparatory and consolidating work on mental arithmetic with children of secondary school age – especially those who are in need of visual support. In Part One it was recommended for work with children who have problems with symbolic understanding (Chapter 1), or with organizational tasks (Chapter 2), or who suffer from a memory deficit (Chapter 3).

Description

The Slavonic abacus (sometimes called the Russian abacus) is a didactically well-thought-out version of the bead frames one can find in toy shops. There are 100 movable beads in two colours, strung horizontally on rods, so that 100 is grouped in rows of 10 times 10 beads. The actual activity consists of isolating various quantities by pushing them from one side to the other.

The apparatus is turned into a mathematical aid – superior to the common play version – by the use of the two different colours, which are so arranged that any quantity between 1 and 100 can be 'subitized' (i.e. recognized at once *as a whole*). The colours provide the important sub-grouping of five both horizontally and vertically: on the first five rows the first five beads start with one colour and the second five are of the second colour. This then changes in checkerboard fashion so that rows 6 to 10 start with five beads of the second colour (see Chapter 1, Figure 1.3). This makes subitizing of quantities over five possible.

Advantages

Working with the abacus is truly 'multi-sensory' work. Language, vision and active handling are all involved, the latter especially reducing anxiety and aiding concentration (cf. Hatano, 1982; Sharma, 1995).

Further, the beauty of the apparatus is that quantities are never seen in isolation but always in the context of 10 or 100 and that, with the help of the visual break at five in both directions, every number can be identified as a whole. Thus, 'seven' is learned visually from the very beginning as:

'five-and-two' = 'three-missing-from-ten'.

Moreover, all 'complementary numbers' up to 100 can be 'read off' the abacus simultaneously:

if 25 is shown by pushing 'two-times-ten-and-five' to the left, the complementary number 75 can be seen as 'fifty plus two-times-ten-and-five' on the right (see Figure 2.4.1).

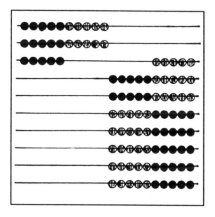

Figure 2.4.1: Complementary numbers 25/75 on the Slavonic abacus

Numbers are thus seen as two-dimensional geometric shapes: as 'quantity pictures' rather than as points on a visually fairly unimpressive number line.

The way in which the Slavonic abacus uses the 'natural' break at the number 'five' is important: in recent systematic Japanese studies this number has been shown as the 'privileged anchor' for young children when they start to work with numbers (Yoshida and Kuriyama, 1991).

Such findings have found their application in Japanese teaching by 'suidou-houshiki' (the 'water supply method'), here known as the Japanese 'AMI (Association of Mathematical Instruction) Method of Tiles' (Ginsburg,

1989: 203), where cardboard or plastic squares ('tiles') are used and where the '5-unit tiles' are one of the main cornerstones. This corresponds with my suggestions of using only a selection of Cuisenaire rods (i.e. 1-, 5-, and 10-rods) for some teaching (see Chapter 1 and Unit 3).

Finally, the Slavonic abacus is a manipulative apparatus for elementary mathematics which comes in one piece rather than consisting of many small parts, as most good materials for early number work do. It means that there is no clutter, no lost parts, organization is easy and there is no time-consuming clearing. This is certainly an advantage that every infant teacher will soon recognize; it makes the apparatus especially useful for quick consistent daily sessions.

How to make a Slavonic abacus

Adapting an abacus that has been bought

The easiest way is probably to buy a toy abacus with 10 × 10 horizontally arranged beads, and then paint the beads so that the colours show the characteristic distribution of the Slavonic abacus. The two colours should be similar but distinctive (e.g. tone-in-tone red rather than bright red and white). If the colours are too different the *gestalt* of a number is somewhat spoiled and the visual impact weakened.

Making a wooden abacus

It is not too difficult to make an abacus. Whatever the dimensions, there is one crucial measurement to consider – its width. The rods between two uprights should be double the length of 10 beads pushed together. This ensures that there will be room enough to give a clear visual image, not only of the number the child is asked to push aside, but also, simultaneously, of the number which is its complement to 100 (e.g. 25 is pushed away and 75 is clearly left to see; see Figure 2.4.1; also Chapter 1, Figure 1.3). If the rods are not long enough, the two numbers will visually merge into each other. Such clear, simultaneous exposure of the two numbers at an early age will help to establish a firm knowledge of complementary numbers, knowledge which is of especial value when one has to give or receive money in change.

The following is an example of a 'cutting list':

base board: 36 × 10 × 2 cm;
two uprights: 31 × 5 × 2 cm;
10 dowelling rods: 34 cm long with a diameter of about 6 mm (depending on the hole in the beads);
100 beads (16 mm).

The uprights can be either set into the base board (in this case: add thickness of base board to length of uprights) or screwed on from the underside (countersunk) of the base boards. The beads are painted as outlined above (best done before assembling!).

Note that wooden beads are not cheap. If one wants to make more than one abacus for group work, one could buy a bead cover used over car seats. There will be enough beads for several pieces. It may, however, be necessary to adjust the dimensions of the abacus to the beads.

Making an 'executive' abacus for older children

Sometimes an older pupil may consider work with a bead frame 'babyish'. One should then point out that many adults in Russia, Japan and China still use a form of abacus and that an experienced abacus user can rival a computer in speed and accuracy. One can also make a smart smaller version of an abacus by using metal nuts (50 brass nuts and 50 steel nuts) and paint the wooden structure black. It is important to counteract the weight of the metal nuts by using fairly heavy hardwood for the base.

Safety regulations

According to European and United States safety regulations, any child *under three years* of age ought to be *supervised* when playing with a normal-sized abacus because the beads can come off and become a 'choke hazard'. This applies to all types unless there are no screws and the beads have a diameter of at least 35 mm. On a personal note, I would not deprive any child under three from playing with an abacus, but I would certainly supervise the child.

How to use the Slavonic abacus

The actual activity consists of isolating various quantities by pushing some beads from one side to the other. As an introduction, a young child should spend a period playing about with the frame, pushing beads along for fun, discovering or making patterns.

After such a 'playing about' period one ought to start work by establishing the habit of always starting an activity with all beads on one side.

- The following descriptions will be fairly difficult to follow, unless one actually has an abacus at one's side.

It is debatable whether one should start with all beads on the right or with all beads on the left. If at the beginning all beads are on the left, one pushes them across 'with the grain' as it were – from left to right, as in writing. However, the quantity picture emerging on the other side will then appear in the reverse order from the one commonly used when writing and drawing. I therefore prefer to start with all beads on the right, which will make the quantity emerge as it would when writing or drawing quantities in a conventional way, although the pushing movement will be from right to left. In the end one can use both ways, which will add to flexibility in perceiving numbers, but at the beginning and with very impaired children it is best to use only one. A child sometimes shows a preference for one way or the other at the experimenting stage; if one intends to work individually with the child rather than in a group, one could adopt his method, at least at the beginning.

Examples of activities

The order of the exercises suggested here is only meant as a guide and ought to be adjusted according to the child's experience.

It is assumed that some less structured work with counters has already been done. All exercises can be followed by more of the same kind before a new kind of exercise is started (i.e. they can be repeated with different numbers; for instance, where I use '3' in the first example, the exercise can be adapted and used for all numbers up to 9 or 10).

In the following, the two different colours or colour tones are called 'Colour A' and 'Colour B'; brackets indicate what should be discussed or what one can expect the child to do or to say.

Numbers from 1 to 10

– Start with all beads on the right

   Show 3 (i.e. push three to the left).

   Show 3 on the next row.

   And the next – and the next – (etc. up to the tenth row).

– Push all the beads back to the right (or better: let them slide with a nice click by lifting the left-hand side a little).

   Show 3 again.

   Show 3 on the next row.

   Show 3 on the next – up to the fifth row.

– Look along the rows you have just done.

   How many 'Colour A beads' are there on the right on each row? (2)

   How many 'Colour B beads' are there on the right on each row? (5)

How many altogether on each row? (Yes, 2 and 5 = 7.)

Show 3 and 7 down to the tenth row.

– Leave your 3s where they are, push the 2s in the middle, leave the 5s on the right.

Say what you see. (3 and 2 = 5; 2 and 5 = 7; 3 and 7 = 10.)

Slide all beads back to the right.

Thus all complementary numbers to 5 and to 10 as well as individual number bonds can be practised as shown above. If a child counts individual beads, let him do so at the beginning. He will tend to give up doing so by about the third row. Encourage him gently to move quantities of beads simultaneously, 'the fast way', all the time.

Working with full 'tens'

– Start with all beads on the right

Let's count in tens (push full rows of ten from right to left, starting at the top and counting: one ten, two tens, three tens, etc.).

It is advisable to continue to call tens 'tens' for some time – for example 'two tens' rather than 'twenty'; however, if the children mention the 'proper names', these can be used in parallel since their meaning is constantly emphasized through the visual representation of the beads that are handled. One can actually use the exercise to introduce the 'proper names' if and when this is wanted.

– Let's count the tens back into their places (push full rows of ten from the left back to the right while counting).

Count down in rows of tens again (from right to left). Let's have a 'rest' after 'five tens'. Look at the beads (the colour scheme is reversed). Let's go on with six tens, seven tens, eight tens...

– Let's now count them back from bottom to top; the bottom row is now 'one ten'.

It is tempting to let the child count them backwards too (going upwards with: ten tens, nine tens, eight tens, etc.). I would avoid such counting at this early stage because the bead picture that the child will see while handling the rows is somewhat confusing: one sees eight tens on the left while saying nine tens and handling the nine tens row.

– Let's make patterns of two-tens (two tens on the left, two tens on the right, two tens on the left, etc.); see Figure 2.4.2a below.

How many two tens? (5)

How many 5s in two tens? (4)

- Slide all beads back to the right.

    Can you make a different pattern of two tens?

Some other patterns are given in Figure 2.4.2b and c.

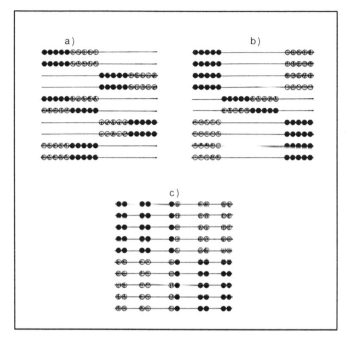

Figure 2.4.2 a – c: Examples of patterns with 20 on the Slavonic abacus

- Have we still got 5 'two tens'? (We must have, because . . . : we always have the same number in our frame – 100).

Perhaps this is the time to introduce the number word 'hundred' if it has not been done already.

- Slide all beads back to the right. Let's start again:

    Count in two tens, using two fingers.

    Count in three tens; try to use three fingers.

    What happened? (there's one ten left).

- Count in five tens: try to use your hand, or a long pencil, or a small ruler.

    What can you say about five tens?

- Make patterns with full tens.

If it seems suitable, all patterns made on the abacus can be 'recorded' with dots in two colours on pre-cut squared paper, to take home or to make a collection.

Dividing the field of 100

In some of the work with full tens, 100 was divided into five sets of 'two tens'. This can also be done with numbers other than full tens. The one that springs to mind first is 25. A child who has seen 100 broken up into 25s on the abacus will perhaps have a picture of it in his mind for the rest of his life and will always know that $4 \times 25 = 100$.

– Show 50 on one side, 50 on the other.

Divide each 50 into two parts (there are two obvious ways of doing this: either two tens and five; or 5 times 5: discuss both).

– Make 40s (again, there are two ways).

How many 40s in a 100? What is left?

How many 5s in a 40?

Some numbers are obviously more suitable than others for such work. As a more advanced example, Figure 2.4.3 gives some symmetrical patterns (a and b) and some unsymmetrical ones (c and d), showing 12 in 100. Such exercises are an excellent way to provide natural repetition in number bond skills. Again, the work can be recorded on squared paper as pattern pictures and, at a later stage, in figures as an equation (100 divided by 12 equals 8; 4 left).

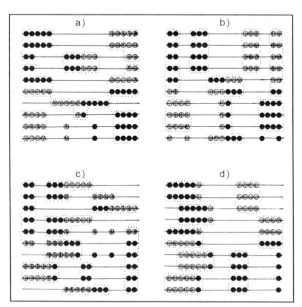

Figure 2.4.3 a–d: Patterns of 12 in 100 on the Slavonic abacus (8 × 12 and 4 single beads left)

Note: the patterns become clearer when shown on an actual abacus, especially if the beads are tone-in-tone colours

Working systematically with number bonds 1 to 10

Knowledge of number bonds from 1 to 10 is essential for all mental arithmetic which does not rely fully on memorization; here it is practised on a visual basis which one hopes will result in useful mental pictures. Such work can be done using the first line of the abacus only. For young children it may be worth making a special 'first-line-abacus' with ten large beads. Start with all beads on the right (this is not essential here but one might just as well establish the habit).

(a) Number bonds of ten (complementary numbers)

- Show 2.

   What is left? (expected answer: 3 'Colour A beads', 5 'Colour B beads'; 8 altogether; 2 and 8 = 10).

   Show 8: (two left: 8 and 2 = 10).

   Show any number you like, I tell you what is left.

   I will show any number I like and you tell me what is left.

   Let's do the same again but now at 'high speed'.

If this has been done on a 'first line abacus', the teacher should now change over to a full abacus where each row is used as a 'first line'; ensure the child understands that one is looking at each line separately now, rather than at the field of 100.

- I'll make ten number stories adding up to ten, you read them off (e.g. 3 + 7; 5 + 5; 8 + 2; 2 + 8; etc. until all ten rows are divided in two parts).

   Read them off 'the other way round', starting from the right.

   You make some, I'll read them off.

Such sets of ten stories can be recorded on paper, either as coloured dots, or later in figures. One might get the odd little joker who makes ten stories of the same kind. This should be taken as a good joke and good practice of the one specific number fact, but if he does it again, tell him that it is really a bit boring and you expected all sorts of stories in a set of ten.

(b) Working with full 'tens' again

One can now do some exercises of the kind shown under number bonds above, but here with full tens:

– Show 2 tens.

How many tens up to 100? (20 and 80 = 100).

(c) Number bonds with a break at five

This is to some extent a repetition of the exercise above ('show 7'). But now the child is asked to look at the larger of the two complementary numbers and to 'break it up in 5 and the rest'. The child will probably have done this more intuitively in the exercises above; now it is practised systematically, either on the full abacus or on a 'first line abacus'; thus the exercises are all done in the 'frame of ten' with two numbers in focus and a third (complementary) simultaneously perceived (e.g. 10: $5 + 2 = 7 \rightarrow 7 + 3$).

In the following instructions the phrase '3 Colour A beads' stands for something like '3 red beads' or '3 dark beads': thus, in practice, the work will be less complicated than it may appear in the answers below:

– Show 8.

Tell me what beads it is made up of (3 'Colour A beads', 5 'Colour B beads'; 8 = 3 and 5; or if one looks at it from different sides: 3 and 5 = 8; or 5 and 3 = 8).

In these cases, where 'five' is one of the components, the colours are a definite help. This may be different in other cases, as shown in the next exercises.

– Show 8.

Break it up into two colours again (5 and 3).

Can you break it up in different ways? Try it (e.g. starting with four: 4 and 4 = 8; 2 and 6 = 8).

This can be done with all numbers and with full tens. Verbal or written work can take various forms. Something like the following can be 'read off' the abacus and recorded on paper.

$4 + 4 = 8$; $8 + 2 = 10$; $4 + 4 + 2 = 10$

$2 + 6 = 8$; $8 + 2 = 10$; $2 + 6 + 2 = 10$

$30 + 40 = 70$; $70 + 30 = 100$; $30 + 40 + 30 = 100$

Complementary numbers to 100

Knowledge of the complementary numbers to 100 is again an essential part in applied mental arithmetic, such as giving or receiving change out of a decimal money system like the US dollar, or the British pound.

By showing any number on the Slavonic abacus one can 'read off' the complementary number from the bottom. This was done with full tens above; now it will be done with numbers in between. For instance:

–   Show 46 (4 tens and 6 more).

    How many are left on the right? (go upwards, starting with the full tens and then looking at the rest, i.e. 54).

    100 = 46 and 54, or

    46 and 54 = 100 (see Figure 2.4.4)

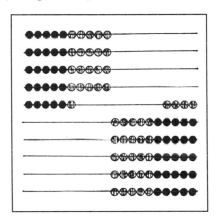

Figure 2.4.4: A pair of complementary numbers in the field of 100: 46/54

Work can then be done as above, for example:

–   I will show you a number: 81.

    What is the other number you can see on the abacus? (Answer: '19')

    Together they make a hundred; say them both (Answer: '81'/'19')

This can be practised in short daily sessions with any number between 1 and 100. At one stage the child can be encouraged to close his eyes after a first quick look and read the complementary numbers off his 'mental abacus'. One can also cover the right-hand side with a piece of cardboard or cloth, expose a number on the left and let the child 'guess' the number left behind on the right. In the end it should be established that, while the units always add up to 10, the tens add up to 9 tens (why?). Perhaps some extra consolidation work with complementary numbers to 9 (i.e. unit bonds of 9; tens bonds of 90) will be of help at this stage.

Adding (mainly single digit numbers which transgress the 10-barrier)

Adding single digit numbers under 10 is so obviously easy that I will concentrate on additions that transgress the 10-barrier.

This is the beginning of trying to establish a 'standardized' method of early mental arithmetic with the visual support of the abacus. The suggested procedure is as follows:

– Show 64

> We want to add 8. Push 8 into the middle. You have to go over two lines.
>
> Check that you have eight (6+2=8; or – checked with the help of the colours: 5+3=8).
>
> When you are sure you've got 8, push them towards the 64 in two movements; say what you are doing and what you see (64 add 6 = 70; add 2 = 72).

Thus the 'standardized' verbal version should be something like:

> 64 add 8
>
> 64 add 6 = 70
>
> and 2 = 72.

This could in the end be contracted to the verbal (and finally mental) version of:

> 64 add 8: 70 → 72

If one wants to work with a parallel written version one could start as follows:

> 64 + 8
>
> 64 + 6 = 70
>
> 70 + 2 = 72

This means that the child becomes increasingly familiar with number bonds. They can be checked by looking vertically at the triplet of 8/6/2. I would insist on good organization of the written version on paper, with the plus and equal signs lined up and with the use of a small ruler for underlining the question and answer. I think it is worth spending some time making children write all number work neatly right from the beginning. They will understand the reason if it is explained that checking is essential in all number work, and that this is made easy when things are neat (cf. Whitburn, 1995: 358).

Subtracting (mainly single digit numbers which transgress the 10-barrier)

This can be done the same way as adding:

– Show 64.

 We want to take away 8. Push 8 into the middle. You have to go over two lines.

 Check that you've got eight (4 + 4 = 8).

 When you are sure you've got 8, push them to the right and away from the 64 in two movements; say what you are doing and what you see (64 take away 4 = 60; take away 4 = 56).

Thus the 'standardized' verbal version should be something like:

 64 take away 8
 64 take away 4 = 60
 60 take away 4 = 56.

In the end this can be contracted verbally to:

 64 minus 8: 60 → 56

The parallel written version would be:

 64 − 8
 64 − 4 = 60
 64 − 4 = 56

The same vertical check of the triplet (here: 4/4/8) should be made.

  With this the possibilities on the Slavonic abacus are probably almost exhausted, although some limited multiplication and division work is possible. It would make sense now to go over to the two-dimensional paper abacus, on which all the work suggested above can be consolidated. The aim is still to build up a 'mental abacus' in the child's mind that can represent arithmetical work inside the decimal system. Further work is also possible, which is better done with the paper abacus than with the Slavonic abacus (like adding and subtracting full tens to and from any two-digit number, e.g. 28 + 10; 47 − 30; also 47 +/− 35; 47 +/−39). However, if the child is keen, occasional work with the beads on the Slavonic abacus is appropriate as a relaxing consolidating activity. A description of the paper abacus (how to make it and how to work with it) is given in the next section.

Paper Abacus

The paper abacus can take the place of the Slavonic abacus described in the previous section when such an apparatus is not available. It can also consolidate and extend the work on the Slavonic abacus. Likewise, it can be used as a new starting point for older children who have failed to understand the decimal system. It was recommended in Part One (Chapters 1, 2 and 3).

Description

The paper abacus is a two-dimensional adaptation of the Slavonic (bead) abacus It consists of two parts: a square card with 100 dots and a coloured or clear transparent overlay (acetate). The 100 dots are arranged in rows of ten with a break at five in both directions. The overlay is cut in such a way that any quantity from 1 to 100 can be exposed (see Chapter 2, Figure 2.2).

Advantages

Work with the paper abacus is based on the same principles as work on the Slavonic bead abacus and it shares most of its didactic possibilities. It lacks the appeal of movable beads and the pattern-making possibilities, but this is compensated for by the following advantages:

    it is less bulky;
    it makes no noise;
    it is easier and cheaper to make so that every child can certainly have his personal abacus;
    it can be on hand at all times (kept flat in the child's exercise book);
    and, most of all, in certain ways it is mathematically more flexible, as will be shown below.

How to make a paper abacus

The base card with 100 dots

Figure 2.4.5 shows a home-made card that can be photocopied.

> The break at 'five' is shown through a gap. The photocopy with the dots is cut out and glued on a somewhat larger card. To enhance the appeal of the abacus, this can be coloured and can show the child's name or can display a small appealing sticker to mark it as the child's personal one. It is advisable to cover the finished card with transparent self-adhesive film. If one wants to make a more elaborate version, coloured self-adhesive round dots (roughly the same size as those used for marking library books) can be used, but with only one colour per card. Any drawing or sticking of the dots must be precise (mark out lines for the position of the dots!).

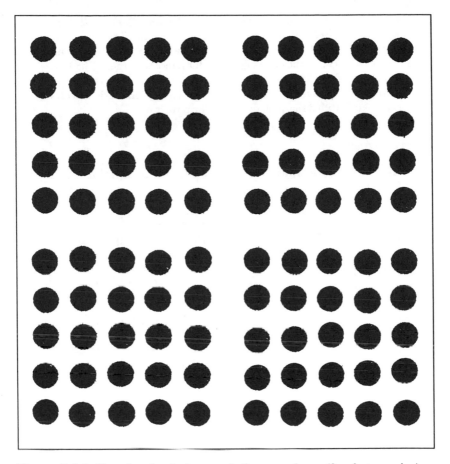

Figure 2.4.5: Template for the base card of a paper abacus (for photocopying)

The overlay

This is made of clear acetate sheeting. I have cut up coloured acetate pockets, which are easily available, but any transparent sheeting can be used. The measurements are crucial here; they must be precise and be related to the size of the dots. I will give the measurements for the base card as shown in Figure 2.4.5.

(a) *Width*: the minimum width of the overlay is twice the area covered by the dots, which in the example means twice 10 cm. It is advisable to add about 2 cm on each side so that the child can hold the overlay on both sides without obscuring the dots (perhaps more space could be allowed for younger children). In all cases it is good to reinforce both sides with folded Scotch tape or similar material to make the handling area stronger.

(b) *Height*: the minimum height is 10 cm to cover the dots. This means that an overlay for the 100 dots shown in Figure 2.4.5 is 24 cm × 10 cm, including 'handles'.

(c) *Cut*: the cut is made on the left-hand side (see Chapter 2, Figure 2.2). It has
to be fairly precise, so that it can expose one row of the dots clearly. In the
example here it is 1 cm deep and half the width long (i.e.10 cm long, or
12 cm if one includes the extra allowance for handles on the left-hand side).
The right angle in the middle of the cut must be as true as possible. It
should be marked out with a sharp pencil; the cutting can be done with scis-
sors or a knife with a sharp blade along a firm ruler.

A 'smart version'

For older children a smart version may be more suitable (see Figure
2.4.6).

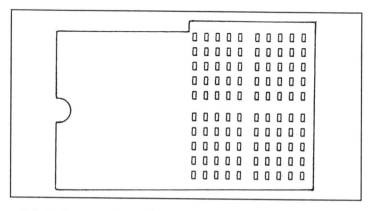

Figure 2.4.6: 'Smart version' of a paper abacus

It is made as follows:

The 100 dots are made with the help of a computer. They ought to cover a
square of about 85 mm; see Figure 2.4.7 which is suitable for photocopying.
    The square is cut out and glued on a piece of white card. Again, it is
advisable to cover the card with clear self-adhesive film. The card should
just fit into a small plastic pocket (160 mm × 115 mm for A6 cards), which
comes with an opening on one of the smaller sides and normally with a
semicircle cut out as a grip-hole on the open side. The pocket is used as the
overlay. The cut is made accordingly. Here it is 8 cm long (i.e. half the
length), starting at the open (left-hand) side, and 7 mm deep. When
cutting, both sides of the pocket are best cut simultaneously. This results in
an additional opening half way down one of the longer sides, adjoining the
original opening.

In order to expose a quantity, the pupil takes the card out of the
pocket and works with pocket and card in the way described below.
For storage the card goes back into the pocket. This unobtrusive set
can be kept in the pupil's maths book. The pupil should be encouraged to use it whenever he needs to check or to work out a number
problem visually.

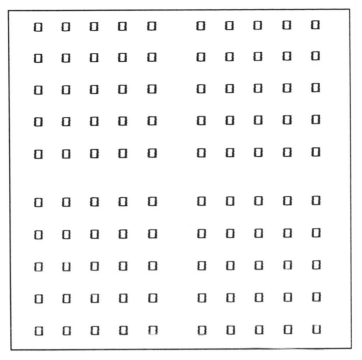

Figure 2.4.7: Template for a base card: 'smart version' of a paper abacus

Working with a paper abacus

Setting

At the beginning of the session the child puts the card on his desk and holds the overlay with both hands at the ends; the side with the cut-out is on top towards the left. He puts the right-hand side of the overlay over the dotted square, covering all dots, now ready to expose any number by sliding the overlay towards the right along the row (exposing units), or downwards, row by row (exposing tens), or both (i.e. first along and then down, exposing tens and units).

I will give one example in more detail, followed by a full list of possibilities in key sentences only. Some of the exercises will be similar to those listed in the section on the Slavonic abacus and the section on quantity pictures.

The following example shows how one could work with one number (number 25). It assumes teacher-directed group work, but individual work can proceed in the same way. For individual introductory work it is best if the teacher or other carer sits beside the child with her own paper abacus, which will allow the child to imitate the adult and the adult to check the child's work.

Example:25

The teacher takes the lead:

– Show 25 (the child shows 25).

   What is 25 'made of'? (the child responds with 'two tens and one five').

   Go to the next full ten. How many do we need to get to the next full ten? (5)

   What is the next full ten? (30)

   Can you say it in a whole sentence, starting with 25? (25 and 5 more 'gets us to 30'; or: 25 plus 5 equals 30)

– Show 25 again. How many do we need to 100? (75)

   Can you say the sentence? $(25 + 75 = 100)$

   Go from 25 to 55. Do it the quick way (the child slides down three rows and sees 55 exposed).

   How many rows of ten did you slide down? (3)

   Can you say the sentence? Twenty-five + . . .? $(25 + 30 = 55)$

– Show 25 again. How many 5s can you see in your 25? (5)

   Look at your covered 75. How many 25s can you see? (3)

   Can you say the sentence about 3 times 25? (three 25s make up 75; or: 3 times $25 = 75$; or: a 75 has three 25s)

   How many 25s can you see in your 100? (4)

– Let us count in 25s (the child shows and says: 25/50/75/100).

   Let us count in 5s. We will have a bit of a rest after each 25-station (the child shows and says: 5/10/15/20/25 – rest; 30–35 . . . and so forth, up to 100).

Similar exercises in the field of 100, focusing on one number at a time, are especially suitable for short daily exercises.

The following is a collection of exercises for the teacher to choose from. The order of the exercises is to be taken as a guide; however, those in the section on identification should be done first as an introduction, so that the child is familiar with the 'field of 100' before being asked to do arithmetical operations in it.

In contrast to the example with 25 above, it is assumed here that each exercise on the list is explored with a variety of suitable numbers before the next exercise is tackled. The number '64' is chosen randomly.

Identification of numbers

The teacher (or any other supervising carer) sits next to the child (children), each with a paper abacus.

1. Teacher   says: show 64

   Child   shows 64 and repeats number; checking is done by looking at teacher's abacus.

2. Teacher   shows 64 and says: look what I have.

   Child   shows 64 on his abacus and names it.

3. Teacher   shows an Egyptian number (only if such numbers have been used).

   Child   shows the same number on the abacus and names it.

4. Teacher   shows written number word 'sixty-four' (only if the child has learned to read it).

   Child   shows the number on the abacus and names it.

5. Teacher   shows written numeral 64 (only if the child is familiar with conventional written symbols).

   Child   shows the same number on the abacus and names it.

Operations (approximate order of difficulty)

The following examples will be given increasingly in outline. It is essential to remember that verbal input by teacher and verbal repetition by pupil should be as extensive as possible (as spelled out above in 'identification of numbers').

1. $6 + ? = 10$ (for complementary numbers to 10)

   For the child this means: show 6, look at remaining quantity on first row and say '6 and 4 is 10'; or '6 plus 4 equals 10'

2. $60 + ? = 100$ (for complementary numbers to 100)

   For the child this means: show 60, look at remaining quantity and say '60 + 40 = 100'

3. $64 = ?$ $(60 + 4$ i.e. analysis of numbers)

   show 64 and say something like: 'sixty-four means six tens and four more'; or '64 is made up of 60 and 4'

4. $64 + ? = ?ty$ $(64 + 6 = 70$ i.e. filling up to the next full ten)

   show 64 and look for the answer: $\ldots + 6 = 70$

5. $64 + ? = 100$ (complementary numbers to 100)

   read picture from bottom upwards (36)

The pupil should now realize that the units always add up to 10 but the tens to 90.

6. 50 + 10 = 60 (adding 10)

   go down one row

7. 60 − 10 = 50 (subtracting 10)

   go up one row

8. 64 + 10 = 74 (adding 10 to a number with 10s and units)

   down one row

9. 64 − 10 = 54 (subtracting 10 from a number with 10s and units)

   up one row

10. 60 + 11 = 71 (adding eleven to full tens)

    one row (ten) down, one place (unit) forward to the right

11. 60 − 11 = 49 (subtracting eleven from full tens)

    one row up, one unit backwards to the left

12. 64 + 11 = 75 (adding eleven to a number with tens and units)

    see item 10

13. 64 − 11 = 53 (subtracting eleven from a number with tens and units)

    see item 11

14. 64 + 3 = 67 (adding units within the row)

    go forward to the right

15. 64 − 3 = 61 (subtracting units within the row)

    go backwards to the left

16. 5 → 10 → 15 → 20 etc. up to 100 (counting in fives)

    go forward in fives (pattern emerges!)

17. 2 → 4 → 6 → 8 etc. up to 100 (counting in twos)

    go forward in twos (pattern!)

18. 4 → 8 → 12 → 16 etc. up to 100 (counting in fours)

    go forward in fours (pattern goes over the 10-boundary)

19. $60 + 9 = 69$ (adding nine to a full ten)

    down one row $\rightarrow$ 70; and one unit backwards to the left $\rightarrow$ 69

20. $60 - 9 = 51$ (subtracting nine from a full ten)

    up one row $\rightarrow$ 50; and one unit forward to the right $\rightarrow$ 51

21. $64 + 9 = 73$ (adding nine to a number with tens and units)

    as item 19: down one row $\rightarrow$ 74; one unit backwards to the left $\rightarrow$ 73

22. $64 - 9 = 55$ (subtracting nine from a number with tens and units)

    as item 20: up one row $\rightarrow$ 54; one unit forward to the right $\rightarrow$ 55

23. $64 + 7 = 71$ (adding *with* transgression over the full ten (in three or two steps))

    (a) knowing or finding out the complement to full 10 (6),

    (b) decomposing 7 into 6 + the rest (1),

    (c) adding the rest, i.e.:
        show and say: $64 + 6 = 70 \rightarrow$ (think: $7 = 6 + 1$) show and say: $70 + 1 = 71$; or, faster, show and say: plus 6 $\rightarrow$ 70, plus 1 $\rightarrow$ 71

24. $64 - 7 = 57$ (subtracting *with* transgression over the full 10 (three or two steps))

    show and say: $64 - 4 = 60 \rightarrow$ (think: $7 = 4 + 3$) show and say: $60 - 3 = 57$;

    or, faster, show and say: minus 4 $\rightarrow$ 60, minus 3 $\rightarrow$ 57.

25. $64 : 2 = 32$ (32/32: sharing an even number evenly by two – halving visually)

    30 for you, 30 for me; 2 for you and 2 for me: each 32

26. $65 : 2 = 32\frac{1}{2}$ (33/32: sharing an uneven number evenly by 2 – halving visually)

    30 for you, 30 for me; 3 for you and 2 for me (be kind to your partner): 33 for you, 32 for me

27. $74 : 2 = 37$ (37/37: sharing a number with uneven tens evenly by 2 – halving visually)

    30 for you, 30 for me; 5 for you, 5 for me (35 each); 2 for you, 2 for me: 37 each

28. $32 \times 2 = 64$ (doubling a number less than 50 *without* transgression over a new 10)

    add the same tens (30) $\rightarrow$ 62; add the same unit (2) $\rightarrow$ 64

29. $36 \times 2 = 72$ (doubling a number less than 50 *with* transgression over a new 10)

    add the same tens (30) $\rightarrow$ 66; add the same unit (6) in two steps:

    $66 + 4 = 70; 70 + 2 = 72$

30. $64 + 23 = 87$ (adding a number with tens and units *without* transgression)

    down two rows $\rightarrow$ 84; 3 units forward to the right $\rightarrow$ 87

31. $64 - 23 = 41$ (subtracting a number with tens and units *without* transgression)

    up two rows $\rightarrow$ 44; 3 units backwards to the left $\rightarrow$ 41

32. $64 + 27 = 91$ (adding a number with tens and units *with* transgression over 10)

    down two rows $\rightarrow$ 84; 6 units (i.e. complement to 4) to next full 10 $\rightarrow$ 90; forward 1 unit (analysis: $6 + 1 = 7$) $\rightarrow$ 91

33. $64 - 27 = 37$ (subtracting a number with tens and units *with* transgression over 10)

    up two rows $\rightarrow$ 44; backwards 4 units to full ten $\rightarrow$ 40;

    backwards from full 10 by 3 units (analysis: $4 + 3 = 7$)

    $\rightarrow$ 37

Once the child has understood the procedures and reached some proficiency with the paper abacus, these exercises ought to be done in short daily sessions. It is hoped that in the end the child will have developed a 'mental abacus' which can help him in all mental arithmetic, either to solve elementary problems or to check memorized arithmetical knowledge. The following section on quantity pictures provides consolidation work.

Quantity Pictures

Quantity pictures were suggested in Part One for use with children with difficulties in symbolic understanding and in organization (see Chapters 1 and 2). The pictures aim at making the decimal system accessible through visual means. Their main use is for work with numbers 1 to 100, but they also have their place for work up to 1000. The materials can be used independently or for extending and consolidating the work done on the Slavonic abacus and the paper abacus (see above).

Description

As the name suggests, the materials are 'pictures' of quantities. The quantities are presented in the 'field of 100' (i.e. in a decimal order), mirroring the Slavonic abacus with its rows of ten and the visual break after five in both directions. The pictures can be easily drawn on paper and stuck on cards or presented in booklets. Figure 2.4.8 shows a quantity picture of 64 (see also Chapter 1, Figure 1.4 and Chapter 2, Figure 2.1).

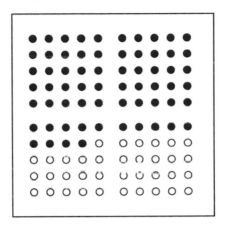

Figure 2.4.8: Example of a quantity picture (64) in the frame of 100

Advantages

The pictures make it possible to work in yet another way with quantities in the structured frame of 100. Whereas the Slavonic and paper abacus display changeable quantities, quantity pictures show only one particular quantity, fixed on paper, ready for use by the child, with or without assistance.

Sets of about 10 to 20 cards with a single quantity picture lend themselves to many activities. They can be used for games and matching exercises as well as for individual arithmetical paper-and-pencil work at different levels of difficulty.

'Sums' can be practised in all forms, with at least one part of the equation still represented in such a way that the child cannot forget what the number symbol stands for. They thus provide a mediating tool between concrete and more abstract numerical written work. The materials – booklets as well as cards – are easily stored and managed; they can be renewed or extended as the need arises without much effort or cost. The work can be fast, involving a minimum of writing.

How to make sets of quantity picture cards

The easiest way is to use computer print-outs of the kind shown in the previous section (Figure 2.4.7).

> The dots of a particular quantity are coloured in with a felt-tip, either dot by dot, or – perhaps later or after intensive work with the Slavonic or paper abacus – with full tens and full fives as single transparent lines drawn through the dots with a highlighting pen. The pictures are then cut out and glued on slightly larger cards (making a frame of about 1 cm around the picture) and preferably covered with thin self-adhesive transparent film for durability.
>
> Alternatives:
>
> (a) 5 mm squared paper with the breaks at five represented by a line of empty squares in both directions; or
>
> (b) photocopies of the template shown in Figure 2.4.9; this will give larger cards which are perhaps better for the younger child.

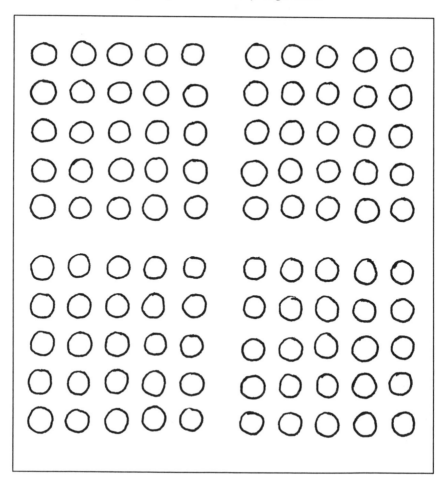

Figure 2.4.9: Template for large quantity pictures (blank)

In all cases it is advisable to mark the top of the cards in a way that shows where the top is, even when they are face down. Cutting the right-hand corner off diagonally is a good way to do this. In order to be able to check written work easily it may also be helpful to number the cards; it is best not to do this on the back of the cards, in case the cards are used for the game of 'Memory' (see below). One ought to have various sets for different purposes.

Examples of sets and their specific use

Single sets

These are sets of about 20 cards each, showing quantities more or less randomly chosen from 1 to 100. Some sets should include all full tens and some zero and hundred.

They could be used for

(a) supervised identification of numbers: the child looks at the quantity and names it;
(b) supervised 'speed identification': when the pupil has reached a certain level of proficiency he names the numbers against the clock (a daily record can be charted so as to make progress obvious);
(c) ordering by size of quantity (checked by supervisor at the end);
(d) semi-formal arithmetic (i.e. starting from a quantity picture): adding/subtracting a given number; halving and doubling (for details see below under procedures).

Sub-sets of single sets (sets with special selections of quantities)

Such sets may be helpful for semi-formal arithmetic. One may want a set with low units so that one can add a given number without transgression over ten (e.g. 64 + 5); or one set with high units (68 − 5); or with low tens (24 + 60); or with quantities under 50 (doubling). However, I have found that if extensive work has been done beforehand with both the Slavonic and the paper abacus, such a selection is not always necessary since the pupil has learned to cope with exceptions. For example if the child comes to a number problem that is not within his experience (perhaps a card showing 24 and the task is to subtract 30), he can just draw a line instead of giving an answer.

Procedures for semi-formal arithmetic with single sets

The cards are first put into the proper order (from 1 to x). The child is then given a number that he is asked to add or subtract (or with which he is to perform any other task). Only the number of the card and the answer are written down (see Figure 2.4.10). It is advisable to have prepared answer cards with which checking or self-checking can take place quickly.

	No.	Quantity shown	Given task	Written answer
a)	1 2 3 etc.	24 3 99	add 6	1. = 30 2. = 9 3. = 105 (or: = over 100)
b)	1 2 3 etc.	24 3 99	subtract 6	1. = 18 2. = -3 (or: --) 3. = 93
c)	1 2 3 etc.	24 3 99	halve	1. = 12 2. = 1½ 3. = 49½
d)	1 2 3 etc.	24 3 99	double	1. = 48 2. = 6 3. = 198 (or: over 100)
e)	1 2 3 etc.	24 3 99	make your answer 50	1. 24 + 26 = 50 (or: +26) 2. 3 + 47 = 50 (or: +47) 3. 99 - 49 = 50 (or: -49)

Figure 2.4.10: Examples of work with quantity pictures

Double sets

These consist of 20 cards, ten of which show randomly chosen quantities, from 1 to 100, drawn in one colour. The other ten show the same quantities but are drawn in a different colour (if one wants to economize, it is possible to use 10 cards of a standard single set and make an identical set in another colour; the drawback of this is that cards have to be sorted out more frequently).

These can be used for:

(a) matching; or
(b) playing the game of 'Memory' ('Pelmanism').

A full description of the game was given in Unit 3 above. One ought to remember that for young children or children with memory difficulties it is best if the second set has the quantity pictures stuck on card of a different colour from the first set; the sets are then put on the table in two parts and each turn includes one card of each colour.

This eases the demand on memory. The level of difficulty can also be monitored by the number of cards in the set. It is important to insist on the clear naming of the quantity at each exposure.

Special matching sets

Each set consists of two sub-sets; one is a selection of quantity pictures, the other is a set of cards which have to be specially prepared or selected to be matched to the first (i.e. the task is different from just matching quantity picture with quantity picture as described above). I suggest the following sets:

(a) a set with complementary numbers to 100 (e.g. if the first set contains a quantity picture of 25, the matching set must contain a quantity picture of 75);

(b) a set of matching number words (e.g. if the first set has a quantity picture of 64, the matching set must have a card with 'sixty-four' in letters);

(c) a set of matching number figures (e.g. if the first set has a quantity picture of 50, the matching set must have a card with '50' as a figure).

The sets could be used for the following:

(a) matching (as with all matching tasks, young children will get special satisfaction from the feeling of having successfully completed a job when they see that the last pair 'fits');

(b) playing the game of 'Memory' (Pelmanism) which can be quite demanding with these sets, especially with complementary numbers.

Task card sets

These are sets of cards with arithmetical tasks; each set has its own level of difficulty. Some examples are shown in Figure 2.4.11. One gives the child a card with a suitable quantity picture (e.g. 64 which incidentally could be used for all four cards shown in Figure 2.4.11) and asks him to perform the tasks listed on the task card.

Difficulties can be controlled through the choice of the card and also through the choice of the quantity picture. It is advisable to number the tasks and let the child likewise number the tasks in his answers. This will make checking the work easier. However, in order to avoid the child spending precious learning time on mere writing, one could have heaps of small pre-printed sheets ready with the numbers of the tasks (1 to 10) on them. Then the child only has to write the answers next to each number.

	card a)	card b)	card c)	card d)
No:				
1.	+4	+20	+27	+12
2.	+6	-20	+19	-54
3.	-2	-50	-55	halve
4.	+3	+30	-27	-36
5.	-4	-60	-36	+36
6.	+2	-40	+28	+20
7.	+1	+10	-17	+18
8.	-1	+ 0	+17	-44
9.	-3	- 0	-48	-43
10.	+5	-10	-15	+ 8

Note: for all examples the quantity card from which to work is assumed to show 64
Key:
a) Tasks involve units only; no transgression over ten
b) Tasks involve full tens only
c) Tasks involve tens and units with transgression over ten
d) Mixture of all

Figure 2.4.11: Examples of task cards showing different levels of difficulty

Booklets

Booklets with quantity pictures are recommended to complement the sets of cards. They can be used in some of the ways outlined above, but I suggest using them mainly for short regular revision work as paper-and-pencil exercises. The tasks can be assigned spontaneously according to the needs of the day, for example:

Write down the number for each picture.

Find the complementary number to 100.

Add 20 to all numbers.

Take 17 away from all numbers.

Double all numbers.

Make the answer 44.

Working with Blank 100-Squares

The use of blank 100-squares was specifically suggested in Chapter 2 for children with organizational difficulties. Work with such squares aims at enabling a child to build up a clearly structured image of the 'field of 100' as a representation of the decimal system, and to link the cardinal aspect of numbers with the ordinal. The squares are easy to make and expendable. They are also useful as a grid for making quick number sketches.

How to make blank 100-squares

To make blank squares one will have to cut squared paper into 10 × 10 squares. The individual squares must be big enough for a child to write a two-digit number into each with ease. The square is then divided into four equal parts by a horizontal line and a vertical line (both should be fairly strong).

Examples of exercises

The place is given, the number has to be found

The blank is prepared with marked squares (e.g. outlined with colour) and the child has to write the appropriate number into each marked square (Figure 2.4.12 gives examples of such prepared squares).

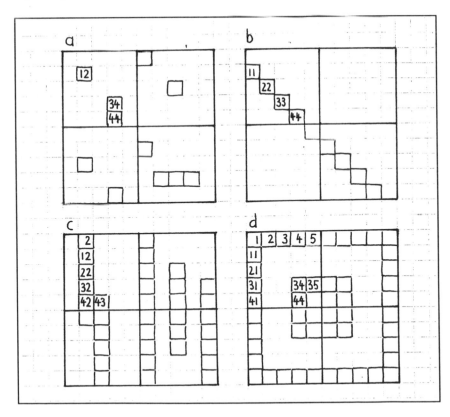

Figure 2.4.12 a–d: Examples of blank 100-squares with marked positions to be filled in

The number is given, the place has to be found

The child has to write the given numbers into the appropriate square on the blank:

(a) give a set of random numbers (e.g. 5, 19, 23, 40, 56, 76, 81, 82, 99);
(b) give a set of numbers not quite so randomly (e.g. 11, 22, 33, 44, etc; or: 2, 12, 22, 32, 42, etc.);
(c) ask the child to fill in all even (or odd) numbers; or all numbers that can be evenly shared by 10 or 5, and perhaps 4 or 3;
(d) ask the child to fill in all numbers which contain the figure 5 (i.e 5, 15, 25, 35 45, 50; 51, 52, 53, etc.).

'Testing' (for fun and to increase competence)

These are further exercises of the type given above, but without pre-marking. They need closer supervision, because some clever Dick (or his female counterpart), if left alone, would rightly think of easier ways of doing them, which would limit their value as 'tests': The instructions would be something like this:

(a) let's go back one by one and row by row (100, 99, 98 etc. to 91; 90 to 81; and so forth, ending with 1);
(b) let's go clockwise around the outside of the square, starting with 1 (ending with 11);
(c) let's go around anti-clockwise, starting with 1 (ending with 2);
(d) let's zig-zag down the square from one line to the other – no 'jumps' – but going one row from left to right, next row from right to left, next one left to right, and so forth. (i.e. starting from left to right with 1, 2, 3 up to 10; from 10 down to 20 and backwards right to left with 19 to 11; from 11 down to 21 and forwards left to right with 22, 23, etc.);
(e) let's go around in circles: starting with an outer frame (as under (b) above); then filling in one inner frame after the other, until we come to filling in the last four numbers in a solid square (i.e. 45, 46, 56, 55);
(f) 'the ultimate': let's go like a snail's house, starting at 45 and going 46, 56, 55, 54, 44, 34, 35, 36, 37, 47, and so forth, until we end up at 1 with the outer squares on three sides left empty.

After such supervised exercises the 'real' test can take place. One now wants to find out if the child can fill in a full 100-square correctly. If enough practice has been given, this should be easy. It is advisable to repeat such tests at regular intervals, perhaps every first day of a new month, or the first day after each holiday.

Transparent Overlays for Place Value Work

The transparencies are meant for pupils who find the place value system difficult to understand. They were suggested in Chapter 1 for children who have difficulties with symbolic understanding; they would also be useful for other children doing advanced work.

Description and advantages

Let us assume that a child wants to write down a number like 'one thousand and twenty-four' in figures. He might be tempted to follow the oral pattern. Thus he writes first '1' and then '24' ('124') which means he omits the 'place value marker' nought for the empty 100-column. With the help of the transparencies the child can overlay and 'build up' the number from its components (1000 + 20 + 4). When he looks at the superimposed transparencies he may realize the necessity of 'nought' as a place marker.

Chapter 1 describes how to use this teaching aid. The following is just a description of how to make a full set.

Materials

One will need:
(a) about four sheets of fairly stiff clear acetate (the stronger kind of transparencies for overhead projectors are suitable);
(b) a black permanent marker pen for writing on acetate;
(c) some coloured marker pens (likewise permanent) or some small round self-adhesive stickers ('dots'); four or five different colours are needed.

How to make the overlay

My suggestions are:

(a) Cut some 45 small rectangles of about 10 cm × 5 cm (the overlays). Only 37 will actually be needed for the set but it is a good precautionary measure to have a few spare ones in case some get lost or are spoilt during preparation. The cutting can be done with a paper trimmer or guillotine.

(b) Mark the right-hand bottom corner with a coloured dot, either with a marker pen or with small self-adhesive coloured stickers, making sure that the dots are in the same position on all overlays. One will need to mark nine overlays with each colour: for example, nine with a yellow mark for the numbers 1 to 9; nine with a blue mark for the full tens 10 to 90; nine with a green mark for the full hundreds 100 to 900; nine with a white mark for the full thousands 1000 to 9000; and one with a red mark for 10,000. Figure 2.4.13 gives an example of such a marked transparency.

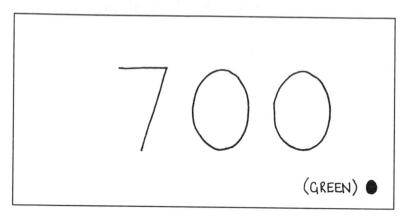

Figure 2.4.13: Example of transparency in actual size (with coloured mark in right-hand corner)

The purpose of the coloured marks on the right is twofold: they ensure that the transparencies can be easily positioned exactly one on top of the other, and the colour coding makes it easier for the child to find a number with a certain value.

(c) Write the figures on the transparencies with the black marker. It is best to start with 10,000. This figure is then taken as the 'template' for the position of the other figures. It is important that all figures are correctly positioned. For example, the tens must occupy the same place as the two last noughts on the 10,000 transparency.

(d) In order to be able to build up any number (up to 19,999) one will have to write nine units-transparencies, nine tens-transparencies, etc.

If one works with a child who has severe difficulties, an additional set of 'blanks' can be helpful (e.g. an overlay with '000' and a green mark for 'no-hundred'). For an example of both, the four single components and the overlaid number 1024, see Chapter 1, Figures 1.9a and b. Although it is advisable to make the full set in one go, it is of course possible to use only a selection of the overlays (e.g. up to 100 or 1000), depending on the child's need.

Unit 5
Money and Time

The 'Money Machine' (A Practice Game)

This game can be used when a child or a group of children need to consolidate their skills in adding up various amounts and different values of money coins. It is designed as a means of 'overlearning' such skills on a daily basis in an efficient but playful way. It was especially suggested for that purpose in Chapter 1.

Advantages

The 'machine' is a means of supplying a small number of money coins at random for children to work with. It differs from other ways of supplying money values randomly (e.g. commercially available money cards, money dominoes, money dice sets) in that the work can be done by actually handling individual coins (mostly play coins). In this respect it is closer to reality than money cards, money dominoes and dice, which show pictures on card in a fixed selection or, as in the case of the dice, give the values in figures (e.g. 2p, £1). Thus work with the money machine can be considered an intermediate step in levels of abstraction, and it would make sense to start with the somewhat clumsy machine and go from there to cards and finally to the dice with figures.

This intermediate step is especially valuable for children with problems with symbolic understanding. In controlled home or therapy sessions one could use real coins if it is considered beneficial to the child.

Setting

The game can be played with two or more players; however, as in most educational games, the smaller the number of players, the more frequent the turns and the greater the practice value. One of the players must be competent in adding up money and should be able to act as a supervisor. The players sit around a table.

Description of the apparatus and how to make it

The machine may strike the reader as a rather weak 'Heath Robinson' affair, but I can guarantee that it works. It consists of a tube, two 'stoppers' and a lid or cork (see Figure 2.5.1). One will also need some plastic playing coins.

(a) *Tube:* This should be about 30 cm long with a diameter slightly larger than the diameter of the largest coin (e.g. 3 cm for a British 50p piece). At the bottom end there must be two slits halfway through the tube. One slit is fairly near the bottom and the other is about 2 cm higher than the first.

(b) *Stoppers:* Two flat pieces of plastic are inserted into the slits. These should fit easily into the tube, go at least halfway through the tube and protrude about 4 cm (see Figure 2.5.1).

(c) *Lid:* The other end of the tube (top end) should be closed with a lid or a cork.

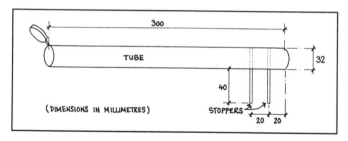

Figure 2.5.1: The 'money machine' and its parts

Scrap version

This can be made as follows:

Take a cardboard tube (e.g. middle of a roll of kitchen paper);
find a cork to fit the tube;
cut two slits at the bottom end (see above);
find or cut two small thin plastic pieces to fit through the slits.

Procedure

Both stoppers are fully pushed in and the tube is randomly filled with a collection of play money coins. The lid is closed.

The first player pulls out the top stopper, shakes the tube and puts the top stopper back. There are now some coins trapped between the two stoppers. The player removes the lower stopper which results in the trapped coins falling on the table. The 'fall-out' is added up and the lower stopper replaced.

It is now the next player's turn to do the same. The winner is the one with the highest fall-out. When the tube is empty, it is simply refilled. Players are encouraged to check each other while adding up.

Variation

For more mature players who can cope with longer games and can lose fairly gracefully, one can keep a record (in writing or with tokens) of the number of winning 'fall-outs' for each player (not the actual sums at this stage, because that would involve long additions). Thus one finds the overall 'winner of the day'. The game ends when the tube is empty. In this case one has to ensure that the number of turns is equal (sometimes some fall-outs of the last round will have to be nullified).

Using Supermarket Bills to Develop Money Skills

As the title suggests, the materials are meant for children who need practice coping with early money skills (see Chapter 1). Using such bills has the advantage that they are easily replaceable and can be adapted to many levels of arithmetical skills. However, some reading skills are desirable.

Description of materials

Supermarkets normally issue receipts which give a detailed, sometimes abbreviated list of items bought, together with their prices. For our purpose, these are cut up into single item strips, and the rather small bits of paper are then glued on cardboard strips large and strong enough to be handled with ease (e.g. 2 cm × 8 cm).

One can select items with different children and different uses in mind, for example:

(a) only those that are dear to a child's heart, for example:

NUTTY BUN LOAF £0.62;

(b) those that are familiar and make easy reading, for example:

RED APPLES £1.25;

(c) those that are of special 'advanced' interest and sometimes fun to puzzle out, for example:

P-NUTS-RAISIN £0.59;

(d) those where the amount is an easy number (e.g. £1.50; £0.40).

The cards may have to be updated as prices go noticeably up (or down). Some children may like to bring their own bills from home to be cut up and used.

Example of activities

Introduction with quantity pictures

With less advanced children one could start as follows:

(a) Select items below £1 and glue them onto a larger card which also shows a quantity picture of the same amount as a visual prop (for 'quantity pictures' see Unit 4). These cards can be used for the operation described below (addition, etc.).
(b) Make a set of cards with quantity pictures only; these must corrrespond to prices as shown on some 'item-and-price cards' (e.g. P-NUTS-RAISIN £0.59); the child matches the selected cards of the item-and-price set with the quantity picture set.

Addition

This could take different forms:

(a) Put item-and-price cards into a bag (or into a wide box, face down). The child picks up two cards at random and adds up the prices of the two items.
(b) Prepare as above. The child picks up three (or four or five) cards, adds up the prices and perhaps checks with the calculator.
(c) Leave the bills whole as they come or cut them up into chunks of about 10 to 15 items. The child then picks three or more items as his 'own shopping list' and works out the price.

Estimation: how much money to take

The child picks up two, three or more item-and-price cards, estimates the likely cost (at first in discussion with carer) and decides how much money to take (rounded up, for example 50p, £1, £5 – not more than necessary). A calculator can be used to check the estimate.

Working out the change

In theory, this can be done in two ways, by subtraction or addition. For example, when the price is £0.64 and the money handed over is £1.00:

subtraction: 100p – 60p (= 40p) – 4p (= 36p): 36p; or
addition: 64p + 6p + 30p (= 100p): 36p.

The child should understand both ways, but one way should in the end be practised as the 'standard' method. Addition is perhaps preferable, since it is the way used by most shopkeepers; it is also the way by which children who are familiar with the Slavonic abacus will find change easiest to work out because they can visualize the procedure.

It is important to stress, especially to children who have a weak memory, that working out (and remembering) the *higher values* correctly (e.g. the tens or full dollars or pounds) is more important than getting the pennies right.

(a) Select some item-and-price cards so that the set only contains items costing less than £1. The child works out the change from £1, if necessary with the help of the Slavonic or paper abacus. For example:

> price 72p: + 8p + 20p = 28p; or:
> I must get more than 20p back.

Perhaps it is worth reminding the child at this point that in all cases of mixed tens and pence the complementary tens add up to *nine* full tens and not, as the pennies, to ten. For example, when the child hears 'seventy...', or sees '72', he should ignore the units for the time being, think immediately of 70 and its complementary number to 90 (i.e. 20) – and know that he must get at least 20p back.

(b) The child works with a mixture of prices that have not been pre-selected. Some can be higher than £1. For example:

> price £3.72; handed over £5:
> £3.72 + 8p (remember 8) = £3.80; + 20p (remember 20) =
> £4; + £1 (remember £1) = £5;
> change: £1.28; or:
> I must get more than £1 back.

List of Unconventional 'Timers'

The use of unconventional 'timers' was suggested in Chapter 1 for children who find the concept of time hard to grasp. The following is a list of 'natural' non-standard timers that could be used to help children understand conventional clock time.

The difference in precision should be pointed out, with the 'sun-timer' perhaps seen as a link between the modern precision clock and 'non-standard' timers. By their nature, the latter should be accepted as being somewhat imprecise and erratic. Any variations in the times shown by 'natural' timers when the same activity is repeated should thus not strike the child as unsatisfactory or confusing. In the case of older children one could repeat an activity with an imprecise 'natural timer' three or more times and find the average.

It is hoped that the following examples may help to generate other ideas that are more suitable to individual circumstances.

Suggestions

(a) *Snail trail.* If one is lucky enough to have a snail track in the playground, field or garden one could watch the snail progressing. While some children play, others take turns observing the snail getting from a point A to a point B. There is, of course, a risk that the snail may change course; it is thus advisable to agree beforehand that the length of a string rather than the straight line from A to B should be the measure. One could use the completion of the track as the sign that the playing session has come to an end or that it is time to go home; in this case the carer should have had a trial session to find out how long roughly the string should be, otherwise playtime may never end.

(b) *Dissolving a sugar cube.* An activity ends when a cube of sugar has dissolved in a glass of water; this takes about 15 minutes if the glass is shaken now and then, over an hour if left undisturbed.

(c) *Flattening of soap bubbles* (produced previously in a bowl).

(d) *Escaping air:* one day from a balloon with a tiny hole, the next day perhaps from the inner tube of a bicycle tyre.

(e) *Water dripping:* from a bottle partly blocked with a cloth (outside or set in a bucket); or from a dripping tap into a jar (set in a bucket) until the jar is full.

(f) *Siphoning water* from one bucket to another; using hoses of various thicknesses.

Such timers can in the end lead to more conventional measures like *sand running through a funnel*, or *an egg-timer*, or *educational sand-timers* of 1, 3 and 5 minutes.

This can in turn lead to the next step: a *sundial* or watching a *second hand* going around a clockface. Finally, an *alarm* clock can be used. This should be a proper clock and not a kitchen timer without an hour dial, where the hand goes anti-clockwise and might thereby confuse children who are still learning to tell the time.

If one uses such timers to measure the periods of 'quiet times', as was suggested in Chapter 1, it is advisable to separate the initial trial with 'invented timers' from such quiet times. Experience has shown that the first experiment is not likely to be very conducive to a quiet period. It is also advisable to appoint a 'monitor' for the day who checks the timer in quiet periods.

Unit 6
Improving Spatial Ability

Introducing Building Blocks

In my opinion, any child will benefit from playing with building blocks. In Chapter 2 they were suggested for young children with organizational problems to foster the development of their spatial/organizational skills. Although the following suggestions are made with the language-impaired child in mind, they are equally suitable for any young child.

How to start

Toy shops offer many different boxes and buckets with good quantities of blocks of all shapes and sizes and in different colours and materials. The initial question is: how many pieces of such sets of building bricks ought one to start with? I suggest that there should be enough to make play productive but not so many that a child loses reach and sight of the pieces. For instance:

- One could start with only three cubes made out of natural wood.
- However, when the *'Montessori phenomenon'* (the intensive interest in a toy for a limited time – see Chapter 2) has worn off, a 'jump' to 20 or more cubes (perhaps 10 natural ones and 10 red ones) may fill the child with wonder and delight and can lead to a host of new activities.
- Next, perhaps, the same amount in a different material could be used (e.g. plastic instead of wood).
- After that one might want to go back to the three plain cubes but add three pieces of a different shape – perhaps three cylinders. 'Octagonal cylinders' are preferable for a young child: such 'cylinders' cannot roll out of reach, and they make a pleasant clatter (to make them, take a suitable square length of wood, chamfer

it on the four long sides so that the ends are roughly the shape of an octagon and cut into suitable pieces.)
– From then on the progression could be: 10 natural cubes and 10 red cylinders – two new shapes using a low number first – later more of the same shape and in different colours – and so forth until the full range of available shapes has been offered.

A quantitatively more restricted but qualitatively superior (and more expensive) set of blocks than normal toy bricks is the *Poleidoblocs G-set* (see below for a full description). They are as good for free play as they are for intuitive learning of first geometrical concepts like faces, edges, and vertices. They can also give experience with equivalences. Thus they offer an extension to the play activities described above.

As it seems to be with all toys – in school or at home – it is probably beneficial to a child if certain sets of building blocks are sometimes kept out of reach and out of sight for a reasonable time, especially when new sets are introduced. The familiar sets can be reintroduced later with a degree of 'newness'. The child may then be able to play in a different, more advanced way with the set.

Poleidoblocs (Description and Suggestions)

Poleidoblocs were suggested in Chapter 2 for work with children with organizational problems.

There are two sets of Poleidoblocs, Set G and Set A; both come in strong wooden boxes which provide almost jigsaw-puzzle-like storage.

> The materials were developed by Margaret Lowenfeld, physician and child psychologist, who in 1928 founded a pioneering neighbourhood clinic for 'nervous and difficult children' in London which, 10 years later, became the Institute of Child Psychology. One of her interests was non-verbal, non-linear thinking in children (Anderson, Thornhill and Smith, no date: 8) The sets have been used in the classroom and for research ever since.

Poleidoblocs G-set (description)

This consists of 54 brightly coloured wooden bricks in basic shapes. By children they are often described as cubes, short blocks, long blocks, slabs, squares, circles, roofs, rollers and cones (in more exact terms they are: prisms of all kinds, cylinders, cones, and square pyramids).

At first sight the set might not look so different from any toy set of coloured wooden bricks. However the shapes (most of them in various sizes) are carefully interrelated in their dimensions. For instance, the largest cube can be built up with triangular prisms, as well as with smaller cubes, or blocks, or slabs.

Activities with the G-set

The blocks can be used in many ways. They are ideal for free play (or 'Free Construction' in Lowenfeld's term) from pre-school age onwards to adulthood; they are excellent for guided play aiming at language interaction, and they can be used in a more structured way for language development, especially with regard to colour, shape and size. Their potential for mathematical development is high in various aspects – number, symmetry and equivalence of area and volume. Although one may be tempted to work in these areas explicitly with the blocks, in my experience this is best done at a later stage with the combination of the G- and A-set. At the elementary stages, ample play of an experimental kind is probably the best foundation for future work, relying on absorption more than explicit teaching.

Poleidoblocs A-set (description)

The Poleidoblocs A-set is not suitable for unsupervised children under three because of small pieces (choke hazard). It is made in plain wood and consists of 140 pieces in 2 basic shapes (various cuboidal prisms and flat 45-45-90 triangles) and in 4, 5, or 6 different sizes (lengths and cross-sections). Altogether there are 21 different kinds of shapes in various quantities (on the whole there are more of the smaller pieces), which make up the 140 pieces. These pieces are all related in size, so that equivalences in length, height, area and volume can be established. They also relate to the sizes of the Poleidoblocs G-set.

Activities with the A-set

Some activities with the A-set are suggested below; they were chosen from many other possible activities because they seem especially suitable for children with combined language and organizational difficulties.

Introducing the A-set

I suggest the following sequence of introductory work:

Show the child the box full of bricks, let him admire the neat fit. Empty the box into a larger cardboard box (not too deep) and let the child explore the different pieces in free construction play; the larger box enables the child to see and to pick out more easily all the pieces he may want. Perhaps repeat such free constructions for a number of sessions, working out of the larger box, being careful not to lose any pieces.

When the child has had some experience with the bricks, ask him to fit the pieces back into the proper box. This is rather like completing a challenging jigsaw puzzle and requires some skill and perseverance, and probably some help. There is actually an outline pattern of all shapes at the bottom of the box to aid re-packing; but perhaps one ought to let the child start as he likes, even if he ignores the pattern.

For a child with a weakness in organization this is a good opportunity to experience the benefit of planning ahead. He will find that it is best to sort the pieces into 21 heaps of identical pieces first, and then start with the largest pieces rather than haphazardly.

On the whole, children seem to get some satisfaction out of this clearing up job because, if done carefully, it will end with a perfect result. A few sessions doing just such jigsaw work, perhaps against the clock, can be useful.

Naming the pieces

During such introductory work the child will become familiar with the pieces. A need to distinguish the pieces by names might also have become obvious, so that a dialogue like the following may occur: 'Can I have more of the long ones?' 'Which long ones?' 'The fattest'. I suggest that naming of pieces should now be done in a systematic way as a rather challenging language task that might take several sessions but will in the end be recognized by the children as a necessary step towards further work.

I have tried the naming task in language sessions with a small group of three boys aged 10 to 11 who showed signs of weak organizational skills and included one pupil with a fairly severe spatial disability. The specific task was to name the 21 different pieces in such a way that all could be discriminated by their names, more or less without ambiguity. Since all pieces can be measured in inches or half-inches, using inches to describe them would have been the obvious way. However, the pupils did not seem to realize that all pieces were interrelated by inches, and I did not tell them at that stage.

The main challenge lay in the fact that most pieces come in four sizes rather than three (the latter would have suggested the use of the familiar 'Goldilocks' pattern: 'big', 'middle size' and 'little'). After the first still very ambiguous attempts the names of 'father, mother, big brother, little sister' were suggested, which meant one had something like a 'fat square daddy-rod', or a 'thin square little-sister-rod'. Later the 'step' idea was tried out ('fat square step-1-rod') which caused problems because the small cube did not fit into the system. Since numbers were now part of the naming game, I finally suggested looking at the measurements of the rods and at the possibility of describing them by numbers. This led to a lot of measuring, some insights about the relations of the rods, and a set of names with numbers only. Thus the 'fat square daddy-rod' was now called '5 × 1 × 1'. Although there was agreement that this was the way the names could best be explained to outsiders, when the pupils were given a choice in the following sessions they mostly preferred to use 'their' names.

Testing games

The different names were tried out at various stages. The aim was to see whether each piece could be recognized unambiguously. For each of the different pieces a card was written with its name on (21 cards for one set). The following describes such games, which all involve labelling and organization.

Game 1: Collecting pieces for construction

(a) The pack of cards is placed in the middle of the table with the writing facing down.

(b) The players take turns in taking a card from the top, reading it out loud, putting the card face upwards back on a second heap (spent cards), and picking out the right piece.

(c) The pieces are kept in front of each player until the cards are all taken.

(d) The cards are shuffled and put back, face down.

(e) The procedure is repeated: it can be repeated as long as there are pieces left in the box. Later rounds will have 'missed goes', since not all pieces will be available any longer; if time is limited one agrees beforehand on just two or three repeats, which means leaving pieces in the box.

At the end, every player constructs something with the random heap of pieces he or she has collected. Exchanging one piece for another by mutual agreement may be allowed. Before packing away, the members try to guess or find names for the various buildings on the table.

Game 2: Who can make the longest line?

The first four steps and the procedure are as for Game 1 above, but instead of free constructions each player makes a line at the end. The player with the longest line is the winner.

The number of repeats will depend on the number of players (so with 3 players and 21 cards everybody will get 7 pieces in the first round; this may be enough, because the length of the table may not allow more pieces to be lined up). If there are more than 3 players, further rounds may be required.

Game 3: Who can make the highest tower?

This game is more or less Game 2 in the vertical. The difference is that motor skills will play an additional role, since not all children will be equally able to put difficult pieces on top of each other. It is best to restrict pieces according to the ability of the group, perhaps starting with just three pieces for each child. The winner is the one who can make the highest tower without any piece tumbling down.

This game provides good opportunities to make the pupils realize the value of organizing the pieces according to their size first.

Game 4: Who can make the largest rectangle?

The game follows the rules from Game 2, except that the players are asked to make a rectangle at the end. This can be made easier if each player is provided with a board which has 1" squares drawn on it. The winner is the player who has completed a rectangle with the lowest number of pieces left. The children will probably soon realize that winning a card with a triangle is useless, unless one has two that are the same (or two smaller ones that make up a larger one).

Game 5: Who has the most wood (largest volume)?

The same rules as in Game 2 are followed, but at the end a comparison of volume is made. This version will probably need some preparatory work, comparing the volume of the pieces in terms of equivalences; it can be fascinating and very instructive. Perhaps having a set of scales on hand may be helpful: this can serve as an additional checking device and may in the end resolve arguments.

Game 6: X is trump

Finally, a short and easy game. The players agree on one piece as the 'trump piece' (e.g. the 'tiny cube', of which there are 24; or the 'double flat piece', of which there are only 4). Cards are taken in the same way as in Game 2. The winner is the player with the most trump pieces. This game, though not very exciting, may be useful as quick reinforcement when time is short, since it can be stopped at any time.

In all games described above, the level of difficulty can be controlled by using different selections of pieces and cards. One could, for example, make an easy start by using only three sizes of each piece for naming and for playing. I suggest that under these circumstances one does not start with showing the full box but that one builds up to it.

'Sharing out'

Besides playing games, a number of other activities are possible, with and without naming and card-writing. Just 'sharing out' may be more suitable with children who cannot yet bear to lose. Again, this activity can be graded for difficulty by using only a certain selection of pieces at a time.

The procedure would be as follows: one puts a heap of pieces (either selected for length, for cross-section, for shape; or taken randomly) in the middle of the table. These pieces have to be shared fairly, either by length (perhaps limited to pieces with the same cross-section), by area (perhaps excluding the pieces with a 1" × 1" cross-section) or, most interestingly, by volume.

Such an activity will give good opportunities for language work of a less systematic kind.

Summing up

Working with Poleidoblocs on whatever level will provide valuable and mostly pleasurable opportunities for helping children to improve their ability to organize materials, to learn to discriminate shapes by manipulation, and to talk about shape, size, number and spatial relationships.

At all times, work with the materials is also valuable as a diagnostic tool for the teacher concerned with spatial ability. This was brought home to me through work with Daniel, where it became clear in a task described under Game 2 (longest line) that he, at the age of 10, had failed to recognize the constancy of solid shapes under positional changes, as Figure 2.6.1 shows.

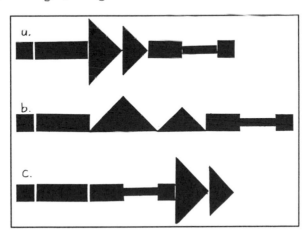

Figure 2.6.1a–c: Example of Poleidoblocs as diagnostic tool (spatial ability). Key:
a) a first attempt at making the longest possible line with a set of blocks (boy, 10yrs)
b) solution (not shown to the pupil)
c) second attempt (after encouragement)

Drawing Activities for Special Purposes

Specific drawing for numerical work was mentioned in Chapter 2 and Unit 3. The suggestions here are limited to drawing activities that are low in numerical content but which have the advantage that they can be combined with specific concept and language work. Although the *numerical* content may be low, the activities should benefit the understanding of *spatial/geometrical* aspects of mathematics, as all drawing can be expected to do.

> Compare, for example, Paul Klee's Pedagogical Sketchbook (1968); or Gombrich (1984: 14), who describes how the English painter Walter Crane (1845–1915) ingeniously taught the drawing of a man or a horse by breaking up the figure either into circles and ovals or into squares and other rectangles, according to the personal styles of his students.

Chapter 2 proposed that drawing activities could be used for children with spatial/organizational difficulties. Some suggestions were made which combined drawing with language work. Here are same additional suggestions.

Concept drawing

The aim is to establish a concept by linking language and drawing; it is not meant to be an 'art' lesson. The activity is shared by carer and child. An example was given in Chapter 2 (the concept 'tree'). Following on from the example my suggestions are:

(a) *Repetition:* 'Let's see if we can still do it' (aim at improving the organization of the drawing over the whole of the paper; aim at better relative proportions of the parts).

(b) *Additions:* encourage the children to be more specific, and to give more detail (e.g. 'apple tree' versus 'pear tree').

(c) *Combining in teamwork:* let the children cut all their trees out and glue them on paper to make a large picture of a wood or an orchard.

Other topics that I have used for concept drawings (in most cases quite successfully, as far as I remember) are:

> a tomato plant;
> a person;
> parts of a windmill (inside and outside parts separately first; followed by a full picture, well structured as to size, position on paper etc.);

parts of a bicycle (first 'listing' all the parts, then deciding how they fit together);
rubbish that one might find in a canal (first 'listing' it all, then 'organizing' it into separate 'containers');
buildings;
boundaries (walls, fences etc.);
water (rivers, ditches, puddles etc.).

Comprehension drawing

The aim is to assist concentrated listening to stories and to develop comprehension as well as visual/spatial skills by drawing a series of selected episodes from the story.

Peter and the Wolf

The following is a specific example of a lesson which uses Prokofiev's musical version of *Peter and the Wolf* for comprehension drawing. Preparations, initial instructions and procedures could apply to other stories too.

(a) *Preparation:* Check the tape and tape recorder beforehand. Allow enough time for the session. Preferably arrange seating so that everybody can see everybody else's drawing. Each person (carer included) has a large piece of paper in front of him/her, which is divided into 40 numbered sections (e.g. an A2 sheet folded into 20 sections and numbered; one can either use one sheet on both sides which gives 40 sections, or 2 single sheets with 20 sections each). Each person will need a pencil and there should be a box with spare pencils at hand.

(b) *Initial instruction:* This is a key-word summary of how one could introduce the story before playing the tape:

> We are going to do some kind of 'speed drawing' today. We will listen to a story and draw it fast in 40 pictures (like a cartoon). Listen to the tape; you will hear the story teller first; when the music starts, draw what you have heard on the first section of your paper. When the music stops, you should also stop drawing and listen again. When the music starts, start drawing again on next section . . . Don't worry if you can't finish the picture in a section; I'm sure you will have drawn enough to remind you of what happened in the story. You are welcome to look at what I am doing if you have forgotten what to do. Have fun!

(c) *Procedure:* The story then starts with the story teller saying 'In this story you will hear about a bird'. This is followed by

Prokofiev's 'bird's music' (repeated whenever the bird appears in the story) during which everybody draws a bird. Thus the story is followed through until it comes to an end with '. . . because the wolf in his haste had swallowed her alive.'

Again, this is a shared activity and the 'team-leader' should join in and draw with enthusiasm, casting happy encouraging glances at everyone. With regard to the results, it surprised me how well even children with comprehension difficulties managed to capture the essence of a section with a few lines (compare Chapter 2, Figure 2.11a–c).

Other stories

Peter and the Wolf seems 'ready made' for such comprehension drawing, probably in an unsurpassed way. A similar musical piece is Carl Orff's *Christmas Story* (but I have not tried it myself). Mostly one will have to make tapes of suitable stories oneself. This has the advantage that one can choose a story with an individual child or a certain group of children in mind, and that one can monitor the length of the music period and thereby the time the children have for drawing.

Possible extension work

One could make a book by selecting pictures from all the drawings (add text). Another suggestion is to keep the picture sequences so that children can use them later as a basis for retelling the story to someone else. Such picture sequences thus provide language-impaired children with the necessary support for the difficult task of structuring a story for retelling.

Pattern Blocks

The use of pattern blocks in connection with written instructions was suggested in Chapter 2 for children whose language difficulties are combined with weak spatial ability. The materials can also benefit older pupils with reading problems. More generally, it is my experience that most children, with or without specific difficulties, like to make these patterns and probably gain in spatial skills or reading skills from the activity.

The suggestions made in Chapter 2 are extended below. They contain the following: advice on how to make sets of pattern cubes (in cardboard or in wood); a description of instruction sheets; examples of patterns; procedures; and how to work with a commercially produced alternative set.

How to make sets of 4 × 4 pattern cubes

Cardboard cubes

The cheapest way of making a set is to make cubes out of thin cardboard, scored and cut.

> The six 'standard' shapes (see Chapter 2, Figure 2.12) can easily be drawn and painted onto the cardboard while this is still a flat 'net'. Figure 2.6.2a shows the simplest way of making a paper cube; Figure 2.6.2b shows a way which results in a surprisingly strong cube and is therefore more suitable for class work.

It is advisable to keep the set of cubes in a flat box or tray (see below).

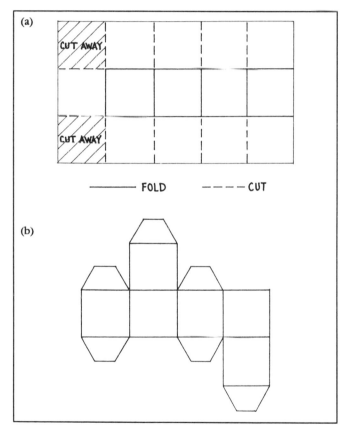

Figure 2.6.2 a–b: Two ways of making cubes from cardboard

Wooden cubes

A more permanent set can be made of wood.

> Here one can either take cubes from existing building blocks (or counting-sets), 16 of one kind, or one can buy a square section of wood (beech is

ideal) and cut the cubes off as precisely as possible (or have them cut by the wood merchant). Small cubes are suitable for older children, but for young children (under three) the size of a cube must not be less than an inch (25 mm) according to European and US toy safety regulations (choke hazard).

A cube of 3 cm³ is, in my experience, a good size for all. For such a cube the 'cutting list' for the necessary wood will be (in cm) $3 \times 3 \times 50$; however, 50 cm is the minimum and I suggest buying a somewhat longer square section to make some spare cubes, either for replacement cubes or to allow for an accident during production.

The shapes of both kinds ought to be painted with non-toxic paint (some acrylics and gouaches are non-toxic, but children's round water colour blocks will also do). Use high-quality masking tape for straight lines; cut a template for curved lines. A coat of non-toxic varnish is advisable for all paints on wood; it is certainly necessary for gouaches and children's paint.

The shapes on the six sides of each individual cube are best distributed in a consistent manner (use a die as model and assign a number to each pattern, e.g. 1 = natural, 6 = fully coloured, 3 = triangles etc.).

If wooden cubes are used it is advisable to use the end-grain sides (i.e. the sides where the cube was cut from the square) for the fully natural and fully coloured sides (this ensures even colours for the rest of the patterns, since the end-grain always has a slightly different colouring).

I suggest making a small tray to hold the cubes (for storing and for building up the pattern picture). This can be made with small square wooden rods and hardboard for the base. Make the inside of the tray about 1 cm larger than four of your cubes, so that the cubes can be handled with ease inside it. Alternatively, use a flat box or a lid with the right dimensions as a tray.

Instruction sheets (example for 4 × 4 blocks, six shapes)

Chapter 2 provided an illustration of the shapes (Figure 2.12) and an example for part of an instruction sheet used with such blocks. The work was done in rows and the result was a picture ('flying fish', Figure 2.13). Here is a second example where one works in columns and where the result is a pattern rather than a picture. The instruction sheet is shown in Figure 2.6.3; it assumes that the colours are red and natural. The resulting pattern ('How many squares?' – a visual puzzle) is shown in Figure 2.6.4a. Figure 2.6.4b–d gives three more examples of possible patterns and pictures to make.

These examples are only given as a 'source of inspiration'. It is good fun to make one's own. The descriptions for the instruction sheets are not so much fun. However, as the same phrases are

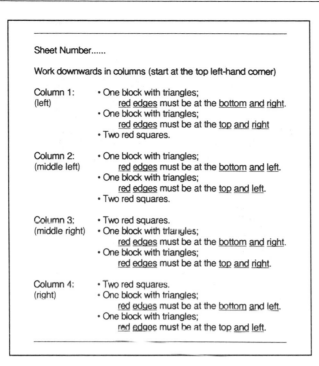

Sheet Number......

Work downwards in columns (start at the top left-hand corner)

Column 1:   • One block with triangles;
(left)   red edges must be at the bottom and right.
               • One block with triangles;
                  red edges must be at the top and right
               • Two red squares.

Column 2:   • One block with triangles;
(middle left)   red edges must be at the bottom and left.
               • One block with triangles;
                  red edges must be at the top and left.
               • Two red squares.

Column 3:   • Two red squares.
(middle right)   • One block with triangles;
                  red edges must be at the bottom and right.
               • One block with triangles;
                  red edges must be at the top and right.

Column 4:   • Two red squares.
(right)   • One block with triangles;
                  red edges must be at the bottom and left.
               • One block with triangles;
                  red edges must be at the top and left.

Figure 2.6.3: Example of instruction sheet for block patterns

constantly repeated, a word processor loaded with the standard phrases can be used. It is best to make a full set of such pictures with instructions, graded for complexity and designed for repeated use. I found it useful to have a set of 20 pictures and 20 corresponding instruction sheets, all in the same format and with the same vocabulary.

In setting up the picture and writing the instruction sheet one has to decide whether to work in columns or in rows. This is a matter of convenience; I have worked in both directions and found that the children could cope with both. If one feels that this can lead to unnecessary confusion, one can describe all patterns in just one way, which will sometimes result in slightly longer instructions.

Another question may arise: does one build up the pattern picture from the top or from the bottom? Children seem to differ in their preferences. Building upwards with blocks (free-standing vertical) often seems natural for a young child, but it is more difficult when following instructions. The reason is that reading has to be done unconventionally from the bottom line upwards (both with the row-by-row and with the column-by-column instructions). It also takes more dexterity; and a quiet place is necessary. For introducing the

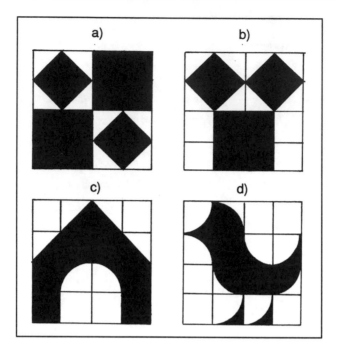

Figure 2.6.4a–d: Examples of some block patterns (including the result of Figure 2.6.3)

work and for standard classroom work the simplest way seems to be: top-down, left to right and working flat into a special tray. This is the way the suggested instruction sheets are organized, but the child can still try other ways.

Procedures

Introduction

In school it is best to introduce the work with a group session where the instructions are given orally by the teacher and the work is supervised. In all cases some help will be required during the first two or three individual exercises. After that the child may have to ask a question now and then, but on the whole my experience has been that because of the constant repetitions in the actions required and in the phrases and vocabulary used (e.g. 'red sides must be at the bottom') even children with spatial and reading comprehension problems are soon able to do the tasks unaided.

Preparation

The carer has to create and draw a pattern and write the instructions down, preferably in a standardized manner. If a set of previously planned and produced patterns is available, a picture and the respective instruction sheet are selected for the child.

The exercise

A set of blocks is put in front of the child, and the instructions are given, either orally or on a written instruction sheet. If the children follows the instructions properly, he will end up with the same picture or pattern as was planned. If he has made a mistake, it will usually be obvious at a glance. He can then correct the result, either intuitively by visual 'clozure', followed by a check through the instructions, or directly by reading the instructions again.

The session ends either with the carer discussing the picture with the child and letting the child find a name for it; or by giving him the title of the picture together with a check-card on which the picture is drawn, so that he can compare the picture on the card with his result.

Some children prefer to know the name of what they are going to build beforehand; in this case one can give the child a list with the titles of the available pictures to choose from.

Most children will become quite proficient at the task and enjoy the independence. They will feel confident with the self-checking device and they will normally be pleased with the visibly perfect, definite completion of the task.

If there are severe reading problems, one can practise the sight vocabulary through flashcards alongside the activity. Sometimes it may help children to use a marker card to show the line at which they are working.

Children vary in their interests in pattern, however, and I would not use this activity with every child. Most seem to be keen and want more and more, even when one may think that they don't need it any more. In that case, some may be able to make up their own patterns and write down the instructions in the same standardized way for use by a friend. A written list of the vocabulary or phrases needed may be given to them for this purpose.

Work with a commercially produced alternative set (Lego-Dacta Mosaic Set)

The activity is the same; the difference lies in the materials. The full Lego-Dacta Mosaic Set comes in five colours (plus white as the background colour) and has nine different shapes instead of 6 (including the white background square). The shapes are illustrated in Figure 2.6.5.

The set is part of the LEGO range, made of strong plastic. Each piece is a cube on which a pattern is shown on one side only (i.e. similar to pattern tiles). There is a fixing device on the underside which makes it possible to fit the pieces firmly onto the special Duplo building plates (see Appendix for suppliers). The pieces are easy to handle and need not necessarily be fitted onto the base. Only a selection of the set is needed. This means that there is a choice in respect of the grid size and colour.

I used a grid with 5 × 5 blocks for which I needed 44 pieces for 20 different pictures (one colour only, plus white as background). One should preferably choose one of the stronger colours (e.g. white/red or white/black rather than white/yellow).

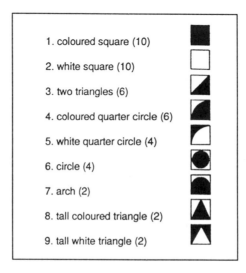

1. coloured square (10)

2. white square (10)

3. two triangles (6)

4. coloured quarter circle (6)

5. white quarter circle (4)

6. circle (4)

7. arch (2)

8. tall coloured triangle (2)

9. tall white triangle (2)

Figure 2.6.5: The shapes of the Lego-Dacta Mosaic Set

The 5 × 5 grid and the greater variety of shapes offer an opportunity for more complex pictures, which may appeal to older children.

The procedures are the same as those for the home-made blocks outlined above. It is advisable to keep the special selection of mosaic pieces in a separate box. The child then works from this box either into a tray (or a suitably sized other box), or onto the special Duplo building plate which can be cut to size. In the latter case the plate with the pattern can be put up vertically on the wall as a picture for a day or two.

For my own work I made a set of 20 pictures and 20 corresponding instruction sheets. The vocabulary consists of 40 generally useful words restricted to 15 different phrases – less than the vocabulary one normally finds in the first booklets of a primer set. This makes the activity very suitable for older children who have reading problems and who therefore need a lot of repetition on the same level.

An example of an instruction sheet is given in Figure 2.6.6. The resulting picture is shown in Figure 2.6.7a. Three additional examples of pictures to make are shown in Figure 2.6.7b–d.

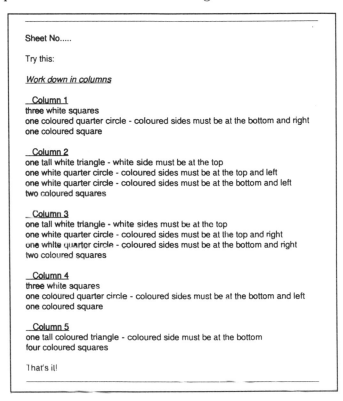

Sheet No.....

Try this:

Work down in columns

 Column 1
three white squares
one coloured quarter circle - coloured sides must be at the bottom and right
one coloured square

 Column 2
one tall white triangle - white side must be at the top
one white quarter circle - coloured sides must be at the top and left
one white quarter circle - coloured sides must be at the bottom and left
two coloured squares

 Column 3
one tall white triangle - white sides must be at the top
one white quarter circle - coloured sides must be at the top and right
one white quarter circle - coloured sides must be at the bottom and right
two coloured squares

 Column 4
three white squares
one coloured quarter circle - coloured sides must be at the bottom and left
one coloured square

 Column 5
one tall coloured triangle - coloured side must be at the bottom
four coloured squares

That's it!

Figure 2.6.6: Example of an instruction sheet for picture-making with the Lego-Dacta Mosaic Set

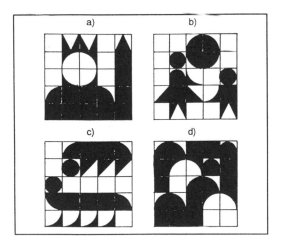

Figure 2.6.7 a–d: Four examples of pictures with the Lego-Dacta Mosaic Set, including the resulting picture of Figure 2.6.6. ('King of the Castle')

Work with Tangrams

Chapter 2 suggested the use of these materials for work with children who have organizational problems combined with weak spatial ability. However, Tangram sets are known as a mathematical puzzle that all generations can enjoy. Used in specific ways as described below, they have been found particularly useful for older children with reading problems and for children in whom one wants to develop 'speech for self' – language directed to oneself rather than to someone else (see Chapter 2).

The materials

Tangrams are defined and illustrated in Chapter 2. Sets are available in plastic or wood from educational suppliers or craft shops.

> An especially useful book about Tangrams is the one by Joost Elfers (Penguin, 1984) which includes an introduction, history, bibliography, over 1600 shapes and pictures to make, solutions, and a small plastic Tangram set in a tray. Another fine booklet is a small Tarquin publication by Millington (1986) which includes a cardboard cut-out of the puzzle pieces.

The following will give examples and details of two kinds of work that were suggested in Chapter 2: making Tangram pictures by following oral or written instructions; and using Tangram pictures to develop 'speech for self'.

Making Tangram pictures by following instructions

Tangram pictures, which are normally built by looking at a model picture, are made here by following oral or written instructions. A prepared instruction sheet is used. A full example of such a sheet is given in the example below. This gives the instructions for making a goose (similar to many possible pictures of geese given in Elfers, 1984). Figure 2.6.8 gives the example of the instruction sheet, Figure 2.6.9 the resulting picture.

The possibilities for Tangram designs are almost unlimited. Writing the instruction sheets is tedious but can be made easier with a word processor. The choice of pictures will normally be a compromise between the child's interest and the ease with which the pictures lend themselves to verbal instructions.

Advantages

Listening comprehension training can be combined with spatial training (the carer reads the instructions to the child in suitable

Tangram No.....

1.
Take the two large triangles.
  Make a large parallelogram with them.
  Place the parallelogram so that the shorter sides are horizontal.
  Place it so that the top leading corner is on your left.

2.
Take the piece which has the shape of a small parallelogram and put it above
the large parallelogram (made of the two triangles).
  Place it so that the two shorter sides are horizontal;
  - the top leading corner must be on the right;
  - the bottom leading corner must touch the left-hand triangle on the
    very left.

3.
Place the square directly above the small parallelogram;
  - one side must rest against the short free side of the parallelogram.

4.
Place the medium-sized triangle above the square;
  - the longer side must be at the bottom
  - the right half of the longer side rests against the top of the square,
  - and the left half of the longer side stays free.

5.
Place the two small triangles next to each other under der large right triangle.
  Place them so that one of the shorter sides is vertical and on the right;
  - the other short side must be horizontal and at the bottom;
  - both must touch the large triangle with their right-hand top corner
  - and look like feet.

Figure 2.6.8: Example of instruction sheet for a Tangram picture (goose)

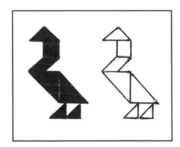

Figure 2.6.9: The result when the instructions in Figure 2.6.8 are followed (Tangram picture of a goose)

chunks). Written comprehension training can be combined with spatial training (the child reads the instructions himself).

In both cases the pictorial model of the Tangram can be given as a check-card at the end (or earlier if the child seems to be completely 'stuck'). Even without the possible benefits for spatial training, the exercises have been found useful for older children with severe reading and language problems since they need the kind of ample repetition given by the standardized vocabulary of the instruction sheets.

Developing 'speech for self' with the help of Tangram work

The activity is briefly described in Chapter 2. It is another case where an activity that may increase spatial skills can at the same time foster language skills. Here it aims at language development of a special kind: one wants to make the pupil aware that talking to oneself can help to organize one's thought, and the hope is that this may become a habit. For language-impaired children with weak organizational skills the formation of such a habit needs consistent repetitive work, such as Tangrams can provide.

Procedure

The following general order is suggested:

- Prepare the child with some introductory sessions with Tangram pieces.
- Choose a Tangram picture.
- Decide if the picture is to be presented with 'solution lines' or without, depending on the complexity of the picture and the child's spatial ability (work with 'solution lines' is much easier – see Chapter 2, Figure 2.14).
- Present the child with the model of the Tangram picture and a Tangram set.
- Explain to the child that you would like him to tell you what he is doing right through the puzzle.
- The child builds the picture and verbalizes what he is doing, or is encouraged to do so.

Variations in the procedures

At times it seems best if the carer appears to be busy with something else, apparently forgetting the child but still listening 'with one ear'. This could become one of the rare structured situations where the materials alone elicit the language. Encouragement to keep talking, if necessary, should be restricted to the end of the session and the beginning of further sessions.

At other times it may be necessary to remind the child frequently to comment aloud on what he is doing; in such cases it will initially be better to tell him that you would like to know how he is making the picture. This means one does not really bring forth true 'speech for self', but one hopes that in the end the habit of talking to oneself while tackling a problem is formed all the same.

In some cases one may be tempted to turn the activity into 'partner work'. Such work means that the child tries to make another person understand how he is putting down the pieces in order to make a certain picture. The partner, perhaps separated by a make-shift screen, tries to follow the child's instructions and builds the picture simultaneously. This is a challenging task that will take one even further away from true 'speech for self' which is seldom precise enough for such activity. However, it may be useful for initial 'habit formation', and in the end one can contrast such speech with true 'speech for self'.

- One word of caution is relevant for all partner work with learning-impaired children: it is definitely preferable if the partner is a *non-impaired* person with superior skills in the task, otherwise the success or failure of the partnership may not mirror the skill of the child who gives the instructions but rather the weakness of the partner. This can be very discouraging for the instruction-giving child and ought to be avoided.

Lastly, one can use a tape recorder and play it back to the child; one can then try to rebuild the picture to his commentary (with or without the model); this is best done when the carer and the child have a Tangram set each and try to rebuild the picture simultaneously; the atmosphere should not be that of a test but rather that of a happy 'let's see if we can do it' affair. This is probably the best time to contrast 'speech for self' with 'speech for instruction'.

Examples of possible results

Figure 2.6.10 gives the full scripts of taped sessions with two different boys. They were recorded while each boy tried to build up the same Tangram picture from the 'solution model'; they had three practice sessions on previous days without a tape. As the two scripts show, the time they used to finish the picture was almost the same, the language output very different.

The example of A. shows that he was grappling positively, not only with the shapes, but also with the language: for instance, when he put the square to the side of the main sail and called it 'nearly'; or when he described the parallelogram as a 'diamond sort of shape', or when he talked about the 'big middle size triangle'. With B., the younger boy, long pauses occurred. He was, by comparison, the one with slightly fewer spatial problems.

Language recorded in such situations often seems poor. This is partly due to the nature of 'speech for self' which seems to have its

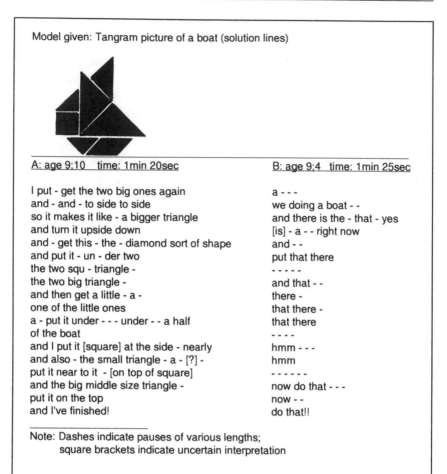

Model given: Tangram picture of a boat (solution lines)

A: age 9;10 time: 1min 20sec	B: age 9;4 time: 1min 25sec
I put - get the two big ones again	a - - -
and - and - to side to side	we doing a boat - -
so it makes it like - a bigger triangle	and there is the - that - yes
and turn it upside down	[is] - a - - right now
and - get this - the - diamond sort of shape	and - -
and put it - un - der two	put that there
the two squ - triangle -	- - - - -
the two big triangle -	and that - -
and then get a little - a -	there -
one of the little ones	that there -
a - put it under - - - under - - a half	that there
of the boat	- - - -
and I put it [square] at the side - nearly	hmm - - -
and also - the small triangle - a - [?] -	hmm
put it near to it - [on top of square]	- - - - - -
and the big middle size triangle -	now do that - - -
put it on the top	now - -
and I've finished!	do that!!

Note: Dashes indicate pauses of various lengths;
　　　square brackets indicate uncertain interpretation

Figure 2.6.10: Tapescripts of 'speech for self' while solving a Tangram puzzle (two boys attending a special school for language-impaired children)

own structure. Some of its features are known to be a drop in volume, a lack of intonational contrasts, and a tendency to omit subject-noun phrases (Wells, 1985: 421). The quality and amount of language produced also tend to be influenced by the difficulty of the task: if it is too difficult, language seems especially poor and patchy; if it too easy, (i.e. if there is no real problem), 'speech for self' does not seem necessary at all. My observation during Tangram sessions was that children seem to forget to give the commentary at a point where 'it clicks' – when they suddenly perceive a possible solution or part-solution. They seem to recognize the emerging picture, and one can assume that the tension of solving the task is more or less over. This, I believe, is of interest because it seems to prove that 'speech for self' is indeed a tool, used mainly as a help in 'tricky' situations, even with children. It may be useful to make the child aware of this with the help of the tape recorder play-back.

For controlling difficulties in this and similar tasks see Chapter 2.

Unit 7
Miscellaneous
Exercises

Examples of 'Distracting' Activities to be Used for Memorizing Sequences

What are 'distractors'?

Distractors, as described in Chapter 3, are activities that are used in parallel with a sequence that is being learned. They have the dual purpose of giving variety to a repetitive task and of promoting its total automatization by testing it under distracting conditions.

The examples in the list below refer to learning the beginning of the counting sequence (1–10 and perhaps to 20), but the same kind of distractors can be used for learning other sequences such as times tables, the letters of the alphabet, or the months of the year.

Such devices can vary widely in difficulty. An early 'distracting' activity might be the building up of the 'staircase' of 10 with rods (1–10 cm long) while reciting the counting sequence in a synchronized rhythm; this is then followed by putting the respective rods back into their container while saying the counting words again. In these two activities there is still an inherent relation between distractor and sequence: numbers and images of quantities increase together. Later the distractor and the sequence to be learned can become unrelated, like doing press-ups while counting.

Distractors can be freely invented, and one can certainly have fun in thinking of new ones. The limit seems to be the imagination of the carer and the attitude and ability of the child. It is no good if the distractors are too difficult, or if they lead the child or the group of children to get out of hand. On the other hand one can use a child's favourite distractor over and over again, if that pleases him and if he seems to progress in the main task.

In the following list of examples, the activities need a supervisor who can count; the description refers to a situation where there is one child and a supervisor, but most can be adapted for a group of children. In all cases it is best if the supervisor joins in the activity with both the counting and the distracting task.

Examples
Distractors where there is a relation to the real task

These exercises should certainly be the first step:
(a) Use a large cardboard box and a heap of counters that are easy to handle (e.g. wooden 1 inch cubes). The players take one counter each for each number in the sequence and let it drop into the box. The task can be reversed, with the players taking the counters out one by one. If there is a group, one has to make sure that the box is wide enough for all hands to take a counter out more or less simultaneously.
(b) Use a stiff piece of string (e.g. a thin plastic washing line) with ten large beads, perhaps five in one colour and five in another (the string should be about twice as long as the total length of beads with a knot at both ends). The beads are moved in 'rosary fashion' from one end of the string to the other while counting.
(c) The same as above but, for a change, use a piece of wooden dowelling with 10 beads, which makes a simple 'first line' abacus. The dowelling should be about 3 inches longer than the length of the 10 beads, with an elastic band as a stopper about one inch from both ends.
(d) Use finger counting, preferably starting with the index finger while the other fingers are held down by the thumb (i.e. index: 1; middle: 2; ring: 3; little: 4; thumb: 5; and the same on the other hand). This gives a clearer image of the numbers 2 to 4 (and 7–9) than starting with the thumb.

Dexterity skills as distractors

These are activities with a more severe distracting effect:
(a) All sorts of clapping: clap hands together ('one'), slap hands flat on your knees ('two'), hands together ('three'), and so forth, with emphasis on every second (odd) number. A more difficult sequence is: hands together ('one') – cheeks ('two') – knees ('three') – hands together ('four'), and so forth, with emphasis on every third number. In theory the sequence of distractors can be extended, in practice this is seldom advisable with children who cannot remember sequences easily.
(b) Use a small but firm bag filled with rice or sand. The bag is thrown to and fro from one partner back to the other (or round a group in a circle). The game starts with one player throwing the bag saying 'one' and the partner throwing it back while saying 'two'; it comes back with 'three', and so forth. One can look at it

as a kind of ping-pong game with number words, the partners take turns in starting with 'one'. Balls of various sizes can also be used, but in my experience the small bag seems the most practical for easy catching and for storing.

(c) Use a ping-pong ball. The child tries to let the ball bounce (lightly!) on the table and to catch it back again; he recites each number to the rhythmic click of the dropping ball. This is a difficult task and not suitable for young or clumsy children.

Physical exercises as distractors

Two suggestions are given, but it is easy to think of more:

(a) Swinging one's arms alternately over one's head.
(b) Squatting down and stretching one's legs one after the other.

Drawings as distractors

There are many objects that can be standardized to a schematic drawing with a set number of strokes. The counting starts with both partners (or all group members) having a sheet of paper and a pencil (crayon, felt tip) in a suitable colour. For instance:

(a) A group of pine trees can be drawn by starting with a green trunk first and then adding some branches on each side while counting rhythmically. The rhythm starts with 'trunk' and is followed by 'one-two-three-four-five-six'; the next tree again: 'trunk-one-two-three-four...' The trees can have more branches than six, by prior agreement.

(b) Houses are drawn. They are suitable for counting up to 'five' or 'six', perhaps more if they have a door and or windows.

(c) Stars and flowers: they are more difficult (drawing is best started with a cross).

For results see Figure 2.7.1.

To give such exercises an extra purpose, it is often possible to combine a number of these repetitive drawings to form a background for wall decorations, perhaps on coloured paper (e.g. a forest, an old town, or a starry sky) to which other things can then be added as a collage (e.g. little Red Riding Hood as the centre of the woods, or angels added to the starry sky).

- Remember that on no account should the distracting activity be so distracting as to seriously hinder the even, correct reciting of the sequence to be learned.

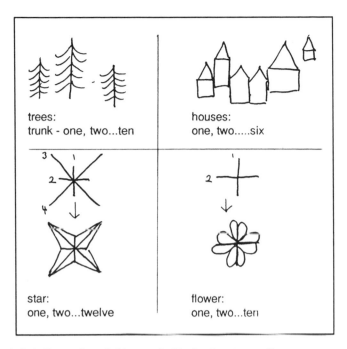

trees:
trunk - one, two...ten

houses:
one, two.....six

star:
one, two...twelve

flower:
one, two...ten

Figure 2.7.1: Examples of objects suitable for drawing as distractors

Exercises for Auditory Discrimination: '-ty' versus '-teen'

In Chapter 4 it was suggested that percussion instruments (improvised or real) could be used with children with auditory discrimination difficulties when they try to distinguish between the number words ending in '-teen' (e.g. 'sixteen') and those ending in '-ty' (e.g. 'sixty'). Such possible exercises are described below.

Materials

One will need:
(a) instruments of different pitch and volume (such as two drums, one large, one small; or a drum and a tambourine; or two boxes, one large, one small; or two pieces of wood in different sizes and a wooden spoon to beat with, etc.);
(b) three different sets of cards:
a selection of quantity picture cards (see Unit 4);
a selection of number word cards (numbers written in letters, for example 'sixteen');
a selection of figure cards (numbers written in figures, e.g. '60');
(c) paper and pencil;
(d) a paper abacus (see Unit 4).

Activities

(a) For the first exercise one will need a large and a small drum and quantity picture cards from 10 to 20. The cards are given to the child in the right order. The teacher/therapist beats on the drum, child and adult count aloud to the rhythm of the drum beat while the child puts down one card after another in keeping with the beats. At thirteen the rhythm changes into two level beats; for twenty – the 'great finale' – the big drum is used, followed by the small drum. One can illustrate the procedure in a kind of rhythm picture as shown in Figure 2.7.2.

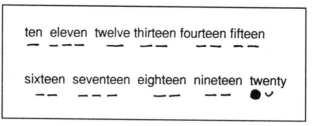

Figure 2.7.2: Rhythm picture (-ty vs -teen)

(b) The quantity picture cards for the full tens (10, 20, 30, etc.) are selected and given to the child in the right order. Counting proceeds as above but now in full tens with the appropriate beat pattern (10 as one beat on the big drum, 20 as 'one big, one small' etc.); 100 can be signified as one big bang or as a short drum-roll. (A word of caution about the drum-roll: it is fun, but one must be confident that the child does not get too excited when it is his turn to beat the drum later as in exercise (d) – he might drum the house down.)

(c) If the child is skilled enough, exercise (a) can be repeated but with changed roles: now the child does the drumming, the teacher shows the cards.

(d) If the child is skilled enough, exercise (b) can be repeated but with changed roles.

(e) Exercises (a)–(d) can be repeated but now with number word cards or figure cards instead of quantity picture cards.

(f) The child has paper and pencil and a set of '-teens' and '-tys' cards (number words or quantity pictures i.e. something where the difference can be *seen*). The teacher drums either a '-teen' or a '-ty' number, the child makes a rhythm picture, finds a corresponding card (any, as long as it corresponds to the pattern) and says the number.

(g) If the child is skilled enough, exercise (f) can be repeated but with changed roles.

(h) A 'minimal pair' is selected, for example, 13 and 30; two corresponding cards (in pictures, words or figures) are put before the child; the teacher says either the one or the other; the child bangs the pattern on the drum, points to the card and says the word (tokens or points can be given for correct responses if the correct responses are more frequent than the errors and the child responds to such an incentive).

(i) The child has a paper abacus with overlay. The teacher says either a '-teen' or a '-ty' number; the child repeats it and shows it on the abacus.

(j) Dictation: the child has paper and pencil. The teacher says either a '-teen' or 'ty' number; the child repeats it and writes it down as a rhythm picture, or number word or figure.

References

Anderson JR (1990) Cognitive Psychology and its Implications. 3rd edn. New York: Freeman.

Anderson V, Thornhill RG and Smith M. (no date). Lowenfeld Poleidoblocs (Handbook): Nottingham, NES/Arnold.

Anghileri J (1991) The language of multiplication and division. In Durkin K and Shire B (Eds) Language in Mathematical Education. Milton Keynes UK and Philadelphia: Open University Press.

Anghileri J (1995) Making sense of symbols. In Anghileri J (Ed) Children's Mathematical Thinking in the Primary Years. London and New York: Cassell.

Ashcraft MH (1993) Cognitive arithmetic: a review of data and theory. In Dehaene S (Ed) Numerical Cognition. Cambridge MA and Oxford UK: Blackwell.

Baddeley A (1990) Human Memory: Theory and Practice. Hove UK and Hillsdale NJ: Erlbaum.

Bath JB, Chinn SJ and Knox DE (1986) Cited in Chinn SJ and Ashcroft JR (1993) The Test of Cognitive Style in Mathematics. East Aurora, New York: Slosson.

Battista TM (1994) On Greeno's environmental/model view of conceptual domains: a spatial/geometric perspective. Journal for Research in Mathematics Education 25, 86–94.

Bednarz N and Janvier B (1988) A constructivist approach to numeration in primary school: results of a three year intervention with the same group of children. Educational Studies in Mathematics 19, 299–331.

Behr M, Erlwanger S and Nichols E (1980) How children view the equal signs. Mathematics Teaching 92, 13–15.

Benton AL (1978) The cognitive functioning of children with developmental dysphasia. In Wyke MA (Ed) Developmental Dysphasia. London and New York: Academic Press.

Bierhoff H (1996) Laying the foundations of numeracy: a comparison of primary textbooks in Britain, Germany and Switzerland. Discussion Paper No 90. London: National Institute of Economic and Social Research.

Binet A and Simon T with marginal notes by Terman LM (1980) The Development of Intelligence in Children. Ltd edn. Nashville USA: Williams.

Bishop AJ (1973) Use of structural apparatus and spatial ability: a possible relationship. Research in Education 9, 43–9.

Bishop AJ (1983) Space and geometry. In Lesh R and Landau M (Eds) Acquisition of Mathematical Concepts and Processes. London and New York: Academic Press.

Bishop AJ (1989) Review of research on visualisation in mathematics education. Focus on Learning Problems in Mathematics 11, 7–16.

Börnsen-Holtman, N (1994) Italian Design. Cologne: Taschen.

Brown, G (1986) Grading and professionalism in ELT. Spoken Language. London: CILT.

Bruner JS (1964) The course of cognitive growth. American Psychologist 19, 1–15.

Bruner JS (1966) Towards a Theory of Instruction. Cambridge MA: Harvard University Press.

Bruner JS and Kennedy HJ (1966) On relational concepts. In Bruner JS, Oliver RR and Greenfield PM (Eds) Studies in cognitive growth. New York: Wiley.

Bryant P (1995) Children and Arithmetic. Journal of Child Psychology and Psychiatry 36, 3–32.

Burroughs GER (1970) A Study of the Vocabulary of Young Children. Educational Monograph 1, School of Education, Birmingham: University of Birmingham.

Buxton LG (1982) Emotional responses to symbolism. Visible Language 16, Special Issue: Understanding the Symbolism of Mathematics. Cleveland, Ohio.

Byers V and Erlwanger S (1985) Memory in mathematical understanding. Educational Studies in Mathematics 16, 259–81.

Campbell JID (1987) The role of associative interference in learning and retrieving arithmetic facts. In Sloboda J and Rogers D (Eds) Cognitive processes in mathematics. Oxford: Oxford University Press.

Carpenter TP and Moser JM (1982) The development of addition and subtraction problem-solving skills. In Carpenter TP, Moser JM and Romberg TA (Eds) Addition and Subtraction: a Cognitive Perspective. Hillsdale NJ: Erlbaum.

Carpenter TP, Moser JM and Romberg TA (Eds) (1982) Addition and Subtraction: a Cognitive Perspective. Hillsdale NJ: Erlbaum.

Chinn S and Ashcroft R (1993) Mathematics for dyslexics: a teaching handbook. London: Whurr.

Choat E (1974) Johnnie is disadvantaged; Johnnie is backward. What hope for Johnnie? Mathematics Teaching 69, 9–13.

Clark HH and Clark EV (1977) Psychology and language. New York: Harcourt Brace Jovanovich.

Clements MA (1980) Analysing children's errors on written mathematical tasks. Educational Studies in Mathematics 11, 1–21.

COBUILD (1987) Collins Cobuild English language dictionary. London: Collins.

Collins K (1982) The structure of learned outcomes: a refocusing for mathematical learning. In Carpenter TP, Moser JM and Romberg TA (Eds) Addition and Subtraction: a Cognitive Perspective. Hillsdale NJ: Erlbaum.

Conti-Ramsden G, Donlan C and Grove J (1992) Characteristics of children with specific language impairment attending language units. European Journal of Disorders of Communication 27, 325–42.

Cromer RF (1991) Language and Thought in Normal and Handicapped Children. Oxford UK and Cambridge USA: Blackwell.

Crystal D (1980) A First Dictionary of Linguistics and Phonetics. London: Andre Deutsch.

Crystal D (1984) Linguistic Encounters with Language Handicap. Oxford, London and New York: Blackwell.

Crystal D (1985) Some early problems with verbs. Child Language Teaching and Therapy 1, 46–53.

Crystal D (1986) Listen to your Child. Harmondsworth, Middlesex UK and New York: Penguin.

Crystal D (1987) The Cambridge Encyclopedia of Language. Cambridge UK: Cambridge University Press.

Crystal D, Fletcher P and Garman M (1976) The Grammatical Analysis of Language Disability. London: Edward Arnold.

Da Costa R (1989) The parents' role in supporting children in education. In Mogford K and Sadler J (Eds) Child Language Disability: Implications in an Educational Setting. Clevedon UK and Philadelphia: Multilingual Matters.

Dantzig T (1962) Number, the Language of Science. 4th edn. New York: Macmillan.

Davydov VV (1982) The psychological characteristics of the formation of elementary mathematical operations in children. In Carpenter TP, Moser JM and Romberg TA (Eds) Addition and Subtraction: a Cognitive Perspective. Hillsdale NJ: Erlbaum.

De Corte E and Verschaffel L (1991) Some factors influencing the solution of addition and subtraction word problems. In Durkin K and Shire B (Eds) Language in Mathematical Education. Milton Keynes UK and Philadelphia: Open University Press.

Dehaene S (Ed) (1993) Numerical Cognition. Cambridge MA and Oxford UK: Blackwell.

Dehaene S (1993) Varieties of numerical abilities. In Dehaene S (Ed) Numerical Cognition. Cambridge MA and Oxford UK: Blackwell.

Dickey A (1994) Popular maths is rooted in reality (Netherlands). Times Educational Supplement, 18 March 1994.

Dickson L, Brown M and Gibson O (1984) Children Learning Mathematics. London: Cassell.

Dienes ZP (1959) The growth of mathematical concepts in children through experience. Educational Research 2, 9–28.

Dienes ZP (1964) Mathematics in the Primary School. Melbourne: Macmillan.

Donaldson M (1978) Children's Minds. Glasgow: Fontana/Collins.

Donaldson M and Wales RJ (1970) On the acquisition of some relational terms. In Hayes JR (Ed) Cognition and the Development of Language. New York: Wiley.

Donlan C (1993) Basic numeracy in children with specific language impairment. Child Language Teaching and Therapy 9, 95–104.

Durant S and Darling E (1993) Architecture and Childhood (exhibition publication). London: The British Architectural Library.

Durkin K and Shire B (Eds), (1991) Language in Mathematical Education. Milton Keynes UK and Philadelphia: Open University Press.

Edwards RPA and Gibbon V (1973) Words your Children Use. 2nd edn. London: Burke.

Elfers J (1984) Tangram: the Ancient Chinese Shapes Game. Harmondsworth UK and New York: Penguin.

Fidelman U (1985) Hemispheric basis for schools in mathematics. Educational Studies in Mathematics 16, 59–74.

Flegg G (1983) Numbers, their History and Meaning. London: Andre Deutsch.

Freudenthal H (1973) Mathematics as an Educational Task. Dortrecht, Holland: D Reidel.

Freudenthal H (1982) Fiabilité, validité et pertinence – critères de la recherche sur l'enseignement de la mathématique. Educational Studies in Mathematics 13, 395–408.

Freudenthal H (1986) On multiplication. Mathematics Teaching 114, 25–27.

Fuson KC and Hall JW (1983) The acquisition of early number word meaning: a conceptual analysis and review. In Ginsburg HP (Ed) The Development of

Mathematical Thinking. London and New York: Academic Press.

Fuson KC (1991) Children's early counting: saying the number-word sequence, counting objects, and understanding cardinality. In Durkin K and Shire B (Eds) Language in Mathematical Education. Milton Keynes UK and Philadelphia: Open University Press.

Fuson KC and Kwon Y (1991) Chinese-based regular and European irregular systems of number words: the disadvantages for English-speaking children. In Durkin K and Shire B (Eds) Language in Mathematical Education. Milton Keynes UK and Philadelphia: Open University.

Gallistel CR and Gelmann R (1993) Preverbal and verbal counting and computation. In Dehaene S (Ed) Numerical Cognition. Cambridge MA and Oxford UK: Blackwell.

Galt Catalogue (1992) Play and Learn with Galt. Cheadle UK: James Galt.

Gardner MK and Clark E (1992) The psychometric perspective on intellectual development in childhood and adolescence. In Sternberg RJ and Berg CA (Eds) Intellectual Development. Cambridge: Cambridge University Press.

Gathercole SE (1993) Word learning in language-impaired children. Child Language Teaching and Therapy 9, 187–99.

Gathercole SE and Baddeley AD (1993) Working Memory and Language. Hove UK and Hillsdale NJ: Erlbaum.

Gattegno C (1963a) For the Teaching of Mathematics. Vol. 3: Elementary Mathematics. Reading UK: Educational Explorers.

Gattegno C (1963b) Arithmetics. Reading UK: Educational Explorers.

Gelman R and Gallistel CR (1978) The Child's Understanding of Number. Cambridge MA.: Harvard University Press.

Giaquinto M (1992) Visualizing as a means of geometric discovery. Mind and Language 7, 382–401.

Ginsburg HP (1977) Children's Arithmetic: the Learning Process. New York: Van Nostrand.

Ginsburg HP (Ed) (1983) The Development of Mathematical Thinking. London and New York: Academic Press.

Ginsburg HP (1989) Children's Arithmetic: How they Learn It and How you Teach It. 2nd edn. Austin TX: PRO-ED.

Gleitman LR and Gillette J (1994) The role of syntax in verb learning. In Fletcher P and MacWhinney B (Eds) The Handbook of Child Language. Oxford UK and Cambridge USA: Blackwell.

Globerson T and Zelniker T (Eds) (1989) Cognitive Style and Cognitive Development. Norwood NJ: Ablex.

Globerson T (1989) What is the relationship between cognitive style and cognitive development? In Globerson T and Zelniker T (Eds) Cognitive Style and Cognitive Development. Norwood NJ: Ablex.

Goffree F (1993) Hans Freudenthal: working on mathematical education. Educational Studies in Mathematics 25, 21–29, Special Issue: The legacy of Hans Freudenthal.

Gombrich EH (1984) The Sense of Order; a Study in the Psychology of Decorative Art. Oxford: Phaidon.

Graham DJ (1987) An associative retrieval model of arithmetic memory: how children learn to multiply. In Sloboda J and Rogers D (Eds) Cognitive Processes in Mathematics. Oxford and New York: Oxford University Press.

Grauberg E (1985a) Some problems in the early stages of teaching numbers to language-handicapped children. Child Language Teaching and Therapy 1, 17–29.

Grauberg E (1985b) Teaching the initial stages of handwriting to children with a language-handicap. Child Language Teaching and Therapy 1, 306–20.

Grauberg E (1986) Feeling at home with number symbols. In Advances in Working with Language Disordered Children (conference papers). London: ICAN.

Grauberg, E (1995) Language and early mathematics – ten years on. Child Language Teaching and Therapy 11, 34–49.

Grice HP (1967) Logic and Conversation. In Cole P and Morgan JL (Eds) (1975) Syntax and Semantics 3 (Speech acts). New York and London: Academic Press.

Griffiths N (1982) Sbardun i Siarad – Pattern for Welsh Learners. 2nd edn. Cyfres Polytechnic Cymru: Gwasg Gomer.

Hatano G (1982) Learning to add and subtract: A Japanese perspective. In Carpenter TP, Moser JM and Romberg TA (Eds) Addition and Subtraction: a Cognitive Perspective. Hillsdale NJ: Erlbaum.

Hatano G, Miyake Y and Binks MG (1977) Performance of expert abacus operators. Cognition 5, 48–55.

Hatano G and Osaka K (1983) Digit memory of grand experts in abacus-derived mental calculation. Cognition 15, 95–110.

Haylock D (1992) Meeting the special needs of mathematically low attainers in the primary school. In Jones K and Charlton T (Eds) Learning Difficulties in Primary Classrooms: Delivering the Whole Curriculuum. Part II: Mathematics. London: Routledge.

Haylock D and Cockburn A (1989) Understanding Early Years Mathematics. London: Paul Chapman.

Haynes, C (1992) Vocabulary deficit – one problem or many? Child Language Teaching and Therapy 8, 8–12.

Haynes C and Naidoo S (1991) Children with Specific Speech and Language Impairment. Oxford: MacKeith Press.

Hiebert J (1988) A theory of developing competence with mathematical symbols. Educational Studies in Mathematics 19, 333–55.

Howson G (1982) A History of Mathematics Education in England. Cambridge: Cambridge University Press.

Hudson T (1983) Correspondence and numerical differences between disjoint sets. Child Development 54, 84–90.

Hughes M (1986) Children and Number. Oxford UK and New York: Blackwell.

Hutt, Ella (1986) Teaching Language Disordered Children – a Structured Curriculum. London: Edward Arnold.

Hyde-Wright S, Gorrie B, Haynes C and Shipman A (1993) What's in a name? Comparative therapy for word-finding difficulties using semantic and phonological approaches. Child Language Teaching and Therapy 9, 214–29.

Jäger RS, and Mayer M. (1988) Differentielle- und Persönlichkeitspsychologie. In Jäger RS (Ed) Psychologische Diagnostik. Munich: Psychologie Verlags Union.

James W (1890) The Principles of Psychology. Vol. 1. London: Macmillan.

Jones K and Charlton T (1992) Learning Difficulties in Primary Classrooms: Delivering the Whole Curriculum. Part II: Mathematics. London: Routledge.

Johnston JR (1992) Cognitive abilities of language impaired children. In Fletcher P and Hall D (Eds) Specific Speech and Language Disorders in Children. London: Whurr.

Karmiloff-Smith A (1992) Beyond modularity: a developmental perspective on cognitive science. Cambridge MA and London: MIT Press.

Katan NJ (1985) Hieroglyphs. London: British Museum Publications.

Kaufman EL, Lord MW, Reese TW and Volkman J (1949) The discrimination of visual number. American Journal of Psychology 62, 498–525.

Kerslake D (1975) Taking time out. Mathematics Teaching 73, 8–10.

Kerslake D (1979) Visual mathematics. Mathematics in School 8, 34–5.

Kieran C (1981) Concepts associated with the equality symbol. Educational Studies in Mathematics 12, 317–26.

Kirchner DM and Klatzky RL (1985) Verbal rehearsal and memory in language-disordered children. Journal of Speech and Hearing Research 28, 556–65.

Klee P (1968) Pedagogical Sketchbook. London: Faber & Faber.

Koppitz EM (1975) The Bender Gestalt Test for Young Children, Vol.II: Research and Application 1963–1973. New York: Grune & Stratton.

Krutetskii VA (1976) The Psychology of Mathematical Abilities in School Children. Chicago: University of Chicago Press.

Lane C and Chinn SJ (1986) Cited in Chinn SJ and Ashcroft JR (1993) Learning by self-voice echo. Academic Therapy 21, 477–81.

Lean G and Clements MA (1981) Spatial ability, visual imagery and mathematical performance. Educational Studies in Mathematics 12, 267–99.

Lesh R and Landau M (Eds) (1983) Acquisition of Mathematical Concepts and Processes. New York and London: Academic Press.

Lester K (1983) Trends and issues in mathematical problem-solving research. In Lesh R and Landau M (Eds) Acquisition of Mathematical Concepts and Processes. New York and London: Academic Press.

Lovell K and Slater A (1960) The growth of the concept of time: a comparative study. Journal of Child Psychology and Psychiatry 1, 179–90.

Lupton E and Abbot Miller J (Eds) (1993) The ABCs of Triangle – Square – Circle: the Bauhaus and Design Theory. London: Thames & Hudson.

Lyons J (1968) Introduction to Theoretical Linguistics. Cambridge: Cambridge University Press.

Luria AR (1969) On the pathology of computational operation. In Kilpatrick J and Wirszup I (Eds) Soviet Studies in the Psychology of Learning and Teaching Mathematics, Vol 1. (The learning of mathematical concepts). Chicago: University of Chicago.

MacFarlane Smith I (1964) Spatial Ability: its Education and Social Significance. London: University of London Press.

Mandler G and Shebo BJ (1982) Subitizing: an analysis of its component processes. Journal of Experimental Psychology: General 111, 1–23.

Mathematical Association 1987: Maths Talk. Cheltenham: Stanley Thornes.

McTear M and Conti-Ramsden G (1991) Pragmatic Disability in Children: Assessment and Intervention. London: Whurr.

Menninger K (1969) Number Words and Number Symbols. Cambridge MA and London: MIT Press.

Michel H (1967) Scientific Instruments in Art and History. London: Barrie & Rockliff.

Miles TR and Miles E (Eds) (1992) Dyslexia and Mathematics. London: Routledge.

Miller G (1956) The magical number 7 plus or minus 2. Some limits on our capacity for processing information. Psychological Review 63, 81–97.

Millington J (1986) Tangrams. Stradbroke, Diss UK: Tarquin Publications.

Morris J (1981) Math anxiety: teaching to avoid it. The Mathematics Teacher 74, 413–17.

Nesher P (1982) Levels of description in the analysis of addition and subtraction word problems. In Carpenter TP, Moser JM and Romberg TA (Eds) Addition and Subtraction: a Cognitive Perspective. Hillsdale NJ: Erlbaum.

Nesher P and Teubal E (1975) Verbal cues as an interfering factor in verbal problem solving. Educational Studies in Mathematics 6, 41–51.

Nesher P and Katriel T (1977) A semantic analysis of addition and subtraction problems in arithmetic. Educational Studies in Mathematics 8, 241–69.

Newman R and Boles M (1992) The Golden Relationship: Art, Math and Nature, Book 1: Universal Patterns. 2nd revised edn. Bradford MA: Pythagorean Press.

Nunes T and Bryant P (1996) Children Doing Mathematics. Oxford UK and Cambridge USA: Blackwell.

Parkin AJ (1993) Memory (Phenomena, Experiment and Theory). Oxford UK and Cambridge USA: Blackwell.

Piaget J (1952) The Child's Perception of Number. London: Routledge & Kegan Paul.

Piaget J (1969) The Child's Conception of Time. London: Routledge & Kegan Paul.

Pollock L and Waller E (1994) Day-to-Day Dyslexia in the Classroom. London: Routledge.

Polya G (1981) Mathematical Discovery. New York: Wiley.

Polya G (1990) How to Solve It. 2nd edn. Harmondsworth UK and New York: Penguin.

Quirk R and Greenbaum S (1973) A University Grammar of English. London: Longman.

Rapin I and Allen DA (1983) Developmental Language Disorders. In Kirk U (Ed) Neuropsychology of Language, Reading and Spelling. New York and London: Academic Press.

Resnick LB (1982) Syntax and Semantics in Learning to Subtract. In Carpenter TP, Moser JM and Romberg TA (Eds) Addition and Subtraction: a Cognitive Perspective. Hillsdale NJ: Erlbaum.

Resnick LB and Ford WW (1984) The Psychology of Mathematics for Instruction. Hillsdale NJ: Erlbaum.

Riley M, Greeno JG and Heller JI (1983) Development of children's problem solving ability in arithmetic. In Ginsburg HP (Ed) The Development of Mathematical Thinking. New York and London: Academic Press.

Robinson R (1992) Brain imaging and language. In Fletcher P and Hall D (Eds) Specific Speech and Language Disorders in Children. London: Whurr.

Rowland T (1995) Between the lines: the language of mathematics. In Anghileri J (Ed) Children's Mathematical Thinking in the Primary Years. London and New York: Cassell.

Ryle G (1973) The Concept of Mind. Harmondsworth, Middlesex UK and New York: Penguin University Books.

Sharma Y (1995) Abacus makes a comeback. Times Educational Supplement, 22 September 1995.

Shuard H and Rothery A. (Eds) (1984) Children Reading Mathematics. London: John Murray.

Skemp RR (1976) Relational understanding and instrumental understanding. Mathematics Teaching 77, 20–6.

Skemp RR (1982) Communicating mathematics: surface structures and deep structures. Visible Language, 16, Special Issue: Understanding the Symbolism of Mathematics.

Skemp RR (1986) The Psychology of Learning Mathematics. 2nd edn. Harmondsworth, Middlesex UK and New York: Penguin.

Slocum J and Botermans J (1987) Puzzles Old and New. Wellingborough: Equation.

Smith P (1991) Spatial ability. Topic 5, 1–6. Andover: NFER Nelson.

Smith P (1992) Spatial ability and its role in United Kingdom education. The Vocational Aspects of Education 44, 103–6.

Snowling M and Thomson M (Eds) (1991) Dyslexia: Integrating Theory and Practice. London: Whurr.

Stackhouse J (1989) Relationship between spoken and written language disorders. In Mogford K and Sadler J (Eds) Child Language Disability. Clevedon UK and Philadelphia: Multilingual Matters.

Starkey P and Gelman R (1982) The development of addition and subtraction prior to formal schooling in arithmetic. In Carpenter TP, Moser JM and Romberg TA (Eds) Addition and Subtraction: a Cognitive Perspective. Hillsdale NJ: Erlbaum.

Starkey P, Spelke E and Gelman R (1990) Numerical abstractions by human infants. Cognition 36, 97–127.

Stern C and Stern MB (1971) Children Discover Arithmetic. 2nd edn. London: Harrap.

Stewart I (1995) Nature's Numbers. London: Weidenfeld & Nicolson. New York: Harper Collins.

Stone JB (1988) Intention and convention in mathematics instruction: reflection on the learning of deaf students. In Cocking RR and Mestre JP (Eds) Linguistic and Cultural Influences on Learning. Hillsdale NJ and London: Erlbaum

Teubal E and Nesher P (1991) Order of mention vs order of events as determining factors in additive word problems. In Durkin K and Shire B (Eds) Language in Mathematical Education. Milton Keynes and Philadelphia: Open University Press.

Thiele R (1988) Die Gefesselte Zeit. Leipzig: Urania-Verlag.

Tulving E (1983) Elements of Episodic Memory. Oxford: Oxford University Press.

Van Est WT (1993) Hans Freudenthal. Educational Studies in Mathematics 25, 59–69, Special Issue: The legacy of Hans Freudenthal.

Vergnaud G (1982) A classification of cognitive tasks and operations of thought involved in addition and subtraction problems. In Carpenter TP, Moser JM and Romberg TA (Eds) Addition and Subtraction: a Cognitive Perspective, Hillsdale NJ: Erlbaum.

Walter M (1986) A mathematical memoir. Mathematics Teaching 117, 14–16.

Wells G (1985) Language Development in the Pre-school Years. Cambridge UK: Cambridge University Press.

Wertheimer M (1966) Productive Thinking. London: Tavistock (SSP).

Wheatley CL and Wheatley GH (1979) Developing spatial ability. Mathematics in School 8, 10–11.

Wheatley GH (1977) The right hemispheric's role in problem solving. Arithmetic Teacher 25, 37–8.

Whitburn J (1995) The teaching of mathematics in Japan: an English perspective. Oxford Review of Education 21, 347–60.

White G (1971) Antique Toys and their Background. London: Chancellor Press.

Whitehead AN (1949) The Aims of Education. London: Ernest Benn.

Wittmann J (1967) Theorie und Praxis eines ganzheitlichen Unterrichts. 4th edited edn. W Müller, ed. Dortmund, Germany: Crüwell.

Wood D (1988) How Children Think and Learn. Oxford UK and Cambridge USA: Blackwell.

Wyke M and Asso D (1979) Perception and memory for spatial relations in children with developmental dysphasia. Neuropsychologia 17, 231–9.

Wynn K (1992a) Addition and subtraction by human infants. Nature 358, 749–50.

Wynn K (1992b) Children's acquisition of the number words and the counting system. Cognitive Psychology 24, 220–51.

Wynn K (1992c) Evidence against the empiricist accounts of the origin of numerical knowledge. Mind and Language 7, 315–32.

Yoshida H and Kuriyama K (1991) Learning to count in Japanese. In Durkin K and Shire B (Eds) Language in Mathematical Education, Milton Keynes and Philadelphia: Open University Press.

APPENDIX (MATERIALS)

Cuisenaire Rods, UK: The Cuisenaire Company, Educational Solutions (UK) Ltd, 11 Crown Street, Reading RG1 2TQ. USA: Cuisenaire/Algebricks Rods Educational Solutions Inc. New York, 99 University Place, NY 10003-4555.

Galt Materials, UK: James Galt & Co. Ltd, Brookfield Road, Cheadle, Cheshire SK8 2PN.

Lego Materials (including Lego Dacta), UK: Lego UK Ltd, Ruthin Road, Wrexham, Clwyd LL13 7TQ (also: Galt, NES Arnold and Hope Education Ltd, Oldham). USA: Lego Systems Inc., 555 Taylor Road, PO Box 1600, Enfield, CT 06083-1600.

Naef materials (Ornabo, Palladio, Archiblocks), Switzerland: Naef AG Spielzeug, CH 4314 Zeilingen, Switzerland.

Poleidoblocs, UK: NES Arnold Ltd, Ludlow Hill Road, West Bridgford, Nottingham NG2 6HD. USA: NES Arnold Inc., 899-H Airport Park Rd, Glen Burnie, Maryland 21061-2557.

Records

Belafonte H (1950) Banana Boat (Come Mr Tallyman). Golden Records. RCA Victor Records (LPM 9940).

Waits T (1976) San Diego Serenade. In The Heart of Saturday Night. Electra/Asylum Records UK, K 53035.

Index